THE FAIRCHILD ENCYCLOPEDIA OF ACCESSORIES

THE FAIRCHILD

Encyclopedia
of Accessories

PHYLLIS TORTORA

FAIRCHILD PUBLICATIONS, INC.
NEW YORK

Executive Editor: Olga T. Kontzias

Assistant Acquisitions Editor: Carolyn Purcell

Development Editor: Sylvia Weber

Production Editor: Amy Zarkos

Art Director: Adam B. Bohannon

Production Director: Priscilla Taguer

Editorial Assistant: Suzette Lam

Copy Editor: Chernow Editorial Services, Inc.

Cover & Interior Design: Adam B. Bohannon

Cover Illustration: Julie Johnson

Library of Congress Catalog Card Number: 2002103885

ISBN: 1-56367- 283-9

GST R 133004424

CONTENTS

PREFACE

The *Encyclopedia of Accessories* is a basic reference that provides a broad overview of contemporary fashion accessories. Not only does the work focus on individual categories of fashion, but it also examines the components from which accessories are constructed. The *Encyclopedia*, therefore, is divided into two sections. It begins with a section on *Components of Accessories*. Here the text explores those materials from which accessories are made or with which they are decorated. The second section, entitled *Accessories*, is divided into numerous categories, each devoted to a specific type of accessory.

Each component and category of accessories begins with a brief introduction to its history and significance to fashion. Structure is described in an "Anatomy" section. Illustrations of common parts accompany this section. Where relevant, the processing and/or manufacturing of components and accessories are explained. Each segment ends with definitions of a lengthy list of terms.

Two appendices are included in the encyclopedia. The first is a list of trade associations serving the various areas related to accessories or their components. The listings include the name of the association, its acronym, the city in which its headquarters is located, and its Web site. Using this information, readers will be able to find information about the objectives of an organization, its activities, and how to make contact with it. Associations for practitioners of crafts or collectors of various types of accessories are not included in this list.

The second appendix is a bibliography of references used in the preparation of this volume and of works useful to those readers who want to explore a topic in greater depth. At the end of this bibliography are listed periodicals devoted exclusively to some accessory or component of accessories. General fashion publications, which periodically cover current developments in accessories, are not included.

For whom will this *Encyclopedia* be useful? The general reader should find it helpful in coming to a greater understanding of accessories and their individual components. It is those who are directly involved with the fashion industry, however, who will be mostly likely to draw on its contents. Through this publication:

(1) Fashion designers will discover some of the many materials and processes used in production and design of accessories, and definitions of the vocabulary applied to various styles of accessories. Copious illustrations illuminate the written text.

(2) Manufacturers will be able to clarify and employ appropriate terminology in working with designers and in marketing their products to retailers and the public.

(3) Retailers will be able to evaluate the components of accessories more effectively and identify specific products accurately when ordering. Information about the materials and accessories contained herein can be utilized in advertising and promoting products to prospective customers.

(4) Persons working in the media or in advertising and public relations will be better informed about all aspects of accessories, ranging from the raw materials used to the actual designing, producing, matching, and customer use. They will be working with a single reference work in which illustrations help to clarify terms and their meanings.

(5) Students of fashion will be introduced to the world of accessories and its appropriate terminology and language. Moreover, instructors will be able to provide students with a resource that provides product knowledge about components, illustrations of specific styles of accessories, and a substantial vocabulary.

(6) Fashion consumers will become familiar with the terminology used in the production and sales of accessories so that they can better understand and appreciate what goes into the making of the objects they buy.

(7) Professionals, students, and consumers will find the bibliography of books dealing with specific types of accessories, the list of trade associations, and the appropriate Web sites a useful tool in examining any of the various areas of the *Encyclopedia* in greater depth.

(8) All readers will benefit from clarification and illustration of the terminology related to the entire production and marketing process of the accessory and its components.

It may be helpful to place this work within the context of several other books from Fairchild Books. The *Encyclopedia* deals only with accessories and their components. It is also limited to contemporary accessories, and no attempt is made to include historic terms that are no longer in contemporary usage. The first topic of the Components of Accessories section is *Textiles in Accessories.* Many accessories use at least some textile material in their structure. This section provides a brief overview of textile fibers, yarns, fabrics, finishes, the ornamentation of textiles, and definitions of related terms. The section is necessarily brief. For readers who need a work that is more inclusive, *Fairchild's Dictionary of Textiles,* 7th Edition provides comprehensive coverage of this field.

The Fairchild Dictionary of Fashion, 3rd Edition, is a comprehensive collection of definitions of both contemporary and historic terms related to the entire field of fashion. Its organization into categories provided a conceptual framework for the organization of this encyclopedia.

For a complete overview of historic fashion in which a wide variety of terms are defined within the text, readers may wish to refer to another Fairchild publication: *Survey of Historic Costume,* 3rd Edition.

ACKNOWLEDGMENTS

*T*he *Fairchild Encyclopedia of Accessories* is, in a sense, the offspring of *The Fairchild Dictionary of Fashion.* It is therefore appropriate to acknowledge a debt of gratitude to the late Charlotte Mankey Calasibetta, who originated the *Dictionary of Fashion* and whose conceptualization of that work is incorporated and reflected in many ways in this book. Not only are many of the definitions drawn from her work, but the organization of the work into categories was inspired by her approach to the dictionary. She has left a lasting legacy to scholars, students, and professionals in the field of fashion.

Many individuals participated in this project. Early in its development, Ellen Goldstein, chair, Accessories Design Department, Fashion Institute of Technology, provided much valuable advice about contents and organization. Her input helped to shape the final product.

My husband, Vincent Tortora, developed the guide to pronunciations, helped with proofreading and editing, and, as always, helped to move the work ahead by his encouragement and support.

Work on both the third edition of the *Dictionary of Fashion* and the *Encyclopedia of Accessories* proceeded along parallel tracks. A number of reviewers contributed their expertise to both projects. Thanks are due to Lynda Campbell, Fairfax County Public Schools; Mary Morris, G Street Fabrics; and Robert Woods, Berkeley College for general reactions to definitions. Reviewers of individual categories include Kate Achelpohl, Vision Council of America, Eyewear; Jerry Anderson, The Neckwear Association of America, Ties; Edith Anderson Feisner, The Embroiderers' Guild of America, Embroidery;

Adam Graham, American Gem Society, Gems, Gem Cuts, and Settings and Jewelry; Keith Kaplan, Fur Information Council of America, Furs; Sally Kay, The Hosiery Association, Hosiery; Jeryl Spear, *Salon News* Contributing Editor, Hairstyles and Hair Accessories; and Bella Veksler, Drexel University, Belts, Handbags, Headwear, and Scarves.

Bina Abling, who did the illustrations for the third edition of the *Dictionary of Fashion,* contributed still more lively and clear drawings to this work. Merle Thomason, archivist for Fairchild Publications, once again directed us to needed illustrative material.

The editorial staff of Fairchild Publications, who eased the way for this project with their encouragement, advice, and expertise, included Olga Kontzias, executive editor; Sylvia L. Weber, development editor; Amy Zarkos, production editor; Adam Bohannon, art director; and Priscilla Taguer, production manager. Mary McGarry also took part in the planning stages.

Barbara Chernow, president of Chernow Editorial Services, Inc., was always ready with answers to questions about organization, and Steve Bedney, managing editor, supervised the copy editing.

Libraries to which I turned for assistance were The Briarcliff Manor, NY, Public Library and the Westchester, NY, Library System and its numerous branches, the library of the Fashion Institute of Technology, the Queens College Benjamin Rosenthal Library, the New York Public Library and Picture Collection, and the Port Washington, NY, Public Library. And the appendix that lists trade associations and their Web pages provides some idea of how useful it was to have a research tool such as the Internet.

INTRODUCTION

Accessories comprise those items of dress that are worn in addition to a basic body-covering garment such as dresses or suits. In some cases they complement the basic garment and create an overall aesthetic effect. In other cases they may be purely practical. They are worn on the head, the hands, the feet, or other parts of the body; they may be carried; or they may be attached to another garment.

Accessories are made from a wide variety of materials. Often several different materials may be combined. Not only are accessories constructed from textiles, leather, straw, plastic, or other components, but embroidery, feathers, gems, and other decorative elements may also ornament their surfaces. Some accessories are held together by sewing stitches or may require the addition of closures. The specific substances and elements used to construct accessories and the forms of ornamentation applied to them are discussed in the COMPONENTS OF ACCESSORIES section of this book.

This exploration of components of accessories precedes the examination of various types of accessories because different types of accessories may utilize similar components. For example, both footwear and gloves may be made of leather, and textiles may be used in footwear, gloves, scarves, or handbags. Although gems are generally made into jewelry, they can also be incorporated into watches or belts. Discussion of components includes a brief history of the use of these materials, their composition, and how they are processed. Definitions of various types of components and of terms used in conjunction with their processing, manufacture, and use are provided.

Specific categories of accessories are discussed in the ACCESSORIES section of this book. Each category of accessories generally begins with a brief exploration of the history and significance of this type of accessory to fashion. An explanation and, where relevant, a drawing of the structure of a typical example of one or more of these accessories follows under the heading of ANATOMY. Finally, types of accessories within that category are defined. Where a category includes a wide variety of types of items, i.e., FOOTWEAR, these definitions may be subdivided.

It should be noted that historic terms no longer in use are excluded from this encyclopedia. Readers interested in historic terms for accessories can consult *The Fairchild Dictionary of Fashion,* which includes extensive listings of terms no longer used.

Terms defined in *The Fairchild Encyclopedia of Accessories* appear in the text in lowercase, boldface type (e.g., **diamond, beret**). These terms may appear within the text discussing the item or in a list of definitions. Cross-references are printed in small capitals. If the cross-reference is to another entry in the same component or category, the subheading and the term being cross-referenced are listed, e.g., TYPES OF LACE DEFINED: VAL LACE or ANATOMY OF FOOTWEAR: VAMP. If the cross-reference is to another component or category, then the full heading is given together with the subheading in which the term will be found. For example, FOOTWEAR: TYPES OF SHOES DEFINED: OXFORD or TEXTILES: HOW YARNS MAY BE IMPORTANT: CARDING.)

Two appendices are included in this work. Appendix A provides a listing of trade associations that provide services and information relating to specific accessory types. The Web address is given for many of these organizations. Appendix B is a list of publications consulted in the preparation of this work and others that are useful to those interested in learning more about accessories or their components. It includes both books and periodicals.

COMPONENTS OF ACCESSORIES

TEXTILES
in ACCESSORIES

This discussion of textiles that are commonly used in accessories defines many terms relating to fibers, yarns, and fabrics. Space does not permit an exhaustive list, however, and readers will find that *Fairchild's Dictionary of Textiles*, 7th edition provides a more complete compendium both of current as well as historic terms related to all aspects of textiles.

Textiles make up all or part of the structure of many accessories. In order to understand the role textiles play in such items as headwear, footwear, hosiery, scarves, or handbags, it will be helpful to understand textile fibers, yarns, and fabrics, and become familiar with the terminology used in connection with textile materials.

FIBERS AND YARNS:
THE BUILDING BLOCKS OF FABRICS

Fibers are the raw material from which cloth is made. Cotton, wool, silk, nylon, and acetate are examples of fibers. Fibers alone cannot make a fabric. They are twisted together into continuous yarns that are then woven or knitted or otherwise constructed into a fabric.

Many accessories use fabrics as part or all of their structure. Fabrics are made from fibers. The technical definition of a **fiber** is that it be at least 100 times as long as its diameter. A single fiber looks rather like a human hair.

Fibers can be found in nature. The major **natural fibers** are cotton from the cotton plant, linen from the flax plant, wool and other animal hair from the coats of sheep or other animals, and silk, which is unwound from cocoons spun by silkworms. **Manufactured fibers** are produced from chemicals or other substances by complex industrial processes.

Natural fibers, except silk, are short. Their length ranges from less than an inch to several feet. Short fibers are called **staple fibers.** Silk and manufactured fibers can be continuous for hundreds of meters. Long, continuous fibers are called **filament fibers.** They can be cut into shorter, staple lengths.

Based on their chemical composition and other properties, natural and manufactured fibers have been assigned by the Federal Trade Commission to one of many **generic fiber categories** or families of fibers. These fiber names are used in labeling as required by the **Textile Fiber Products Identification Act (T.F.P.I.A.),** which is a Federal law setting labeling requirements for clothing made of textiles. It requires that they be labeled with generic fiber identification, manufacturer identification, and designation of country of origin. Fibers may also have trademark names. A **trademark** is a word, name, or symbol that has been adopted and used by the owner to identify a product and distinguish it from others. When trademarks have been registered they may not be used by any other individual or firm and are written with the symbol ® or ™. Trademarks may be used in labeling, but are not required, whereas generic names must be given, even if a trademark is used. An example of a generic fiber name is spandex. An example of a trademark name for one type of spandex fiber is Lycra®.

The following is a list of generic fibers frequently found in accessories together with their definitions.

COMPONENTS OF ACCESSORIES: TEXTILES IN ACCESSORIES

Trademarks are not listed because they are subject to frequent changes.

GENERIC AND OTHER MANUFACTURED FIBERS DEFINED

acetate (as´-uh tayt) Generic fiber category established by the FTC for manufactured fibers that are chemical variants of cellulose called cellulose acetate and that are manufactured from cellulose materials, such as wood chips. The term also refers to fabrics or yarns made from acetate fibers. Used in a wide variety of apparel, acetate fabrics have a crisp hand and a high luster. Current trademarks for acetate fiber include Chromespun®, Estron®, and Celanese® acetate.

acrylic (uh krihl´ ihk) Generic fiber category established by the FTC for a manufactured fiber primarily composed of a polymer material called acrylonitrile. Also refers to fabrics or yarns made from acrylic fibers. Acrylic fabrics have a soft, wool-like hand, good wrinkle resistance, wash and dry quickly, and therefore are often used in easy-care apparel products such as sweaters and socks. Current trademarks for acrylic fiber include Acrilan®, Duraspun®, and Creslan®.

cuprammonium rayon Cellulosic fiber regenerated from wood pulp or from cotton fibers too short to spin into yarns. This fiber is no longer manufactured in the United States because it produces high levels of water pollution, but is manufactured abroad and may be found in imported goods. Often used in women's scarves.

elastomer A synthetic material that has the excellent stretchability and recovery of natural rubber. SPANDEX (see under GENERIC AND OTHER MANUFACTURED FIBERS DEFINED), an elastomeric fiber, is an example.

Lycra® See GENERIC AND OTHER MANUFACTURED FIBERS DEFINED: SPANDEX.

lyocell Regenerated cellulosic fiber made by a more environmentally friendly process than rayon. The Federal Trade Commission has designated lyocell as a generic fiber name but classified it as a subcategory of rayon. Trademark names for the fiber include Tencel®, made by Acordis, and Lyocell by Lenzing®.

man-made fibers See GENERIC AND OTHER MANUFACTURED FIBERS DEFINED: MANUFACTURED FIBERS.

manufactured fibers Textile fibers that are not found in nature but are produced through various chemical processes. They may be classified as either **synthetic fibers,** which are created from chemical components (e.g., ACRYLIC, NYLON, POLYESTER, OLEFIN, SPANDEX), or as **regenerated fibers,** which are created by taking natural materials, such as wood chips or very short cotton fibers that cannot be used as textile fibers in their natural form but which can be chemically processed and reformed into useable textile fibers (e.g. RAYON, ACETATE, LYOCELL). Also called *man-made fibers.* See GENERIC AND OTHER MANUFACTURED FIBERS DEFINED.

microfiber Manufactured filament fiber that measures 1.0 denier per filament or less.

modacrylic Generic category of manufactured fiber made from acrylic resins and characterized by soft hand, warmth without bulk, resistance to moths and mildew, easy care, and high wrinkle recovery. Used for knitwear, wigs, and fur fabrics.

nylon Generic fiber category established by the FTC for a manufactured fiber (see under GENERIC AND OTHER MANUFACTURED FIBERS DEFINED) composed of a long chain of chemicals called polyamides. Introduced in 1939 by DuPont and later produced by other manufacturers, nylon fabrics generally have a silky hand, strength, crease resistance, washability, and resistance to mildew and moths. Current trademark names include Antron®, Caprolan®, and Ultron®.

olefin (oh´-leh-fihn) Generic fiber category for a MANUFACTURED FIBER (see under GENERIC AND OTHER MANUFACTURED FIBERS DEFINED) composed of either polyethylene or polypropylene. Manufacturers prefer the term **polyolefin** (pol-ee´ -oh´-leh-fihn). Polypropylene is used for some kinds of apparel, such as activewear products, e.g., hosiery, and is also beginning to be used in other products such as lingerie, bathing suits, and children's clothing. One trademark name is Marvess®.

polyester Generic fiber name for manufactured fibers made of acids and alcohols derived from petroleum. The wide variety of fabrics made from these fibers are easy care, resilient, retain their shape, and are often blended with other fibers. Current trademarks for polyester fiber include Dacron®, Hollofil®, Fortrel®, Micrell®, and Stay Gard®.

polyethelyne See GENERIC AND OTHER MANUFACTURED FIBERS DEFINED: OLEFIN.

polyolefin See GENERIC AND OTHER MANUFACTURED FIBERS DEFINED: OLEFIN.

polypropylene See GENERIC AND OTHER MANUFACTURED FIBERS DEFINED: OLEFIN.

rayon Generic fiber name for manufactured cellulosic fibers regenerated from short cotton fibers or wood chips. Characteristics include a silky hand, shiny lustrous appearance, good dye absorbency, and good draping qualities. Disadvantages include poor wrinkle recovery and a tendency to shrink, unless it is given special finishes to improve performance. *Der.* French, "ray of light."

spandex Generic fiber term for manufactured fibers composed largely of segmented polyurethane, which are stretchable, lightweight, and resistant to body acid. Spandex is not used alone, but in combination with a wide variety of other fibers. Current trademarks include Lycra®, Dorlastan®, and Glospan®.

triacetate (try-ass′-eh-tate) Manufactured fiber regenerated through chemical treatment from wood chips or very short cotton fibers. Used for wearing apparel. Relatively little triacetate is produced at present, none in the United States.

ultrafine fiber Manufactured filament fiber that measures 0.01 denier per filament or less.

viscose rayon (vis′-kos) Rayon fiber regenerated through the viscose process from wood pulp or cotton fibers too short to be spun. This process produces pollutants that are hard to eliminate, therefore production in the United States has been sharply reduced. The fiber is used for a wide variety of apparel because it can be dyed or printed in attractive colors and patterns, drapes well, and is comfortable to wear; however, if not given special finishes, it has a tendency to shrink and to wrinkle.

NATURAL FIBERS DEFINED

alpaca A sheeplike animal of the camel family, related to the llama, native to the Andes in South America. Yarn spun from fleece is lustrous and shiny.

angora Soft fuzzy yarn made from the underhair of the angora rabbit used for knitwear and for trimmings.

camel hair Fibers from the crossbred Bactrian camel of Asia, which produces soft luxurious yarn resistant to heat and cold.

cashmere A fine, soft, downy wool undergrowth produced by the cashmere goat, which is raised in the Kashmir region of India and Pakistan and parts of northern India, Tibet, Mongolia, Turkmenistan, China, Iran, and Iraq. Similar goats can now be raised in the United States. Synonyms include PASHMINA (see under NATURAL FIBERS DEFINED).

cotton Soft white vegetable fiber from ½ to 2 inches long that comes from the fluffy boll of the cotton plant. Composed largely of cellulose, cotton fibers are absorbent, comfortable, and washable and are therefore used in a wide variety of items.

flax Fiber from the stem of the flax plant. Linen fabrics are made from flax fibers.

hair fibers Fibers obtained from the fleece or pelt of an animal.

hemp A coarse, strong, lustrous fiber from the stem of the hemp plant. Cultivation of hemp plants is illegal in the United States because the plant is from the same family as marijuana; however, import and sale of hemp fabrics and fibers is legal, and the fiber is used for making apparel.

horsehair Hair fiber obtained from the mane or tail of a horse.

jute A fiber from the stem of the jute plant, grown in Bangladesh, India, China, and Thailand. Soft, fine, lustrous, and pliable, it becomes weak and brittle when exposed to moisture. It is used in making fabrics such as BUCKRAM and BURLAP (see under WOVEN FABRICS DEFINED).

latex Rubber in natural or synthetic liquid form that is used bare or wrapped with another textile yarn in yarns that stretch.

linen Fibers of the flax plant that are used to make linen yarn and fabrics.

llama Fibers obtained from a member of the camel family, native to high altitudes in Andes mountains of South America. Fiber colors range from white, gray, and light brown to black. The outer coat of the animal is coarse while the under coat is soft.

mohair   Fiber obtained from the hair of the angora goat or fabric made from that hair. The fiber is long, white, and lustrous and comparatively coarse. Durable and resilient, it is used for scarves, stoles, imitation furs, and knitting yarn. *Der.* Arabic, *mukhayyar,* "goat's hair."

organic cotton   Cotton grown without the use of pesticides and chemical fertilizers.

pashmina (pash-mee′-nah)   Synonym for CASH-MERE (see under NATURAL FIBERS DEFINED) used in the 1990s and after to promote fine quality cashmere apparel, especially shawls, stoles, and scarves.

qiviut (kay′-vee-ut)   Underwool of the domesticated musk ox. Spun into yarn, this fine, soft fiber is knitted into a variety of apparel by Eskimo women in Alaska. Sold to tourists and by mail order.

ramie   Strong, soft, lustrous fiber, somewhat similar to linen, from inner bark of *ramie* plant, formerly imported from China. Also called *rhea* or *China grass.*

shahtoosh   Exceptionally soft, fine, and rare wool taken from a Tibetan antelope, the chiru, which is an endangered species. The animals must be killed in order to obtain their wool, and it is illegal in the United States to buy or sell products made from this fiber. Shahtoosh shawls sell for as much as $15,000 on the black market.

silk   Fiber obtained from the cocoon of the silkworm. Noted for its resiliency, elasticity, strength, and luster. Often used to make luxurious fabrics. **Raw silk** is silk fiber reeled from cocoon while still containing the gum or sericin that gives it a rough, slightly sticky feel. **Tussah** (tuss′-ah) is coarse, irregular silk from wild Asian silkworms that is used to make PONGEE and SHANTUNG (see under WOVEN FABRICS DEFINED). The silkworm, the fiber, the yarn, and also the fabric made from the yarn are all called by the name tussah.

vicuña (vi-koon′-yah)   Hair fiber from the vicuña, a species related to the llama. It is one of the softest fibers known. Colors range from golden chestnut to deep fawn. In spite of attempts to domesticate the animals, most of the fiber must still be obtained by hunting and killing them. The Peruvian government limits the number of animals that can be hunted,

therefore the fiber supply is very limited and very expensive.

wool   **1.** Animal fiber from fleece of sheep or lambs. Fabrics made from wool are warm, resilient, have good absorption, and good affinity for dyes. Disadvantages include tendency to shrink and poor resistance to moths unless treated. May be knitted, woven, or felted, which is possible because of a microscopic structure of scales on the surface of the fibers. May also be blended with other fibers. **2.** The Wool Products Labeling Act of 1939 expanded the definition of wool to include ANGORA or CASHMERE, ALPACA, LLAMA, CAMEL HAIR, or VICUÑA (see under NATURAL FIBERS DEFINED).

HOW YARNS MAY BE IMPORTANT

Fibers must be held together in some way. This may be done by twisting fibers together to form a **yarn.** In fabrics not made from yarns, heat, adhesives, chemicals, or some other process that bonds the fibers may hold fibers together.

Fibers can be twisted into yarns of many different types. One of the most important aspects of a yarn is how tightly it is twisted. In general, the more tightly a yarn is twisted, the finer and stronger it will be; however, when yarn is twisted past a certain point, the yarn tends to kink and lose strength. These basic principles of yarn structure are used to produce yarns and fabrics with different appearances and characteristics.

The process of creating a yarn by twisting fibers together is called **spinning.** As part of this process, fibers must be made parallel. Continuous filament fibers emerge from the fiber formation process in parallel strands and require some twisting to form them into a cohesive yarn. **Carding** is the first step in making staple fibers into yarns. The fibers are separated, straightened out somewhat, and formed into a weblike mass, after which the web is drawn out and twisted to form a yarn. **Combing** is an optional step in which carded fibers are subjected to further straightening and alignment, formed into a strand of fibers, and given a greater or lesser amount of twist to form them into a yarn. Combed yarns have fewer fibers on the surface, are smoother, and can be finer yarns than those that have only been carded.

Yarns are generally divided into two types: simple and complex, or fancy, yarns. A **simple yarn** is one with a uniform diameter and even surface. One of these yarns is called a **single yarn.** Several simple, single yarns can

single yarn   ply yarn

be twisted together to form a **ply yarn;** several ply yarns can be twisted together to form a **cord yarn.** A **fancy yarn** is made to have a more decorative appearance, and often uses several different yarns together to create interesting effects.

cable/cord yarn

The kind of yarn used will affect the appearance of the fabric into which yarns are woven or knitted. If a simple, single, tightly twisted yarn is used to create a fabric, it will have a smooth, regular appearance. If a complex yarn with an uneven surface is used, it will have an uneven and irregular appearance.

Size of silk and manufactured filament yarns is measured in **denier** (den-yer′). The low numbers represent finer yarns, the higher numbers the heavier yarns. A new numbering system based on the metric system is called the **tex system** and is intended to replace older, more complex systems. The tex number of a fiber or yarn is the weight in grams of one kilometer length. As with denier, the lower the number, the finer the strand.

TYPES OF YARNS DEFINED

blended yarn   Yarns that are composed of two or more fibers mixed together and then spun to form one yarn, e.g., cotton fibers and polyester staple. When such a yarn is used to make a fabric, the fabric possesses some of the qualities of both fibers.

bouclé yarn (boo-klay′)   A rough, curly, knotted yarn made by twisting together two fine-foundation threads with a thicker yarn that is delivered in such a way as to cause the thick yarn to twist up on the surface.

bouclé yarn

chenille yarn   Yarns with a fuzzy surface with short fibers projecting on all sides.

core yarn   Yarn made with a heavy center cord around which is wrapped finer yarns of different fibers, e.g., synthetic rubber core wrapped with

rayon, cotton, or silk to improve absorption and feel.

crepe yarn (krape)   Yarn that is given a high twist during spinning. The yarn is stiff, wiry, and contracts during finishing giving pebbled surface to fabrics.

crewel yarn   Two-ply, loosely twisted, fine-worsted yarn used for embroidery.

doupioni (doop-ee′-on-ee)   Yarn or fabric made from silk yarn reeled from double cocoons or two interlaced cocoons in which the silk is intertwined. Yarn has uneven slub, rather than being smooth, giving a decorative texture to the fabric. Also spelled *douppioni, doppione.*

handspun yarn   Yarn made with different types of spindles or hand-spinning wheels—making it less regular in appearance than machine-made yarns and adding texture and interest to the woven fabric.

lisle yarn (lyle)   A two-ply cotton yarn made of long staple fibers that are combed, tightly twisted, and sometimes given further treatment to remove all short fuzzy fibers. Often used in hosiery.

Lurex®   Trademark for a decorative metallic fiber and yarn made of aluminum-coated plastic to prevent tarnishing.

marl yarn   Yarn made from two or more different-colored strands of fiber or two or more different-colored yarns, producing a mottled effect in fabrics woven or knitted from this yarn.

merino wool   High-quality wool yarn made from fleece of merino sheep, which has short, fine, strong, resilient fibers, and takes dyes well.

metallic yarn   **1.** See TYPES OF YARNS DEFINED: LUREX. **2.** CORE YARN made by twisting thin metal foil around another yarn. See under TYPES OF YARNS DEFINED.

multifilament yarn   Many long, continuous manufactured fibers twisted together to form a yarn.

novelty yarn   Yarns made with unusual or special effects such as nubs, slubs, loops, or some other variation. The preferred term in the textile industry is now *fancy yarn.*

nub yarn   Yarn made with slubs or lumps, knots, or flecks of fibers at intervals—sometimes of different colors giving a mottled effect to the finished fabric.

ratiné yarn (rat′-in-ay)   Spongy, rough, nubby-surfaced yarn with nubs or knots at intervals. *Der.* French, "frizzy" or "fuzzy."

slub yarn Yarn that has thicker areas alternating with thinner. When used as crosswise yarns in shantung and other fabrics, it produces an uneven appearance with elongated thickened places at intervals.

space-dyed yarn Yarns colored or dyed various colors at intervals. When woven into a fabric, they produce a random design.

textured yarn Manufactured continuous-filament yarns permanently heat-set in crimped manner, or otherwise modified to improve its handle, increase bulk, or increase elasticity.

thick and thin yarn Yarns, that are unevenly sized at intervals. When woven into cloth, they add interest.

thread Smooth, tightly twisted yarn made specifically for sewing.

woolen Yarns or woven or knitted fabrics made from wool fibers that are not COMBED, but may be CARDED two or three times. See under HOW YARNS MAY BE IMPORTANT. **Worsteds** are made from combed and carded fibers. Generally, woolens are kinkier and softer than worsteds. Finishing processes for woolens frequently include napping or brushing as the fabrics have a fuzzy warm handle rather than a smooth feel as do worsteds.

DIFFERENT TYPES OF FABRIC STRUCTURES

The fabrics into which fibers and yarns are made are given names based on their specific structure. Taffeta, satin, jersey, and crepe are examples of fabric names. These fabrics can be made from any fiber, although traditionally certain fibers have been used for certain fabrics. So, for example, taffeta or satin is most likely to be made from silk or from acetate. Crepe might be made from wool, silk, viscose rayon, cotton, or a blend of several fibers.

WOVEN FABRICS

Fabrics can be constructed from yarns either by weaving, knitting, crocheting, or knotting. **Weaving** is the interlacing of yarns on a machine called a loom. A set of lengthwise yarns (**warp yarns**) and a set of crosswise yarns (called **weft**, **filling**, or **woof**

yarns) are interlaced. This interlacing can be done in a number of different patterns.

A **plain weave** is a simple interlacing in which in one row, one crosswise yarn crosses over one lengthwise yarn, then under the next, then over the next, and so on across the fabric. In the second row, the first crosswise yarn goes under the first lengthwise yarn, over the second, and so on. In the third row, the pattern of the first row is repeated.

This simplest of constructions can be used to create many effects. By varying the colors of the yarns used in the crosswise directions, stripes can be created. If the color of the lengthwise yarns is also varied, checks or plaids can be made. By using fancy yarns with thicker and thinner areas, shantung— a fabric with a rough, uneven surface—can be made. Alternating larger and smaller yarns will make a ribbed fabric. Many commonly used fabrics are created using this basic weave.

even plaid

uneven plaid

Other basic weaves include the **twill weave** and the **satin weave**. In twill weaves, crosswise yarns cross over more than one lengthwise yarn before they interlace. There are numerous patterns of interlacing that are used in twill weaves, but always the point of interlacing is regularly spaced, so that a diagonal line can be seen as one looks at the surface of the fabric. In satin weaves, crosswise yarns cross a number of lengthwise yarns before interlacing, and the spacing is arranged irregularly so that no pattern of interlacing can be seen. For this weave, yarns that are made from lustrous, shiny fibers such as silk, acetate, or nylon are often used, so the fabric is usually characterized by a beautiful surface luster.

These three basic weaves are used to create a wide variety of complex weaves as well. The more complex weaves found in fabrics with woven patterns such as brocades or damasks require complex machinery that can put together the basic weave patterns in many ways.

In descriptions of woven textiles, certain technical terms may be used. Fabric has a lengthwise and crosswise direction or **grain**. The direction in fabrics diagonal to the lengthwise or crosswise directions is called the **bias**. When woven fabrics are pulled in

bias

the bias direction, they exhibit greater stretch than in the other directions. The **face** is the right side of a fabric—as opposed to **back,** or reverse side. It generally has a better appearance. Some fabrics are **reversible** and may be used on both sides.

In the textile-industry **fabric count** refers to the number of lengthwise (warp) and crosswise (filling) yarns in a square inch of woven fabric. This number is expressed by first writing the number of warps then the number of fillings, e.g., 72 × 64 would mean 72 warps and 64 fillings per square inch. When a heavier yarn is used in either the lengthwise or crosswise direction, a ridge is formed and the fabric is said to exhibit a **cord** (lengthwise) or **rib** (crosswise) effect.

WOVEN FABRICS DEFINED

antique taffeta   Crisp taffeta that may have irregular slubs throughout in imitation of 18th-c. fabrics. Also made in iridescent effects with lengthwise and crosswise yarns of different colors.

astrakhan/astrakan   1. Fabric with a heavy, curly pile made to imitate karakul lamb fleece. May be woven or knitted. Used as trimming or for men's hats. **2.** See WOVEN FABRICS DEFINED: KARAKUL CLOTH and FURS: TYPES OF FURS DEFINED: KARAKUL.

basket weave   Variation of plain weave, made by weaving two or more crosswise yarns over and under same number of lengthwise yarns to produce a checkerboard effect.

basket weave

batiste   A plain-weave, lightweight sheer fabric usually made of cotton or a cotton/polyester blend. Made in a variety of colors and printed designs.

bengaline   Heavyweight fabric characterized by large corded effect in the crosswise direction. Often made of lustrous fibers and used for millinery and ribbons.

bird's-eye   Fabric woven in linen or cotton on a loom with a DOBBY ATTACHMENT (see WOVEN FABRICS DEFINED: DOBBY WEAVE) in small diamond design with dot in center. Crosswise yarns are heavier and loosely twisted to make fabric more absorbent to use for diapers. Also called *diaper cloth.*

broadcloth   1. Closely woven plain weave fabric with a fine rib in the crosswise direction. Usually made from cotton or cotton blends but can also be made of other fibers. **2.** Wool or wool blend fabric made in plain or twill weave with a napped (brushed) surface that is brushed in one direction.

brocade   A heavy fabric with a complex, raised pattern that is woven on a JACQUARD (see under WOVEN FABRICS DEFINED) loom. Electronic or mechanical controls in this loom can manipulate yarns to combine into many different types of weaves in a single fabric. Often made with decorative and lustrous yarns.

brocatelle   Medium-weight dress fabric woven on a JACQUARD (see under WOVEN FABRICS DEFINED) loom with a pattern that stands out in high relief, giving a blistered effect. Some fabrics give the appearance of being quilted. Made of filament yarns on its face and with cotton yarns in the backing.

buckram   Loosely woven, heavily sized fabric in a plain weave used for stiffening. Similar to CRINOLINE (see WOVEN FABRICS DEFINED) but heavier and much stiffer. Sizing will wash out, making fabric unsuitable for washable products.

burlap   Loosely constructed, plain woven fabric made of jute or other minor bast fibers. Originally considered a utility fabric for bags and sacks. Now sometimes embroidered and used for handbags and items of apparel.

calico   Plain weave, light- to medium-weight cotton or cotton-blend fabric usually printed with very small designs such as flowers or geometric forms. Also see DESIGNS AND SURFACE EFFECTS DEFINED: CALICO PRINT.

cambric   Fine, closely woven cotton fabric made with mercerized yarns given a calendered finish. May also be made of linen and used for handkerchiefs. *Der.* From Cambrai, France.

challis (shal'-lee)   Soft, plain weave fabric made of wool, rayon staple, cotton, or manufactured fiber blends. Supple and lightweight, it is often printed in small floral patterns.

chambray (sham'-bray)   A broad class of plain weave fabrics made with colored yarns in the lengthwise direction and white yarns in the crosswise direction. May be a plain color, striped, or checked. Usually made of cotton, manufactured fibers, or a blend of the two.

chamois cloth (sham-wah′) Soft cotton fabric that is either knitted or woven. Made with a fine soft nap in imitation of chamois-dyed sheepskin. Should not be shortened or confused with CHAMOIS (See under LEATHER: TYPES OF LEATHER DEFINED) as this refers to leather and a leather-tanning process.

chiffon Thin transparent fabric made in a plain weave. It drapes well and is made from tightly twisted or CREPE YARN (see under TYPES OF YARNS DEFINED). Originally made in silk; now also made in manufactured fibers. Dyed solid colors or often printed in floral designs. Used for sheer dresses, blouses, and scarves. *Der.* French, *chiffe,* "rag."

China silk Soft, lustrous silk fabric in a plain weave that may have slight texture due to use of irregular yarns. Made in China and Japan; originally handmade in China as early as 1200 B.C., the name is also applied to machine-made fabrics of a similar type.

chino (chee′-no) Durable cotton, firmly woven with a fine steep twill and dyed a yellowish-tan or khaki color. Contemporary versions are also dyed in many colors. Originally used for summer uniforms for the U.S. Army, by the 1950s the fabric had been adopted by teenagers for school and general wear, particularly for pants. Now used for a wide variety of casual clothing.

chintz Medium-weight cotton or blended fabric with a glazed or shiny finish that may be a plain color or printed with floral, bird, or other designs. Originally a fabric for slipcovers and draperies; now also used for variety of apparel items. *Der.* Indian, *chint,* name for a gaudily printed fabric of cotton.

ciselé velvet (seez-el-ay′) A fabric with a raised pattern of velvet figures on a satin ground formed by cut and uncut loops—with the cut pile being higher.

corduroy (kohr′-duh-roy) Strong durable woven fabric with vertical stripes of cut pile that are formed by an extra system of crosswise yarns. The lengthwise stripes may be made in various widths. Those that are very narrow are called **pinwale**. Usually made of cotton or a cotton blend. The name is thought to derive from the French *corde du roi,* meaning "cord of the king."

covert cloth **1.** An extremely firm, durable twill weave fabric with a characteristic mottled look achieved by twisting lengthwise yarns spun from two strands—one dark and the other light. Crosswise yarns are the same or of a dark color. **2.** Imitated in all cotton.

crash Coarse, loosely woven fabric made in a variety of weights with irregular yarns giving it an uneven texture. Usually made in plain weaves of cotton, cotton blends, or linen.

crepe (krape) A general classification of fabrics made from almost any fiber and characterized by a broad range of crinkled or grained surface effects.

crepe de chine (krepp deh sheen) **1.** Fine, lightweight silk fabric with a crepe texture made by using highly twisted yarns in the filling and more warps than filling yarns. *Der.* French, "crepe of China."

crepe-back satin (krape) Lightweight fabric with a smooth, lustrous, shiny finish on the face and a dull crepe appearance on the back. May be used with either side as the exterior. Made in a satin weave with silk, rayon, or manufactured fiber for the lengthwise yarns, and a crepe twist crosswise yarn. The fabric has twice as many lengthwise as crosswise yarns. Also called *satin-back* and sometimes called *satin-faced crepe.*

crinoline (krin′-uh-lyn) Heavily sized (see SPECIAL FINISHES DEFINED: SIZING) open-weave cotton fabric.

damask A broad group of fabrics with elaborate woven floral or geometric designs that are distinguished from the background by contrasting luster and/or color and which are reversible. Woven on a JACQUARD (see under WOVEN FABRICS DEFINED) loom, the design of the fabric is often made in a satin weave. Because of their decorative aspects, damask fabrics are often used for evening wear.

denim Sturdy, serviceable fabric woven in the TWILL WEAVE (see under WOVEN FABRICS DEFINED) traditionally made with indigo blue or brown lengthwise yarns and white crosswise yarns. It is now made in many color variations and in novelty striped and figured patterns. Used for sportswear and occasionally in high-fashion items. *Der.* French, *serge de Nimes,* a fabric made in Nimes, France. Also called *dungaree.*

dimity   A range of lightweight, sheer fabrics usually made of cotton or a cotton blend characterized by lengthwise cords made by bunching or grouping several yarns together. Less often, a checked effect is made by grouping crosswise yarns together as well.

dobby weave   Weave forming small repeated geometric patterns that is made on plain loom with **dobby attachment,** a mechanical or electronic device that enables a loom to produce small repeating designs of not more than 8 to 30 rows of crosswise yarns. More complex and larger patterns can be made on a JACQUARD loom (see under WOVEN FABRICS DEFINED).

doeskin fabric   Any of several types of fabric made to simulate the texture and appearance of sueded doeskin leather. The fabrics may be made from napped wool, rayon, manufactured, or cotton fibers, and woven or knitted.

dotted swiss   Crisp lightweight fabric ornamented with regularly spaced dots that are created either by clipped sections of extra crosswise yarns that interlace with lengthwise yarns or flocked dots of fiber glued to the fabric surface.

double cloth   Heavy fabric consisting of two separate fabrics woven at the same time and having another binder yarn that moves from one layer to another to hold them together. Such fabrics are usually reversible, in which case they are referred to as **double faced.**

double-faced satin ribbon   Ribbon woven with satin face on both sides.

drill   Durable cotton fabric made in a twill weave and similar to DENIM (see under WOVEN FABRICS DEFINED).

duchesse   Lightweight lustrous satin fabric made of silk or rayon and dyed solid colors. Also called *duchesse satin.*

duck   A broad term for a wide range of strong, firm, plain weave fabrics that is usually made of cotton, linen, or cotton blended with manufactured fibers.

faille (file)   Fabric with a flat-ribbed effect running crosswise, it is flatter and less pronounced than GROSGRAIN (see under WOVEN FABRICS DEFINED). Lengthwise yarns are finer and more plentiful in order to cover the heavier filling yarns. Originally made in silk—now made of silk, wool, cotton, manufactured yarns, or combinations of yarns. Used for trimmings and hats.

fishnet   Coarse mesh fabric made in LENO WEAVE (see under WOVEN FABRICS DEFINED). Major uses include scarves and trimming.

fleece   A fabric with a thick, heavy, fleecelike surface; it may be a PILE fabric (see under WOVEN FABRICS DEFINED), or simply one with a NAP (see under SPECIAL FINISHES DEFINED), and may be woven or knitted.

foulard   Soft lightweight silk or manufactured fiber fabric, usually made in a twill weave and surface-printed in a small design. Used for scarves and neckties. Also see ACCESSORIES: SHAWLS, SCARVES, AND HANDKERCHIEFS: TYPES OF SCARVES DEFINED.

gabardine (gab´-uhr-deen)   Durable, closely woven fabric with diagonal ridges created by a warp-faced TWILL WEAVE (see under WOVEN FABRICS DEFINED) and made from wool, rayon, or other fibers and blends. Wool gabardine has a firm hand, is made with worsted yarns, and is given a clear finish. *Der.* From word used for a cloak or mantle in the Middle Ages.

gauze (gawz)   **1.** Sheer open weave fabric used for trimmings and costumes made in the LENO or PLAIN WEAVE (see under WOVEN FABRICS DEFINED) of silk, cotton, rayon, and other manufactured fiber fabrics. **2.** Plain open weave fabric, similar to lightweight muslin made of loosely twisted cotton yarns. Sometimes given a crinkled finish. *Der.* From Gaza, a city in the Middle East.

georgette/georgette crepe/crepe georgette   Fine sheer silk fabric made in the plain weave with twisted or creped yarns in both lengthwise and crosswise directions.

gingham   Yarn-dyed, checked or plaid fabric made of cotton or cotton blended with polyester. May be made of coarse yarns or of combed yarns in a high-count fabric. **Checked ginghams** are two-colored effects made by using two colors, or one color and white, for groups of yarns in both the warp and filling. **Plaid ginghams** are yarn-dyed designs of several colors. **Zephyr ginghams** are made with fine, silky, mercerized yarns.

grosgrain (groh´-grayn)   Fabric with a large rib that is made by grouping several crosswise yarns together. Made originally in silk, now made mostly with rayon or acetate warp and cotton or rayon filling. Also made entirely of cotton. Used for ribbons, sashes, trim on dresses, bows, neckwear, hatbands, and millinery trimming.

herringbone Pattern made of short, slanting parallel lines adjacent to other rows slanting in reverse direction, creating a continuous V-shaped design like the bones of a fish. Used in tweeds, embroidery, and in working of fur skins.

high-tech fabrics/hi-tech fabrics Fabrics made from manufactured fibers with special performance characteristics (e.g., water repellence, strength, stretch, heat resistance). Such fabrics have been used for fashion goods, especially in the area of clothing for active sports. Also called *high performance fibers.*

homespun Fabrics made from handspun yarns and woven on a hand loom. Most are plain weave, loosely constructed, heavy wool fabrics made of coarse, uneven yarns. Contemporary versions are now made from manufactured and wool blends with automatic looms and imitate the texture and appearance of the handmade fabrics.

honeycomb Any fabric that forms a series of recessed squares similar to a waffle and is made either in a honeycomb weave or knit.

hopsacking A broad classification of fabrics made in loosely constructed plain weave of coarse uneven yarns. The fabric was originally found in sacks made from coarse undyed jute or hemp into which hops were put during harvesting. Made in cotton, spun rayon, and manufactured fibers. Coarse varieties also called BURLAP (see under WOVEN FABRICS DEFINED).

Irish linen Fine quality of linen fabric woven from flax grown mainly in Northern Ireland. Used for handkerchiefs and apparel.

jacquard (ja-kard′) A system of weaving (and the fabrics made on this loom) that, because of a pattern-making mechanism of great versatility, permits the production of woven designs of considerable size. Invented by Joseph Marie Jacquard in France in 1801, the loom controls each lengthwise yarn separately by use of a pattern on a punched card or, in newer looms, by an electronic device. Some of the most widely used jacquard fabrics are BROCADE, DAMASK,

warp

filling

jacquard fabric

and TAPESTRY (see under WOVEN FABRICS DEFINED).

jaspé (jas-pay′) Cotton or cotton blend fabric with narrow woven stripes of coloring that shade from light to dark, or a knitted fabric with crosswise ribs, which achieves this effect.

jean Durable fabric made of carded yarns, primarily of cotton or cotton blend, in a twill weave. It may be bleached, dyed a solid color or printed. Used in blue for overalls and work pants, such pants were given the name of *blue jeans.*

karakul cloth (kar′-ah-kul) Heavyweight pile fabric, similar to ASTRAKHAN (see under WOVEN FABRICS DEFINED), woven in imitation of BROADTAIL LAMB fur or PERSIAN LAMB (see under FURS: TYPES OF FUR DEFINED).

khaki (ka-key) Fabrics of a dull, yellowish tan color, whether serges, drills, or whipcords, are called by this name. Used by the Armed Services of France, England, and the United States as far back as 1848. After World War I, the United States added an olive drab tint that is now government issue for armed forces. *Der.* Hindu, "dust color or earth color."

lamé (lah-may′) Any textile fabric woven or knitted with metallic yarns to form either the background or the pattern. May be made in JACQUARD (See under WOVEN FABRICS DEFINED) or rib weave. The metallic yarns are frequently coated with a fine polyester film that prevents tarnishing. *Der.* French, *lamé,* "leaves of silver or gold."

lawn Sheer, lightweight, high-count cotton fabric made in a plain weave of fine-combed yarns. May be dyed or printed, given a soft or a starched finish, and ironed.

leatherette Misnomer for fabrics made in imitation of leather.

leno weave Open weave with two lengthwise yarns locking around each crosswise yarn in a figure-eight design. Also called *doup* and *gauze weave.* MARQUISETTE (see under WOVEN FABRICS DEFINED) is one of the most widely used leno weave fabrics.

loden cloth Dense, water-repellent coatings and suitings woven by people of the Tyrol, a section of Austria and Germany. Made of local wool in a deep olive green color, sometimes with the addition of camel's hair, these fabrics are used for winter sportswear.

loom   A mechanical device on which cloth is woven. Looms may be hand-operated, now used mostly for crafts, or automated for use in the textile manufacturing industry.

madras (mah-drass')   Fabric woven in a variety of structural patterns, e.g., stripes, cords, plaids, dobby, and jacquard, from cotton or cotton blends, usually made with combed yarns and mercerized (see SPECIAL FINISHES DEFINED: MERCERIZATION). Stripes and plaids are yarn-dyed and may bleed. Sometimes this is considered an asset, as it tends to soften the sharp plaid effect. Such fabrics are called **bleeding madras.** *Der.* Imported from the city of Madras in India.

maline (mah-leen')   **1.** Extremely fine, soft silk, rayon, or cotton net with hexagonal holes used primarily for millinery. Sometimes used over feathers on hats to keep them in place.

marquisette (mar-kee-set')   Fine, transparent, netlike fabric with good durability. Made with cotton, silk, or synthetic yarns in the LENO WEAVE (see under WOVEN FABRICS DEFINED), which prevents the crosswise yarns from slipping.

matelassé (mat-lass-ay')   Luxurious fabric with a blistered or embossed effect made on the JACQUARD or DOBBY loom (see under WOVEN FABRICS DEFINED) in a double-cloth weave. Front and back of cloth are actually separate fabrics fastened together with extra crepe yarns that form the raised pattern. Genuine matelassé will not become flat looking, as the raised portion is woven in and is quite different from an inexpensive embossed design (see SPECIAL FINISHES DEFINED: EMBOSSING). Made from many different fibers. Cotton may have a quilted effect, others a blistered effect. *Der.* French, "cushioned or padded." Also spelled *matellassé.*

melton   Heavy, durable, coating fabric that looks somewhat like wool broadcloth and has a hand similar to felt. Originally made of heavy woolen yarns or wool crosswise and cotton lengthwise yarns. Now made in combinations including manufactured fibers. Compactness of the fabric makes it warm and protective against wind penetration. *Der.* Named for Melton Mowbray, a town in Leicestershire, England.

mesh   Knitted or woven fabric in an open weave, such as LENO (see under WOVEN FABRICS DEFINED), producing a net or a screenlike effect.

Also see KNITTED FABRICS DEFINED: MILANESE KNIT.

metallic cloth   Any type of fabric made with metallic yarns or using metallic yarns in the crosswise direction and other yarns lengthwise. Formerly yarns such as silver tarnished, but now they may be coated with a fine film of tarnish-resistant polyester.

moiré (mwa-ray')   Stiff, heavy-ribbed fabric with a watered effect that is made of silk or manufactured fibers. The design is applied with heated rollers that flatten some of the heavy crosswise yarns, thus changing the light reflection. The pattern is not permanent on silk, but is permanent if made with heat-sensitive fibers. *Der.* French, "watered."

moleskin fabric   Durable cotton fabric with a suedelike nap in a satin weave made with coarse cotton yarns and a large number of crosswise yarns. Fabric should be called *moleskin fabric* to distinguish it from the fur by the same name. Used for sportswear and work clothes. *Der.* Arabian, *molequin,* "old fabric."

mousseline   Transparent, lightweight fabric made in the plain weave and similar to chiffon. Often made of silk.

muslin   Plain-weave cotton or cotton-blend fabric made in many weights from very fine and sheer to coarse and heavy. Higher qualities have combed, mercerized yarns (see SPECIAL FINISHES DEFINED: MERCERIZATION) and may be either dyed or printed. Such fabrics are lustrous, long-wearing, washable, and soft to the touch. Coarser qualities have carded yarns, may have a variety of construction counts, and are used for sheets and pillowcases.

nacré velvet (nah-cray')   Velvet fabric with an iridescent or changeable effect caused by using one color yarn for the background and another color for the pile. Used for evening wear.

narrow fabric   Any nonelastic fabric such as tape, ribbon, or webbing, not more than 12″ wide, woven on narrow looms with selvages on both sides. Bias binding and seam binding are not included in this classification.

organdy   Light sheer cotton fabric with a permanently crisp feel. If made of manufactured fibers, it is crease resistant; if made of natural fibers it will wrinkle. Made in an open weave of fine, high-quality combed yarns, the fabric may be dyed, printed, or embroidered. Used for dresses, collars, cuffs, millinery, aprons, interfacing, and neckwear.

organza   Lightweight, thin, transparent fabric that is stiff and wiry. Made in the PLAIN WEAVE (see under WOVEN FABRICS DEFINED) of manufactured filament or silk yarns, this fabric has a tendency to crush, but is easy to press. Used for millinery, trimmings, and neckwear.

ottoman   Heavy luxurious fabric with broad, flat, crosswise ribs or wales. Made from silk, acetate, rayon, cotton, or wool with crosswise cord yarns of cotton. Lengthwise yarns are finer and more are used so that they cover the crosswise yarns completely on both sides.

oxford cloth   Men's shirting fabric made in a basket weave, sometimes 2 × 2 and sometimes 4 × 2. Yarns may be all combed or all carded with crosswise yarns coarser than lengthwise. Better grades are mercerized (see SPECIAL FINISHES DEFINED: MERCERIZATION). The fabric may be bleached, dyed, have yarn-dyed stripes, or small fancy designs. *Der.* Originally produced by a Scottish firm along with fabrics labeled Yale, Harvard, and Cambridge, which are no longer important.

panne velvet   (pan-ay′) VELVET (see under WOVEN FABRICS DEFINED) that has had the PILE (see under WOVEN FABRICS DEFINED) pressed down in one direction, giving it a glossy appearance. Originally made with wool or silk pile and raw silk ply yarns; later with silk ground and flattened rayon pile.

paper taffeta   Crisp lightweight TAFFETA fabric (see under WOVEN FABRICS DEFINED).

peau de soie   (po de swah′) Heavyweight satin with a fine filling ribbed effect on the reverse side made of silk or manufactured fibers. Piece-dyed and given a dull luster—better grades are reversible. Used for shoes, dresses, evening gowns, and wedding dresses. *Der.* French, "skin of silk."

percale   Plain-weave, lightweight fabric made in a great variety of qualities. Originally made of cotton, better qualities now may also use blended yarns of polyester staple with the cotton. Finest qualities are high count and made with combed yarns. Other percales are of low count, made of carded yarns, and sized to add body to the fabric. All types may be dyed or printed.

pile   Cut or uncut loops of yarns that stand erect on fabric to form all or part of the fabric surface. Either length-
pile fabric

wise or crosswise yarns can be used to produce this thick soft surface. May be uncut as in TERRYCLOTH or cut as in VELVET, VELVETEEN, and CORDUROY (see under WOVEN FABRICS DEFINED).

piqué   (pee-kay′) group of durable fabrics characterized by corded effects either lengthwise or crosswise. *a)* plain piqués in the United States are made with lengthwise cords. **Pinwale piqué** is a variation with smaller ribs. *b)* Piqués made in England have cords in the crosswise direction. *c)* **Waffle piqué** is made in a HONEYCOMB pattern (see under WOVEN FABRICS DEFINED). *d)* **Birdseye piqué** has a diamond-shaped pattern woven in dobby pattern. *e)* **Embroidered piqué** is plain piqué that has been embroidered with the SCHIFFLI MACHINE (see under EMBROIDERIES AND SEWING STITCHES: ROLE AND FUNCTION OF EMBROIDERIES AND SEWING STITCHES IN ACCESSORIES). All types are used for handbags and neckwear.

plain weave   A basic weave in which one crosswise yarn passes over the first lengthwise yarn, then under the next lengthwise yarn and continues across the width of the fabric to pass over one yarn and under another. In the next row, the crosswise yarn passes under the first lengthwise yarn, then over the next lengthwise
plain weave diagram

yarn, and so on. In the third row, the pattern of the first row is repeated. The resulting interlacing of yarns is like a checkerboard pattern.

plissé   (plee-say′) Lightweight cotton with a pebbly surface given a creped appearance by applying caustic soda with rollers, thereby causing the fabric to shrink in those areas, while the untreated areas remain the same size. The result is a crinkled appearance. Pressing will remove the crinkle. Also known as *crinkle crepe* and *plissé crepe.*

polished cotton   Most any plain-weave cotton fabric, e.g., SATEEN, CHINTZ (see under WOVEN FABRICS DEFINED), given a glazed finish to make it shiny and lustrous. Some finishes are permanent, particularly those of the resin type. If the finish is made by starching and ironing with a hot roller, it is not permanent.

pongee (pon-gee′) Light- to medium-weight rough-textured silk fabric made from wild silk and usually left in natural color. Originally hand-loomed in China, later machine made. Warp yarns are finer than the filling, causing a slight rib formed by the uneven texture of the yarn. *Der.* Chinese, *penchi,* "woven at home."

poodle cloth Knitted or woven fabric characterized by small curls over the entire surface. Similar to ASTRAKAN fabric (see under WOVEN FABRICS DEFINED but made with looser curls like the coat of a poodle dog.

poplin Medium-weight durable fabric with crosswise rib effect made with cotton or blends of cotton and polyester. Better qualities use combed yarns in both directions. A water-resistant or water-repellent finish may also be applied to fabrics used for rainwear.

rep Fabric with closely spaced crosswise ribs that may be made from a variety of fibers. Used for neckties and women's wear.

ribbon Long narrow strip of silk, cotton, or rayon woven with selvages on both sides. Also made of acetate and then sliced into narrow strips with heated knives that fuse the edges. Used mainly for trimming and for tying hair. Made in a variety of weaves: *a)* cross-ribbed, called *grosgrain* (see under WOVEN FABRICS DEFINED); *b)* with looped edges, called *picot; c)* cut-pile surface, or *velvet* (sometimes satin-backed); *d)* satin, very narrow pink or blue satin is called *baby ribbon.*

sailcloth Durable canvas fabric made in a rib weave. When made in medium weight in cotton or a cotton blend, it is used for sportswear.

sateen Smooth glossy cotton fabric made in the SATEEN WEAVE (see under WOVEN FABRICS DEFINED: SATIN WEAVE) with floating crosswise yarns on the right side, given a lustrous finish, and used mainly for linings.

satin Smooth lustrous silk fabric woven with floating yarns in the warp in many variations: *a)* woven with a crepe back, and called *crepe-back satin* (see under WOVEN FABRICS DEFINED); *b)* finished to be rather stiff in texture and called **panne satin;** *c)* finished with a dull nubbed surface (see TYPES OF YARNS DEFINED: NUB YARN) and a satin back and called **antique satin.** Usually made of filament yarns. *Der.* Name derived from *Zaytoun,* now Canton, China, from which fabrics were shipped in the Middle Ages.

satin weave A basic weave in which the lengthwise, and sometimes the crosswise yarns, float over five to eleven yarns before interlacing. As a result the surface has a smooth feel and a lustrous appearance. When the floats are in the crosswise direction, the fabric is called SATEEN (see under WOVEN FABRICS DEFINED) and this construction is sometimes called a **sateen weave.**

satin weave

seersucker Medium-weight fabric made with lengthwise crinkled stripes alternating with plain woven stripes. Puckering is achieved by releasing the tension at intervals on the lengthwise yarns. Effect is permanent and will not wash out.

serge (serj) Suiting fabric made in an even twill with worsted yarns. Occasionally some woolen yarn is used to provide greater softness. Generally piece-dyed and given a clear finish that becomes shiny with wear. Used for suits, skirts, and pants. *Der.* Latin, *serica,* "silk," indicating it was first a silk fabric; later Italian, *sergea,* "cloth of wool mixed with silk," probably appearing as early as the 12th c.

shantung (shan-tung′) Medium-weight fabric woven with irregular, elongated slubs (see TYPES OF YARNS DEFINED: SLUB YARN) in the crosswise direction caused by yarns of uneven diameter through-out. Originally made of TUSSAH silk (see NATURAL FIBERS DEFINED: SILK) yarn that varied in thickness, texture is now imitated with yarn of various fibers.

sharkskin **1.** Worsted fabric woven in a TWILL WEAVE (see under WOVEN FABRICS DEFINED) with alternating black-and-white yarns in both directions to give a grayed effect. Characteristic feature is the smooth, sleek, clear finish. **2.** Lightweight acetate (sometimes rayon) sharkskin uses filament yarns in a plain, basket, or sometimes jacquard weave to get a smooth sleek appearance. Usually made in white but sometimes dyed. Used for sportswear and uniforms. **3.** See LEATHERS: TYPES OF LEATHER DEFINED.

shetland Soft suiting fabric made of fine wool from Shetland sheep of Scotland. Usually woven in HERRINGBONE PATTERN (see under WOVEN

FABRICS DEFINED). The term refers to the type of wool used.

shoe cloth   Any fabric used in making fabric shoes, shoe linings, or any other part of the shoe. SILK, COTTON, WOOL, and MANUFACTURED FIBERS are all used to make fabrics such as BROCADE, tapestry, slipper satin, FAILLE, NYLON MESH, CREPE, and SHANTUNG. Many of these fabrics are used to make white dyeable shoes. Better shoes are lined with leather, while drill and similar fabrics are used for less expensive shoes. (See definitions of various fabric types under WOVEN FABRICS DEFINED, GENERIC AND OTHER FABRICS DEFINED, and NATURAL FIBERS DEFINED).

silk illusion   Very fine net, similar to TULLE (see under WOVEN FABRICS DEFINED), used for wedding veils.

stretch woven   Woven fabric that has at least 20% stretch in either the lengthwise or crosswise direction or both. Stretch may be obtained by using elastic yarns or by using yarns that have been textured.

surah   Lightweight soft silky fabric made in a TWILL WEAVE (see under WOVEN FABRICS DEFINED) of silk or manufactured yarns. May be woven in yarn-dyed plaids, printed, or dyed in solid colors. Used for dresses, scarves, neckties, and blouses.

taffeta   (taf′-et-tah)   Crisp fabric with a fine, smooth surface made in the PLAIN WEAVE (see under WOVEN FABRICS DEFINED) with a small crosswise rib. Originally made in silk, now made in manufactured filament fibers. *Der.* Persian *tuftah,* "fine, plain woven silk fabric."

tapestry   Heavy fabric, usually with a pictorial design, woven of multicolored yarns on a Jacquard loom in imitation of handwoven tapestries. A heavy fabric, it is used mainly for shoes, bags, and handbags.

terrycloth   **1.** Fabric made in the pile weave with uncut loops and a background weave of plain or twill. Usually made in cotton but now also made from manfactured fibers. Sometimes woven in plaid, dobby, or jacquard patterns of two or more colors. May be yarn-dyed, bleached, piece-dyed, or printed. **2.** A similar pile weave fabric made by knitting, usually called *knitted terrycloth.*

ticking   Sturdy, durable fabric woven in a close SATIN WEAVE or a TWILL WEAVE (see under WOVEN FABRICS DEFINED) with soft filling yarns. Originally used for covering pillows and mattresses, now used for sport clothes.

tie silk   Broad term for fabrics used for making neckties and scarves. Usually distinguished by small designs or stripes and woven in narrower widths than other fabrics. Since neckties are now made of fabrics with all types of fibers, including cotton, polyester, and nylon, the term *tie fabrics* is more accurate.

tissue   Descriptive of lightweight, semitransparent fabric (e.g., tissue gingham, tissue taffeta).

transparent velvet   Lightweight velvet that reflects light, thereby changing color to be somewhat iridescent. Has excellent draping qualities. Usually made with rayon pile, and given a crush-resistant finish.

tulle   (tool)   Fine sheer net fabric made of silk, nylon, or rayon with hexagonal holes. Used unstarched for wedding veils and millinery, and starched for ballet costumes. In the 18th c., all hexagonal netlike fabrics were called by this name. *Der.* First made in 1768 in England by machine; in 1817, a factory was opened in the city of Tulle, France.

tweed   Rough textured fabrics made of coarse wool in yarn-dyed effects. Made in PLAIN, TWILL, or HERRINGBONE weave (see under WOVEN FABRICS DEFINED) in various weights. *Der.* Scotch, *tweed,* "twill," because they were at first handloomed in homes along the Tweed River in Scotland.

twill weave   Basic weave characterized by diagonal wales (raised lines) produced by staggering the points of intersection of lengthwise and crosswise yarns. Wales generally run
right-hand twill weave
upward from left to right, called **right-hand twill,** or from lower right to upper left, **left-hand twill.** Both make a firm, durable fabric.

velour   (ve-loor′)   Soft velvety thick fabric with a cut pile brushed in one direction. It may be made of various fibers and yarns. Originally a woven fabric, now made by either weaving or knitting.

velvet   A fabric with a short, closely woven pile created from extra lengthwise yarns. Usually the pile is cut to create a soft, rich texture, but sometimes patterns are created by cutting some of the pile yarns and not others.

velveteen Cut-pile cotton or cotton-blend fabric in which the pile is made with an extra crosswise yarn. The pile is not more than ⅛″ high and the most durable of these fabrics have twill woven background.

voile (voyle) Lightweight OPEN-WEAVE fabric (see under WOVEN FABRICS DEFINED) made of tightly twisted combed yarns that give it a crisp and wiry feel. Originally made only of cotton but now popular in blends of cotton and polyester.

waffle cloth/waffle pique Cotton fabric made in a honeycomb weave. See WOVEN FABRICS DEFINED: HONEYCOMB.

whipcord Medium- to heavyweight worsted fabric with a diagonal wale caused by the steep TWILL WEAVE (see under WOVEN FABRICS DEFINED). Yarns are hard-twisted and fabric is given a hard finish to make the weave very distinct. Also made of cotton, wool, man-made fibers, or blends.

KNITTED FABRICS

Knitting is the process of making a fabric, or an item of apparel, by the interlacing of loops either by machine or by hand. A crosswise row of loops is called a **course,** while a vertical row is called **wale.** A great variety of stitches and yarns may be used to give textured effects and surface interest. Two major types of knits are made on knitting machines. One is called a **weft knit;** the other is a **warp knit.**

welf knit

Weft knits are made by yarns that run horizontally across the fabric. In the simplest weft knit fabric, known as a **plain knit,** the front and the back of the fabric look different. Hand-knitted fabrics are always weft knits. If one loop is broken, a **run** will form. Many variations of weft knits can be made. Hosiery is made almost exclusively from weft knit fabrics.

warp knit

Warp knits are made so that the yarns interlace vertically, and at the same time yarns move within the fabric so that they interlace with several rows of stitches. As a result, these fabrics are more stable, do not stretch as much, and do not run. Gloves are frequently made from warp knit fabric.

Some types of warp knitting machines can make fabrics that look like lace or crochet.

KNITTED FABRICS DEFINED

double knit Knit fabric in which face and back of the fabric have a similar appearance. Made in a rib knit construction using double sets of needles, the resulting fabric is heavier, has greater dimensional stability, and less tendency to sag or lose its shape than single knit fabrics.

intarsia (in-tar′-sea-a) Decorative colored motifs knitted into a solid color fabric, giving an inlay effect. Patterns on both sides of fabric are identical.

interlock Knit made on a machine having alternate units of short and long needles. Thicker than plain rib knits with good lengthwise elasticity, firm texture, and less tendency to curl at the edges. Similar to JERSEY (see under KNITTED FABRICS DEFINED) but both the face and back of the fabric look alike.

jacquard (ja-kard′) Elaborately patterned knitted fabric produced on a knitting machine that makes a wide variety of stitches.

jersey Classification of knitted fabrics that are made in a plain stitch without a distinct rib. Originally made of wool but now composed of many natural and manufactured yarns, some textured. Also called *plain knit. Der.* From Isle of Jersey, off the coast of England, where it was first made.

knit corduroy Knitted fabric made to have the appearance of corduroy, a pile weave fabric.

knitted terrycloth A pile weave fabric made by knitting that is similar to woven TERRYCLOTH (see under WOVEN FABRICS DEFINED).

ottoman ribbed knit Double-knit fabric with a pronounced wide crosswise rib.

Milanese knit (mil′-en-aze) Machine-made warp knit with diagonal yarns at intervals giving run-resistant openwork effect.

purl knit A weft-knit fabric in which the knitting machine can form stitches on both the front and back of the fabric so that both sides of the fabric can have the same appearance.

raschel knit Type of warp knitting done on a special Raschel machine that can produce a wide variety of complex knit patterns, including lace-like effects.

rib knit Knitted fabric that shows alternate lengthwise rows of ribs and wales on both sides. More elastic, heavier, and durable than plain knitting.

simplex knit A reversible warp-knit, double-faced fabric with the same appearance on both sides. Used for gloves.

stretch-knit fabrics Fabrics knitted with textured or stretch yarns.

tricot (tree′-co) **1.** Warp-knit fabric made with two sets of yarns characterized by fine vertical WALES (see under KNITTED FABRICS DEFINED) on the face and crosswise ribs on the back. When made with one set of yarns, it is called **single-bar tricot. Two-bar tricot,** made with yarns crossing, is run-resistant. Also called *double warp tricot, glove silk.* **Three-bar tricot** has an open-work effect.

wale Knitting term for row of loops or stitches running lengthwise.

NONWOVEN FABRICS

Some fabrics are made by techniques other than weaving or knitting. Fabrics can also be made directly from fibers. One fabric made directly from fibers is felt. **Felt** is made from wool fibers, which have a unique structure with small, microscopic scales. When wool is subjected to heat, moisture, and pressure, the fibers shrink, and these scales become entangled, holding the fibers together. Felt is often used in making hats and other headwear.

After manufactured fibers came into widespread use in the post–World War II period, industrial processes were developed that make it possible to hold fibers together by using heat or chemicals or both. A common use for these nonwoven fabrics is as supporting fabrics in handbags, in headwear, and belts.

Some traditional methods of fabric construction that differ from weaving or knitting use knotting or other forms of interlacing of yarns to create fabrics. One such technique is used to make lace. See LACE as a separate topic under COMPONENTS OF ACCESSORIES.

NONWOVEN FABRICS DEFINED

batting Matted sheets of fibers used in quilting or stuffing. Fibers used include cotton, wool, spun rayon, or FIBERFILL (see under NONWOVEN FABRICS DEFINED).

fiberfill Generic term for a material consisting of fluffy short fibers. Frequently made of polyester and used between two layers of fabric to make quilted fabrics.

bobbinet **1.** A machine-made net fabric with hexagonal meshes. See LACES AND BRAIDS: TYPES OF LACE DEFINED: BOBBINET.

crochet (kro-shay′) Fabric made from a continuous series of loops of yarn constructed by a single-hooked needle. Originally developed in the 16th c. as an inexpensive method of creating a lacelike fabric. Modern textile machinery can create fabrics that have the appearance of crochet.

fusible fabric Nonwoven fabric made up of some fibers that have a low melting point. When heat and pressure are applied, the heat-sensitive fibers melt and the fabric can bond to another fabric or surface.

macramé (mak′-rah-may) Two, three, four, or more strands of cord, string, or yarn knotted in groups to form patterns. Craft used by sailors as a pastime, producing belts and ornaments. Revived in early 1970s by young adults making neckwear, vests, belts, and other accessories. In 1980s, used for belts, handbags, and shoes. *Der.* Turkish *magramah,* "napkin" or "facecloth."

macramé
flat knot

stitch-bonded fabric Fabrics constructed by binding together yarns or fabric webs with stitches like those made in knitting. The earliest trademark name for this process is Malimo®.

Thinsulate® A 60% polyolefin, 40% polyester microfilament insulation providing warmth equal to down or polyester insulations of close to twice the thickness. Does not absorb water.

Ultrasuede® Registered trademark for luxury suedelike fabric made of 60% polyester and 40% nonfibrous urethane in a porous sheet material. Used in a wide variety of apparel.

MULTICOMPONENT FABRICS

Fabrics are sometimes made by combining several fabric structures. **Quilted fabric,** for example, consists of a fiber layer sandwiched between two layers of fabric and held together by hand or machine. **Electronic stitching** can also be done by using heat-sensitive fabrics and a machine that fuses the fabric layers. Among the multicomponent fabrics that may be found in accessories are these:

Gore-Tex® fabric Trademark owned by W. L. Gore and Associates Inc. for a porous membrane that repels water but allows for the passage of moisture vapor. This membrane is placed behind a woven fabric and is widely used in garments for outdoor sports.

laminated fabric A layered fabric structure in which the outer layer is joined to the backing fabric by either heat-sensitive foam or adhesive.

Naugahyde® Trademark of U.S. Rubber Co. for a fabric with a vinyl resin coating on the face and knitted fabric back. The knitted back gives stretch to the vinyl. Used for handbags, shoes, and rainwear.

ADDING COLOR AND DESIGN TO FABRICS

After they are finished and before they are put into a final product, fabrics will frequently have some color or design added. Some of the techniques used to decorate fabrics are discussed elsewhere in the *Encyclopedia.* See COMPONENTS OF ACCESSORIES: EMBROIDERIES AND SEWING STITCHES and OTHER DECORATIVE MATERIALS.

Solid color fabrics are generally created by dyeing. **Dyeing** is the coloring of fibers, yarns, fabrics, furs, and leather with natural or synthetic coloring agents, called dyes, that are relatively permanent. **Printing** is reproducing a color design on fabric either by mechanical means or by hand. The most common methods currently in use in the textile industry are **roller printing,** using as many as 16 engraved metal rollers, and **rotary screen printing,** using perforated, round, metal screens. Hand-printed designs that are often used in crafts include those made by **block printing** and **screen printing** (see under DESIGNS AND SURFACE EFFECTS DEFINED). A fabric-effect motif or a pattern achieved by weaving rather than surface treatment is known as a **structural design.** Designs may be achieved through weaving, using dyed or naturally colored yarns to create a specific effect such as a stripe or plaid or woven figure, and through the use of colored fibers.

DESIGNS AND SURFACE EFFECTS DEFINED

abstract print A pattern or motif not related to natural or real objects. May emphasize line, color, or geometric forms.
abstract print

African print Bold geometric designs inspired by some traditional African prints. Frequently carried out in browns, blacks, and whites.

allover print Print covering the entire surface of the fabric from selvage to selvage in a repeat design. Compare with DESIGNS AND SURFACE EFFECTS DEFINED: BORDER PRINT or PANEL PRINT.

American Indian print Bold, stylized, geometric designs from Native American sources carried out in bright colors.

animal print Designs imprinted on fabrics in imitation of fur of the leopard, giraffe, ocelot, tiger, or zebra.

apron checks A gingham fabric made in even checks of white and another color, designated as 4×4 or 8×8 according to number of yarns used in each check. Originally a fabric used for aprons, by extension, a type of check.

Art Deco print Small geometric prints, frequently outlined in black, inspired by *Exposition International des Arts Décoratifs et Industriels Modernes,* Paris, 1925; reintroduced in the late 1960s. *Der.* French, *art décoratif,* "decorative art."
Art Deco Designs

Art Nouveau print Designs emphasizing curved, waving lines; stylized natural forms of plants, animals, and women; and a strong sense of motion. Inspired by early-20th-c. French art movement called *Art Nouveau.* First revived in late 1960s and seen occasionally since. *Der.* French, *nouveau,* "new art."
Art Nouveau Designs

awning stripe   Wide even bands of one or more bright colors and white, woven or printed on coarse canvas. Formerly used for window awnings, now copied in lighter fabrics for sportswear.

Aztec print   Designs based on Mexican Indian geometric motifs in bright colors usually banded in black.

bandanna print (ban-dan′-nah)   Designs, usually in black and white on a red or navy-blue background in imitation of bandanna handkerchiefs. *Der.* Indian, *bandhnu,* "method of tie-dyeing cloth."

batik   A method of dyeing in which the pattern area is covered with wax and the fabric is placed in a dyebath where the uncovered areas take up the color. Additional colors can be added by selectively covering and uncovering areas of the cloth. Because the wax sometimes cracks during handling, dye leaks through these cracks, and fabrics often show fine lines or streaks in the patterns.

batik print (baa′-teek)   Designs, usually in dark blue, rust, black, or yellow, copied from Indonesian technique of painting with wax before dyeing.

batik print

bayadère stripe (by-yah-deer′)   Horizontal stripes of varying widths in brilliant colors of red, green, blue, and gold. Also called *gypsy* or *Romany stripes. Der.* Hindu, "dancing girl."

blazer stripe   Inch-wide bands of one or several colors alternating with white. *Der.* From striped patterns of some blazer jackets.

block printing   Method of hand-printing fabric by cutting separate wood or linoleum blocks for each color in relief, then inking and printing individual colored blocks.

bookbinder print   Designs copied from multicolored abstract, swirled, and woodgrain designs used formerly on endpapers of expensively bound books.

border print   Print designed so that one selvage forms a distinct border used at the hem of a dress or shirt, or worked into the garment in some other way.

burn-out/burnt-out   Adjective describing fabric or lace that has a patterned effect produced by using yarns of two different fibers and destroying all or part of one of the yarns. Chemicals that dissolve one of the fibers are printed onto the fabric in the design areas. A burn-out pattern effect may be produced on velvet by dissolving parts of the pile but leaving other pile areas and the ground intact.

calico print   Allover print usually of tiny naturalistic sprigs of flowers on a colored background of red, blue, yellow, or black.

calico print

candy stripe   Narrow bands of red on a white background, imitating peppermint candy sticks.

chalk stripe   Narrow lines of white, widely spaced, frequently used on gray, navy, or black flannel.

changeable effect   An iridescent effect in fabric that is achieved by using lengthwise and crosswise yarns dyed different colors. Usually made in silk or lustrous manufactured fibers in fabrics such as TAFFETA (see under WOVEN FABRICS DEFINED) to achieve the most dramatic effect. Synonyms: *glacé* (glahs-ay′), *shot.*

check   A fabric design composed of alternate squares of colors in various sizes usually alternating with white. Design may be similar to checkerboard or any other block design that is geometrical and repeats regularly. A checked pattern may be woven or printed.

checkerboard checks   Even squares of two colors alternating to form a row. Succeeding rows alternate colors. *Der.* From resemblance to a checkerboard. Also called *even checks.*

chiné   See DESIGNS AND SURFACE EFFECTS DEFINED: WARP PRINT.

coin dots   See DESIGNS AND SURFACE EFFECTS DEFINED: DOTS.

discharge print   Design made on piece-dyed fabric by applying with copper rollers chemicals that dissolve and remove the dye in the design area. A white polka-dot design on a navy ground can be made in this manner.

dots   Round spots used as a pattern in regular rows or a random arrangement; e.g., **coin dots,** larger than a dime; **pin dots,** as small as the head of a pin.

double ombré stripe (om-bray′)   Stripes of two colors shaded from light to dark, usually run horizontally, either printed or woven.

duplex print   Fabric with same design printed on both sides to imitate a woven pattern.

even checks   See DESIGNS AND SURFACE EFFECTS DEFINED: CHECKERBOARD CHECKS.

express stripe   Twill weave fabric made with even stripes of blue and white running lengthwise. Originally used for janitors' uniforms, caps, and railroad workers' overalls. *Der.* From overalls worn by railroad workers.

fleur-de-lis (flur deh lee′) French stylized lily design used in heraldry and part of the coat-of-arms of France's former royal family. Often used in formal repeat designs.

fleur-de-lis

flocked print Design made by applying adhesive to fabric in a pattern and affixing tiny fibers. Frequently used to make border prints or flocked dotted Swiss.

floral print Any design using flowers in either a natural or stylized manner (e.g., a daisy, a rose, or sprigs of flowers arranged together in repeat design).

geometric print 1. Circles, oblongs, squares, triangles, or other geometrical forms used in a printed design. **2.** Print with background broken up by using a repeat design of rectangular forms then imprinting another design within each unit.

geometric print #1

gingham checks Yarn-dyed checks of 1″, ½″, ⅛″, or ¹⁄₁₆″ made in a color alternating with white. Also called *apron check.*

granny print Small floral print similar to a calico print. *Der.* Named after prints formerly worn by grandmothers for housedresses at the turn of the 20th c.

gun club checks A three-color, double-check design consisting of a large check over a smaller one used in wool and worsted fabrics.

gypsy stripe See DESIGNS AND SURFACE EFFECTS DEFINED: BAYADÈRE STRIPES.

hairline stripe See DESIGNS AND SURFACE EFFECTS DEFINED: PINSTRIPES.

hand-blocked print See PRINTS, STRIPES, AND CHECKS: BLOCK PRINTING.

hand-painted print Not a print at all but a pattern painted directly on fabric.

hand-screened print See DESIGNS AND SURFACE EFFECTS DEFINED: SCREEN PRINTING.

harlequin checks (har′-leh-kin) Check made of medium-sized, diamond-shaped, colored motifs alternating with white.

heather effect Appearance of fabric achieved by blending dyed fibers with white fibers to produce a mottled appearance. First made in lavender tones similar to the flowers of the heather plant, but now made in many different colors.

hickory stripe Lengthwise stripes, usually blue and white with the blue two times the size of the white, woven in a denim-type fabric. Fancy hickory stripes are white stripes of varying widths on a blue ground. Also called *Liberty stripes* and *victory stripes.* Originally used for janitors' uniforms and workclothes, now used for sportswear.

hound's-tooth/houndstooth checks Irregularly colored ½″ to 2″ checks comprised of a square with points at two corners. Consists of colored checks alternating with white, produced by a yarn-dyed twill weave. *Der.* From resemblance to pointed dog's tooth.

ikat (ee′-kat) **1.** A method of yarn dyeing in which selected areas are knotted or tied so the dye will not penetrate. **2.** Fabrics woven from ikat yarns. The resulting design has a blurry or indistinct appearance. *Der.* Malayan, *mengikat,* "to tie, bind, knot, or wind around." Also see DESIGNS AND SURFACE EFFECTS DEFINED: WARP PRINT.

ikat fabric

Indian print May be a hand-blocked print or a batik as long as it originates in Madras or another city of India. Frequently made with inferior dye that *bleeds* or runs when the fabric is washed.

indigo Blue dye made since earliest time from stems and leaves of *Indigofera tinctoria, Indigofera anil,* and woad plants; a similar synthetic dye now made from coal tar.

iridescent fabric Any fabric made with yarns of one color in the lengthwise direction and another color crosswise. Reflects both colors in the light, e.g., CHAMBRAY (see under WOVEN FABRICS DEFINED).

Japanese print Usually a scenic print featuring pagodas, foliage, and mountains, in a repeat design.

jungle print Designs using animals found in the jungle, e.g., leopards, tigers, and lions.

kente cloth Fabric with woven or printed designs characterized by narrow, brightly colored bands with randomly placed geometric patterns. These fabrics are derived from traditional silk fabrics and their designs are made by the Asante people of Ghana.

kente cloth

COMPONENTS OF ACCESSORIES: TEXTILES IN ACCESSORIES

kente cloth print Fabric printed to imitate woven KENTE CLOTH (see under DESIGNS AND SURFACE EFFECTS DEFINED).

Laura Ashley® print Provincial, small floral designs, typically Victorian, copied from antique designs, printed on cotton fabrics and wallpapers. Originally used for home furnishings, now used for clothing as well. Trademarked by Laura Ashley of England.

Liberty® print Trademark of Liberty, London, for wide range of printed fabrics. The best known are small multicolored floral designs.

medallion print Repeat round or oval design sometimes connected with realistic swags of foliage.

mixture Fabric woven with yarns composed of fibers dyed different colors. Fabric may also be made of yarns that vary in luster.

mola appliqué (ap-plee-kay) A technique for making decorative textiles, associated with the Cuna Native American women of Panama and Columbia, that are created by tacking together two or more layers of fabric of the same size in different colors. Designs are cut out of one or more of the uppermost layers to expose brightly colored lower layers. The edges of the cut fabric are turned under and stitched down to prevent raveling.

mosaic print Print introduced in early 1970s made by tiny square blocks of color arranged in a manner imitating a Byzantine mosaic.

naturalistic print Representation of flowers, shrubs, trees, and birds, arranged in a realistic manner in a repeat design.

ombré stripe Bands of color either woven or printed, usually composed of monochromatic tones of one color running from light to dark.

Op Art print Design, basically geometric, in which lines are "bent" or "warped" to create an optical illusion, (e.g., a checkerboard design formed with some curved lines and squares not all of equal size). *Der.* Became popular in 1964 after an exhibit of Op Art paintings op art print at the Museum of Modern Art in New York City.

paisley print Allover design featuring a shape like a tear drop, rounded at one end and with a curving point on the other. Frequently features rich colors with bold designs outlined in 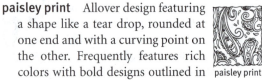 paisley print

delicate tracery and swirls. A printed version of the pattern used in a PAISLEY SHAWL (see under ACCESSORIES: SHAWLS, SCARVES, AND HANDKERCHIEFS: TYPES OF SHAWLS DEFINED).

pajama checks DIMITY (see under WOVEN FABRICS DEFINED) woven with coarser yarns at intervals in both warp and filling to form a checked design.

panel print A large design intended to be used in one length, without repeating (e.g., one panel used for front—one for back of a dress). Usually made with hand-screened process and expensive.

patchwork print A print designed to mimic a patchwork quilt design. Design is printed on fabric, not made with "patches."

pencil stripe Vertical stripes as wide as a pencil line, with wider stripes of background color in between.

photographic print Prints made by coating a photosensitive dye on fabric, then printing a design from a photographic negative.

pin dots See DESIGNS AND SURFACE EFFECTS DEFINED: DOTS.

pincheck Check made of very tiny squares.

pinstripe Very narrow stripes the width of a straight pin woven or printed in vertical stripes placed close together, either white stripes on dark ground or vice versa. Also called *hairline stripes.*

psychedelic print (sy-keh-dell'-ik) Unconventional designs done in extremely vibrant, full-intensity colors (e.g., chartreuse, fuchsia, and purple in bizarre combinations forming flowing patterns on the fabric). *Der.* Inspired by the hallucinations had when under the influence of the drug LSD.

Pucci print (poo'-chee) Design introduced by Emilio Pucci, an Italian couturier, that is highly original and hard to imitate. Pattern is abstract and composed mainly of brilliant unusual color combinations outlined in black, usually printed on knitted fabric. White space is also utilized but the distinguishing feature is the use of exciting and unusual color combinations. *Der.* Prints are inspired by medieval and late Renaissance designs still used in flags and costumes of the famous Palio in Siena.

rainbow stripe Full range of the spectrum hues arranged in bands on the fabric; a multistriped effect made by weaving or printing.

regimental stripe Wide, even-colored stripes on a plain dark background. Used for men's tie fabrics. *Der.* Taken from insignia on British military uniforms in which colors of stripes identify the regiments.

resist printing Method of printing fabric by first applying design to fabric with chemical paste that will not take dye, and then dying the fabric. When chemical is removed, design is left in white against a colored background, e.g., white polka dot on navy ground.

Roman stripe Horizontal stripes, varied in size and color, grouped together with no contrast in background.

Romany stripe SEE DESIGNS AND SURFACE EFFECTS DEFINED: BAYADÈRE STRIPES.

satin stripe Satin-woven stripes alternating with bands of plain fabric.

screen printing Printing process in which a design for each color is etched on separate pieces of pure dye silk or manufactured fiber enclosed in wooden frames. Fabric to be printed is stretched on a long table; each screen is placed individually over the fabric; and dye, applied with a squeegee, is pushed through the etched sections. Process produces especially vibrant colors and unusual designs. When made using silk fabric, called *silk screen printing.*

shadow stripe Indistinct narrow stripes, all in tones of one color family, woven vertically (e.g., navy, light blue, and gray-blue used together).

shepherd's check Small checked patterned fabric usually made of black and white or of white and another color. Made in a TWILL WEAVE (see under WOVEN FABRICS DEFINED) of fine- to medium-quality yarns. Originated from a checked length of fabric about 4 yards long and 1½ yards wide worn in a draped manner by Scottish shepherds in Scotland. Also called *shepherd's plaid.*

shibori (she-bor´-ee) Japanese fabric ornamentation technique created by stitching gathers into fabrics before dyeing. After dyeing the stitched areas may be released to display complex patterns in the areas protected by the stitching.

stenciled print Design made by using cardboard or metal cutouts over fabric, spraying paint or roller printing over them. The uncovered portions absorb the color and form the pattern.

stripes Bands of color or texture of varying widths, making a design in a fabric, either printed on or woven in; may go in horizontal, vertical, or diagonal direction.

stylized print Ideas presented in an abstract, rather than naturalistic, manner, reducing the objects to a design.

tablecloth check Large checkerboard check, 1–3″ in size, usually in red or blue alternating with white. *Der.* Originally used for tablecloths.

tattersall Fabric with an over-check, approximately ½″ square made, with colored lines in both directions, on a white or contrasting ground. Also called *tattersall checks.* Sometimes called *tatersall plaid. Der.* Named after Richard Tattersall, English horseman, founder of Tattersall's London Horse Auction Mart, established in 1776.

ticking stripes Narrow woven dark blue stripes, sometimes spaced in pairs, on a white ground, which is made in a TWILL WEAVE (see under WOVEN FABRICS DEFINED). *Der.* Originally a heavy fabric called *ticking* used to cover mattresses, now used for sport clothes and copied in lighter weights and other colors for clothing.

tie-dyed print Handmade print created by gathering the fabric and tying at intervals, then immersing in dye that does not penetrate the tied areas. When untied, reveals a pattern of irregular designs. Method originated in Dutch East Indies and became popular as a handicraft in the United States beginning in late 1960s. Used on pants, knit shirts, dresses, and even furs. Also imitated commercially by other methods. Called *bandanna* in India.

wallpaper print Tiny floral stripes alternating with plain colored stripes, frequently of pastel colors. *Der.* Made in imitation of 19th-c. wallpaper.

warp print Design printed on warp yarns before fabric is woven, producing a watered effect with fuzzy edges. Also called *chiné* and *ikat.*

warp print

windowpane check Dark horizontal and vertical bars crossing over light background, giving effect of a window divided into small panes. Also called *windowpane plaid.*

yarn-dyed Describing fabric that is woven or knitted from yarns dyed before the fabric is constructed.

SPECIAL FINISHES

At some point during their manufacture, textiles may be given special finishes. A **finish** is a chemical or mechanical process that affects the appearance, hand, or performance of textile fibers, yarns, or fabrics. Finishes are generally applied during the manufacturing process. Some of the finishes that are frequently applied to fabrics used in accessories are listed below.

SPECIAL FINISHES DEFINED

brushing   Pulling up fibers to the surface of knitted fabrics to create a soft texture or nap.

coated fabrics   Fabrics sometimes made non porous and water repellent through coating with various substances, such as lacquer, varnish, pyroxlin, rubber, polyethylene, or plastic resin.

durable finish   Any fabric finish that will withstand laundering, drycleaning, and wear for a reasonable period of time.

durable press (DP)   The name given to a special finish that provides garments with shape retention, durable pleats and creases, durably smooth seams, and wrinkle resistance during use and after laundering. Some of the first fabrics that did not require ironing were called **drip-dry** fabrics.

embossing   A process to produce a raised design or pattern in relief on fabrics by passing the cloth between hot, engraved rollers that press the design into the fabric. In heat-sensitive fabrics, embossing is permanent. In other fabrics, resin finishes are used to give fabrics a durable effect. Velvet or plush fabrics are embossed either by shearing or by pressing certain areas flat.

flame resistant finish   Applied chemical finish that enables fabrics to resist burning. Fabrics treated with such finishes will burn only when placed in a flame, but will self-extinguish rapidly when the source of ignition is removed.

flocking   Method of applying short fibers overall or in a design by first printing fabric with an adhesive and then causing minute pieces of fibers to adhere to the design. When a design is produced, the method is known as **flock printing**.

fulled wool   Woolen or worsted fabrics that have been subjected to the finishing process called fulling, which consists of compressing or shrinking the fabric by use of heat, moisture, pressure, and friction to produce a dense appearance somewhat like felt. Contemporary fashion promotions often use the terms *boiled wool* or *felted wool* to refer to these fabrics.

glazing   Process of pressing fabric with heated rollers to give it a high gloss. Finish may be permanent or nonpermanent.

heat setting   By applying heat and pressure, this process is used to set permanent pleats or creases in fabrics made of manfactured fibers such as NYLON, POLYESTER, and ACETATE. See under TEXTILES IN ACCESSORIES: GENERIC AND OTHER MANUFACTURED FIBERS DEFINED).

mercerization   Finishing process with caustic soda applied to cotton yarn, fabric, or thread, which increases luster, strength, and dyeability. *Der.* Named for John Mercer, calico printer in Lancashire, England, who discovered this process in 1844.

mothproofing   A special finish used on wool fabrics or clothing to make them resistant to moths. Can also be purchased in a spray can for use at home.

napping   Brushing the surface of one or both sides of a fabric constructed from loosely twisted yarns to produce a fuzzy appearance and soft texture. The surface texture is called the **nap** and may be brushed in one direction.

Scotchgard®   Registered trademark of Minnesota Mining and Manufacturing for a fluoride-based finish used on fabrics to repel grease and water stains.

shearing   Process of clipping nap (see SPECIAL FINISHES DEFINED: NAPPING) of fabric to desired length.

shrinkage control   Fabrics woven and finished with processes that make them less likely to reduce their dimensions after washing and dry cleaning.

sizing   Nonpermanent finishing process applied particularly to cotton fabrics to increase weight, crispness, and luster by means of starch, gelatin, oil, and wax. When done at home or in a commerical laundry, the process is called **starching**.

sueding   Creating a nap on one or both sides of a knitted or woven fabric in order to imitate genuine *suede*.

water resistant/repellent Describing clothing of fabric or leather treated to shed water easily and dry quickly—not entirely WATERPROOF (see under SPECIAL FINISHES DEFINED).

waterproof Describing clothing, usually of rubber, plastic, or heavily coated fabric, that cannot be penetrated by water, especially boots. Also see SPECIAL FINISHES DEFINED: WATER RESISTANT/ REPELLENT.

weighted silk/weighting Silk fabric having metallic salts, called weighting, added to it in the finishing process to give the fabric more body so that it drapes better. Since 1938, legislation has required that weighted silk must be identified if fabric has been weighted more than 10% for colors or 15% for black fabrics. Weighting was used in excessive quantities in many silk fabrics of the late 19th c. and early 20th c., which caused many of these fabrics to split and crack. This damage cannot be repaired or prevented. **Pure dye silk** has less than 10% (15% for black goods) weighting.

LACES *and* BRAIDS

HISTORY AND SIGNIFICANCE OF LACE AND BRAIDS TO FASHION

Lace is a decorative openwork fabric made by hand or machine by the looping, braiding, interlacing, knitting, or twisting of thread to form a pattern. Lace and embroidery are sometimes hard to distinguish. Indeed, lacemaking probably developed from CUTWORK EMBROIDERY (see EMBROIDERIES AND SEWING STITCHES: TYPES OF EMBROIDERY DEFINED) in the 15th c. and was an important industry for centuries. Distinctive techniques and patterns that developed in cities and regions were named for the locality. Lace became very popular for collars, cuffs, and ruffs in the 16th c. and was fashionable in the 17th and 18th c. for trimmings and flounces. By the early 19th c., John Heathcoat had invented the bobbinet machine, which made net. This net was used as a background for embroidered and appliquéd laces. Soon after this, John Leavers established a factory in England to make lace by machine. The first lace factory in the United States was opened in 1818 in Medway, Massachusetts. Machine-made lace was used for shawls, parasols, collars, cuffs, and trimmings. In the 20th and 21st c., lace and lacelike fabrics are frequently used as a trimming for accessories and may also be used in gloves, scarves, hosiery, and veils. Handmade lace is now rare, being made mostly for souvenirs and for special-occasion clothing such as high-priced wedding veils.

Braid is yarn, fabric, rope, or straw plaited or woven into a narrow strip of flat or tubular fabric. It is used as trimming or binding, or for outlining lace and embroidery. Various types of braid are used to trim headwear, handbags, gloves, and other accessories. It can also be used to make hats, handbags, and belts.

ANATOMY OF LACE

There are various elements that may be present in a piece of lace. The **ground** is the background as opposed to the designs it supports or surrounds. Two types of ground structure are used: (1) net or mesh, and (2) **bars,** also called **brides,** that may be used to join motifs. Heavier outline threads are called **cordonnets** (kor-dohn-ay′). **Picots** (pee′-koh) are small loops along the edge of lace. The fancy stitches used in needlepoint and bobbin lace for filling enclosed spaces are called **jours** (zhur).

Lace is classified according to the method used to produce it. Although today making lace by hand is practiced by only a few, the modern terminology derives from its handmade origins. **Needlepoint** or **point lace** was handmade by outlining the design with a single linen or cotton thread on parchment paper, holding it with tiny

brides ground
cordonnet
needlepoint lace

stitches to be cut away later, then working the background entirely with a needle. **Pillow** or **bobbin lace** was handmade with small bobbins holding each yarn. A paper design was placed on a small pillow, pins inserted, and yarns interlaced around the pins to form a

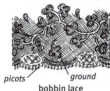

picots ground
bobbin lace

pattern. Designs were also made separately and appliquéd to a handmade net. **Tatting,** a knotted lace, usually narrow, was made by winding thread on a small hand-held shuttle with the fingers making small loops and patterns. Used for edging lingerie, handkerchiefs, etc., this type of trim generally appears on craft items rather than manufactured products. **Macramé** (mak´-rah-may) is a technique in which two, three, four, or more strands of cord, string, or yarn are knotted in groups to form patterns. It is sometimes used to make lacelike fabrics.

macramé
flat knot

A number of lacelike fabrics are also made by warp knitting machines (see TEXTILES IN ACCESSORIES: KNITTED FABRICS: WARP KNITS). These are called Raschel knits, after the name of the machine that makes them. Schiffli embroidery (see EMBROIDERIES AND SEWING STITCHES: ROLE AND FUNCTION OF EMBROIDERIES AND STITCHING IN ACCESSORIES: SCHIFFLI MACHINE) can also be made to look very much like lace.

TYPES OF LACE DEFINED

Lace is used as a component of relatively few accessories; therefore, this is a somewhat abbreviated listing of the most commonly encountered types. For a more extensive listing of lace definitions, see *The Fairchild Dictionary of Fashion* and *Fairchild's Dictionary of Textiles*.

Alençon lace (ah-lan-sohn´) Fine handmade or machine-made needlepoint lace with solid designs on sheer net ground outlined with CORDONNET (see under ANATOMY OF LACE). First made in 1665 and called *point de France,* later in 1678 called *point d'Alençon. Der.* Named for town of Alençon, France.

allover lace Term for wide lace with repeat patterns extending entire width of fabric. Lace purchased by the yard used for clothing.

antique lace Darned bobbin lace made by hand with heavy linen thread on knotted square net with large irregular or square openings. Also called *araneum, opus araneum,* and *spider work.*

appliqué lace (app-lee-kay´) Type of lace made by attaching previously made bobbin or needlepoint handmade designs to machine-made mesh ground. Also called *point d'appliqué.*

baby lace Any narrow, fragile, dainty lace used to trim infants' garments (e.g., baby caps and baptismal gowns).

Battenberg lace Lace made by applying a coarse linen Battenberg tape to the design and connecting the tape with decorative linen stitch by hand or machine. Similar to RENAISSANCE LACE (see under TYPES OF LACE DEFINED), but coarser.

beading Narrow slotted lace or embroidered bands, through which ribbon was pulled.

beggar's lace Inexpensive type of TORCHON LACE (see under TYPES OF LACE DEFINED). Also called *bisette.*

Belgian lace Classification for PILLOW LACES (see under ANATOMY OF LACE) with machine-made grounds from Belgium, including VALENCIENNES, BRUSSELS, and MECHLIN LACES (see under TYPES OF LACE DEFINED).

Binche (bansh) Flemish bobbin lace similar to VALENCIENNES (see under TYPES OF LACE DEFINED) with scroll floral patterns and snowflakes sprinkled on net ground. *Der.* Named for town of Binche, Belgium.

bisette (bee-set´) Inexpensive, narrow, coarse bobbin lace of TORCHON type (see under TYPES OF LACE DEFINED), made in France since 17th c. Same as *beggar's lace.*

blonde lace Fine French bobbin lace with floral pattern on net ground, originally made of unbleached Chinese silk in Bayeux, Caen, and Chantilly; later bleached and dyed black or colors.

bobbinet (bob-in-ett´) Mesh fabric base for lace with hexagonal holes made by hand or machine.

Bohemian lace Bobbin lace characterized by tapelike designs on net ground. Originally handmade in Bohemia from old Italian patterns, now made by machine.

bourdon lace (boor´-dohn) Machine-made net lace with cord outlining pattern and outer edge.

Breton **1.** Lace made by embroidering with colored yarns on net, rather than weaving design, in imitation of ALENÇON LACE (see under TYPES OF LACE DEFINED). **2.** Net fabric with larger holes than Brussels net.

bridal lace Contemporary industry term for lace used to make a wedding dress, for trimming, or for the veil.

Bruges lace (broozh) Fine GUIPURE (see under TYPES OF LACE DEFINED) tape lace of bobbin-type similar to DUCHESSE (see under TYPES OF LACE DEFINED), but coarser. *Der.* Named for city of Bruges, Belgium.

Brussels lace   Needlepoint lace with cords outlining designs made separately and appliquéd to fine net. Formerly handmade, now made by machine.

burn-out lace   Lace that has a patterned effect produced by using yarns of two different fibers and destroying all or part of one of the yarns. Chemicals that dissolve one of the fibers are printed onto the fabric in the design areas. A burn-out effect may be produced on velvet by dissolving parts of the pile but leaving other pile areas and the ground intact.

Carrickmacross lace   (Kar-ik′-ma-cross)   Two types of lace: *a)* GUIPURE type with design cut from fine cambric or lawn and embroidered with fine needlepoint stitches connected by brides, *b)* APPLIQUÉ type with designs embroidered, then superimposed on machine net. See cross-references under TYPES OF LACE DEFINED. *Der.* Made in or near Carrickmacross, Ireland, since 1820.

Chantilly lace   (shan-til′-ee or shon-tee-yee′)   Delicate fragile-looking bobbin lace first made by hand in early 18th c., then later by machine. Has hexagonal mesh and a design of scrolls, branches, and flowers outlined with CORDONNETS (see under ANATOMY OF LACE). Made in white or black with a scalloped edge. Made in Caen and Bayeux during the last half of the 19th c. *Der.* Named for town of Chantilly, France, where it was first made.

Cluny lace   (kloo′-nee)   **1.** Coarse bobbin lace, similar to TORCHON (see under TYPES OF LACE DEFINED), usually made of heavy ivory-colored linen thread in wheel or paddle designs. **2.** Machine-made cotton lace of similar design.

Crete lace   Silk or linen bobbin lace usually made with geometrical designs on colored ground with colored chainstitch along the edge. Made in Crete.

crochet lace   Imitations of lace made by hand using the technique of crocheting in which a continuing series of loops of yarn is made with a single-hooked needle.

darned lace   Term applied to all filet-type lace made by pulling out groups of warps and fillings from fabric and inserting stitches with a needle. Background may also be reworked in buttonhole stitch. See TYPES OF LACE DEFINED: FILET LACE.

duchesse lace   (do-shes′)   Type of bobbin lace characterized by floral designs and a tapelike effect made with fine thread and much-raised work. Designs are made first, then connected by means of BRIDES or BARS (see under ANATOMY OF LACE). When joined together, it gives an allover effect with irregularly shaped spaces between the designs. Frequently handed down from one generation to the next for use on bridal dresses. Originally called *guipure de Bruges.*

Egyptian lace   Knotted lace frequently made with beads placed between meshes.

filet lace   (fil-ay′)   Hand-knotted lace with square holes frequently filled in with colored yarns in darning stitch. Also imitated by machine. Also called *darned filet lace.*

flouncing   Lace wider than edging lace, used for ruffles or trimmings, with one straight edge, the other scalloped. Usually made with one strong thread along straight edge that can be pulled to make gathers.

French lace   Machine-made lace fabrics in imitation of handmade French lace. Included are lingerie laces of the ALENÇON, CHANTILLY, VALENCIENNES types (see under TYPES OF LACE DEFINED.

gros point   (groh pwanh)   Venetian needlepoint lace made in large designs with high relief work. Also called *gros point de Venise* and *point de Venise.*

guipure   (ghee-poor′)   **1.** Heavy tape lace characterized by large showy patterns in needlepoint or bobbin fashion worked over a coarse mesh ground. **2.** Lace with designs that hold the pattern in place.

Honiton lace   (hon′-ih-ton)   Bobbin lace, similar to DUCHESSE, made in England with either motifs made first and appliquéd to machine-made net ground, or lace with round heavy motifs made of fine braid joined together like GUIPURE. See under TYPES OF LACE DEFINED. *Der.* From town of Honiton, Devonshire, England, where lace has been made since time of Queen Elizabeth I.

Irish crochet lace   Handmade lace characterized by raised designs of roses, shamrocks, or other patterns set against a coarse diamond-shaped mesh with heavy scalloped edge. Made in the chain stitch. Copied from needlepoint lace of Spain and

Venice and made in Ireland originally, but later spread to France, Belgium, China, and Japan.

knotted lace   Lace made by hand-tied knots to form a meshlike pattern, e.g., MACRAME and TATTING (see under ANATOMY OF LACE).

lacis (lay-sis)   Original term for square-mesh net that is darned or embroidered; a forerunner of lace.

Lille lace (lihl)   Finc bobbin lace of simple pattern outlined by heavy CORDONNETS (see under ANATOMY OF LACE) on net background with hexagonal holes, similar to MECHLIN LACE (see under TYPES OF LACE DEFINED). First made in 16th c. *Der.* From town of Lille, France.

maline lace (mah-leen')   Stiff bobbin lace with hexagonal mesh ground similar to MECHLIN LACE (see under TYPE OF LACES DEFINED).

Mechlin lace (meck'-lin)   Fragile bobbin lace with ornamental designs outlined with shiny CORDONNETS (see under ANATOMY OF LACE) and placed on hexagonal net ground. *Der.* From city of Mechlin, Belgium, where it was made.

Medici lace (med-ih'-chee)   French bobbin lace, combining closed and open work, one edge finished in scallops similar to, but finer than, CLUNY LACE (see under TYPES OF LACE DEFINED). Also spelled *Medicis* in France. *Der.* For royal Italian family in power from 14th to 18th c.

mignonette lace (min-yohn-et')   Narrow, light, fine, French bobbin lace made in linen thread and worked in small patterns on six-sided mesh ground that resembles tulle. Also called *blonde de fil.*

Milan lace (mee-lan')   Type of bobbin lace, originally made with flat, tapelike, circular designs connected with BRIDES or BARS (see under ANATOMY OF LACE). Popular in 17th c. and earlier made of gold, silver, and silk thread. Later, elaborate designs such as flowers, animals, and figures were used on a mesh ground and made in shaped pieces for collars. *Der.* From Milan, Italy. Also called *Milan point lace.*

Nottingham lace   **1.** Cotton lace made on Nottingham machine. Has a V-shaped mosaic-like pattern and is made in wide width. **2.** Originally a classification of machine-made laces made in Nottingham, England. Now used for laces made on Nottingham machines anywhere. *Der.* From place of origin.

Plauen lace (plow'-en)   Lace made by BURNOUT method—the design is embroidered by SCHIFFLI MACHINE (see under EMBROIDERIES AND SEWING STITCHES: ROLE AND FUNCTION OF EMBROIDERIES AND STITCHING IN ACCESSORIES) in a fiber different from the ground fiber, so when chemically treated, the ground dissolves, leaving lace. *Der.* From Plauen, Germany, where method was invented. Also called *St. Gall* and *Saxony* laces.

point lace   Shortened term for NEEDLEPOINT LACE (see under ANATOMY OF LACE).

point d'esprit (pwanh des-pree')   Open stitch used in GUIPURE lace (see under TYPES OF LACE DEFINED) with loops forming a pattern on a mesh ground.

point de Gaze (pwanh de gahz)   Belgian needlepoint lace with flower designs appliquéd on fine bobbin net, later cut away under the designs.

point de Paris (pwanh de pa-ree')   1. Narrow bobbin lace with hexagonal mesh and flat design. **2.** Machine-made lace similar to VAL LACE (see under TYPES OF LACE DEFINED) with design outlined with GIMP (see under TYPES OF BRAIDS DEFINED).

point de Venise (pwanh de ven-ees')   Type of Venetian needlepoint lace made with padded, raised cordonnets, and edges of designs trimmed with many picots. By late 17th c. also made in France and England. Also called *gros point de Venise.*

point noué (pwanh new-ay')   French lacemakers' term for buttonhole stitch, the basis of all needlepoint lace.

princesse lace (pranh-sess')   Imitation of DUCHESSE LACE (see under TYPES OF LACE DEFINED), done in a fine delicate manner with machine-made designs joined together or applied to net ground.

punto (puhn'-toe)   Term for Italian laces of 16th c. Also applied to Spanish laces. *Der.* Italian, "stitch."

Renaissance lace (ren-ay'-sonse)   Heavy flat lace made with tape laid out in pattern and joined together with a variety of stitches. First made in 17th c. and revived in late 19th c. for fancy work and called BATTENBERG LACE (see under TYPES OF LACE DEFINED).

reticella lace (reh-tee-chel' lah)   First needlepoint lace made by cutting and pulling out threads, then re-embroidering. Developed from cutwork and drawn work done on linen. Early patterns were geometrical and connected by PICOT BRIDES or BARS (see under ANATOMY OF LACE). First mentioned in 1493; very fashionable in 16th c. and widely imitated; still made in Italy. Also called *Greek lace, Greek point, Roman lace, Roman point,* and *Venetian guipure* (ghee-poor′).

rose-point lace   Venetian needlepoint, similar to VENETIAN POINT LACE (see under TYPES OF LACE DEFINED) but finer and with smaller motifs of flowers, foliage, and scrolls. Has more design repeats and connecting BRIDES or BARS (see under ANATOMY OF LACE) and is padded with buttonhole edges and a heavy cordonnet. Also called *point de rose.*

shadow lace   Machine-made lace that has flat surface and shadowy indistinct designs.

Spanish lace   **1.** Lace with a flat design of roses connected with a net background. Used for mantillas. **2.** Coarse pillow lace made with gold and silver threads.

spider work   Coarse open bobbin lace, same as ANTIQUE LACE. See under TYPES OF LACE DEFINED.

stretch lace   Machine-made lace of narrow or full width knitted with extra core yarns that are expandable. Used in narrow width for hems; wider widths used for girdles and foundations.

tambour work   See EMBROIDERIES AND SEWING STITCHES: TYPES OF EMBROIDERY DEFINED.

tape lace   A lace made of machine- or hand-made tape manipulated into a pattern either connected with bars or laid upon a net ground.

teneriffe lace   (ten-err-eef′)   Lace with wheel designs made by winding thread around the top of a small spool about 2½″ in diameter then working back and forth across the circle with a needle and thread. Made chiefly in the Canary Islands. Sometimes called *teneriffe work.*

toile   (twal)   Lace-makers' term for pattern of lace as distinguished from the background. *Der.* French, "cloth."

torchon lace   (tor′-shon)   Coarse inexpensive bobbin lace made of cotton or linen in simple fanlike designs, produced in Europe and China. Also made by machine. Also called BEGGAR'S LACE and BISETTE LACE (see under TYPES OF LACE DEFINED).

Valenciennes lace   (va-lahn′-see-enz)   Hand-made French fine bobbin lace first made in time of Louis XIV. Distinguished by small floral and bow designs made in one with the ground of square, diamond-shaped, or round mesh. *Der.* From Valenciennes, France.

val lace   Abbreviated form for VALENCIENNES (see under TYPES OF LACE DEFINED). This term usually applies to machine-made copies.

venetian lace   Many types of laces and embroidery from Venice including cutwork, drawn work, RETICELLA LACE (see under TYPES OF LACE DEFINED), raised point, and flat point.

venetian point lace   Heavy needlepoint lace with floral sprays, foliage, or geometrical designs made in high relief by buttonhole stitches with motifs connected with BRIDES or BARS and decorated with PICOTS (see ANATOMY OF LACE). Originally made in Venice; later made in Belgium and other countries. Also called *Venetian raised point.* Also see TYPES OF LACE DEFINED: POINT DE VENISE.

youghal lace   (yoo-gahl′)   Irish flat needlepoint lace inspired by Italian laces, particularly Venetian types. *Der.* First made in Youghal, County Cork, Ireland. Also called *Irish point lace.*

TYPES OF BRAIDS DEFINED

ball fringe   Type of braid with little fuzzy balls suspended at regular intervals.

coronation braid   Firmly woven mercerized cord braid, alternately wide and narrow, used to outline a pattern in embroidery or lace. Also used for COUCHING (see under EMBROIDERIES AND SEWING STITCHES: TYPES OF EMBROIDERY DEFINED).

diamanté braid   (dya-mahn-tay′)   Fake sparkling jewels, e.g., rhinestones, sewn on strips of fabric. *Der.* French, "set with diamonds."

embroidered braid   Tape with decorative motifs embroidered at regular intervals that is used for trimming.

galloon   **1.** Narrow tape or braid made of cotton, silk, rayon, wool, or manufactured fibers (sometimes with metallic threads added) used for trimming. **2.** Double-edged lace made in various widths. **3.** Double-edged wide braid frequently made of gold or metallic yarn with jewels sometimes spaced at regular intervals. *Der.* French, *galon,* "braid."

gimp Braid made from heavy core yarn arranged in a pattern and stitched in place to create a raised effect.

Hercules braid Worsted braid heavily corded from ½″ to 4″ in width; several widths often used together.

horsehair braid Permanently stiff coarse braid made originally from horsehair, now of nylon. Used in millinery.

lacet Braid of silk or cotton woven in various widths, frequently with looped edges. Used for trimming and edging, and sometimes combined with crochet work or tatting.

ladder braid Braid with open stitches crossed by BARS (see ANATOMY OF LACE) creating a ladder-like effect that is made with a bobbin.

middy braid Narrow, flat, white braid originally used to trim collars and cuffs on middy blouses and sailor collars.

military braid Flat, ribbed, worsted or gold braid sometimes in twill weave and made in various widths. Used to designate rank on military uniforms and as trimming.

rapolin (rap′-o-lin) Swiss millinery braid made in triple rows and having an uneven surface.

rat-tail braid Silk braid of tubular shape used for trimming.

rice braid Firmly woven, highly mercerized braid with wide parts alternating with narrow, to give the appearance of grains of rice. Used for trimming. Similar to CORONATION BRAID (see under TYPES OF BRAIDS DEFINED).

rickrack Braid usually made of cotton or blends that has a zigzag form. Widths may vary.

Russian braid See TYPES OF BRAIDS DEFINED: SOUTACHE BRAID.

soutache braid (soo-tash′) Narrow flat decorative braid. Used for borders and for allover ornamental patterns. Also called *Russian braid. Der.* Hungarian, *sujtas,* "flat trimming braid."

LEATHER

HISTORY AND SIGNIFICANCE OF LEATHER TO FASHION

Leather is the skin or hide of an animal with the hair removed and the grain revealed by the process of tanning. Animal hides were probably the first materials used for clothing. By using smoke and grease, it was possible to preserve hides and keep them flexible. Accessories made of leather such as shoes, belts, gloves, headwear, and bags for carrying things were practical and durable. When fashion became an important element in the design of accessories of dress, special finishing methods and even techniques for dyeing leathers were developed to enhance their appearance. The popularity of leather has led to the development of artificial leathers, often made from vinyl, a type of plastic that can be extruded into a continuous sheet, or from fabrics that have the appearance and/or textures associated with leather. Such materials are discussed in the following sections of COMPONENTS OF ACCESSORIES: TEXTILES IN ACCESSORIES: NON-WOVEN FABRICS DEFINED: ULTRASUEDE®, MULTI-COMPONENT FABRICS: NAUGAHYDE®, and SPECIAL FINISHES DEFINED: SUEDING; and in OTHER MATERIALS USED IN ACCESSORIES: PLASTICS.

ANATOMY OF LEATHER

In the leather industry, the term **hide** is used to refer to the pelts of larger animals (e.g., horsehide, cowhide), and **skin** to the pelts of smaller animals (kidskin, sheepskin, pigskin). The contemporary method of handling leather includes several steps.

Hair is removed from the pelt (**dehairing**), any remaining flesh is eliminated (**fleshing**), and the hide is cleaned (**cleaning**). The critical step in making leather from hides is **tanning,** or treating the hide with veg-

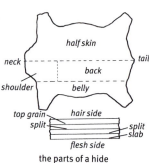

the parts of a hide

etable substances, minerals, oils, or other synthetic substances. The result is a flexible, pliable material.

Tanning methods can vary. Among these methods are:

alum tanning Process used to produce soft, pliable, white leathers. Mainly used for gloves. Primary disadvantage is that leather is not washable.

chamois tanning Treatment of hides by scraping the surface, saturating both sides with oil, and pounding the hide until the oil is absorbed. Also called *oil tanning.*

chrome tanning A mineral type of tanning process for leather. Skins are placed in large revolving drums and are tanned in three to eight hours. The basic ingredients used are salts of chromium. This is the most used process today for tanning shoe uppers, handbags, belts, etc. Before being dyed, leather is a robin's-egg blue color.

combination tanning Leather tanned by using both CHROME and VEGETABLE TANNING methods (see under ANATOMY OF LEATHER).

formaldehyde tanning A bleaching process that can be added to chrome or chamois tanning. Necessary if white leather is to remain white after frequent laundering. See ANATOMY OF LEATHER: CHROME TANNING and CHAMOIS TANNING.

vegetable tanning Tanning process that produces various shades of orange- and beige-colored leathers. Basic ingredients include vegetable products such as bark, leaves, nuts, tannic acid, and twigs. Great disadvantage is the length of time involved for tanning, which runs between four and six months. Also called *bark tanning*.

A machine then splits the leather into two or more layers, including a **flesh side** layer and a **grain side** layer. The **grain** is the markings that appear on the skins and hides when the hair or feathers are removed. Pigskin shows small markings in groups of three. Ostrich skins show a rosette where the quill has been removed. Thin, soft grains used for linings are called **skivers**. The layers or cuts sliced from hides are called **splits**. **Top-grain** is the smooth, hair side of the skin; other splits have a rough surface called **deep-buff**, split, and **slab**. The latter cuts are mainly used to make SUEDE (see ANATOMY OF LEATHER: SUEDING).

The layers are usually dyed either to achieve an even surface appearance or to produce a fashionable color. The surface can also be finished by: **glazing** or **lacquering**, applying a shiny finish; **buffing**, abrading with an emery wheel; **embossing**, impressing a design with engraved metal rollers to imitate another leather; or **sueding**, buffing on the flesh side to raise a slight nap.

TYPES OF LEATHER DEFINED

alligator Leather from alligators with characteristic markings of blocks, rectangles, and circles with cross markings between. Used for shoes, handbags, and belts. Law passed by Congress in 1970 prohibited use in the United States, later rescinded.

alligator lizard Leather from a large lizard with markings like grains of rice and elongated blocks, similar in appearance to hides of small alligators.

alligator-grained Term for alligator-skin pattern EMBOSSED (see under ANATOMY OF LEATHER) or printed on cowhide, calf-skin leather, plastic, or imitation leather.

antelope Rare soft velvety leather made from antelope or gazelle skins, usually SUEDED (see under ANATOMY OF LEATHER). Used for fine shoes and handbags.

antelope-finished lambskin Soft finish applied to lambskin, calfskin, or goatskin in imitation of genuine antelope skin.

antique finish Finish applied to leather giving a shaded effect by dyeing, buffing, wrinkling, waxing, and oiling the surface to resemble old leather.

bating Processing of skins and hides to reveal grain of leather after hair has been removed.

bend Leather term for the best section of leather cut from a whole hide.

boarded finish Leather finish that makes the grain of the leather more pronounced. Hand-processed by folding the leather with grain sides together and rolling it back and forth while pressing it with a cork board.

box calf Calf that has been BOARDED (see under TYPES OF LEATHER DEFINED) in two directions to give it squared markings on the GRAIN side (see under ANATOMY OF LEATHER).

bronzed leather Copper-colored kid or calfskin.

brush-dyeing Coloring of leather by placing skins flesh side down on metal table and applying dye to grain side with brush. Desirable for black kidskin gloves as inside remains white.

buckskin **1.** Deer or elk skins with the grain given a suede finish similar to early skins cured by Native Americans. Second SPLITS (see under ANATOMY OF LEATHER) of deerskin must be called *split deerskin* or *split buckskin*. **2.** Sheepskin treated to resemble true buckskin.

buffing See under ANATOMY OF LEATHER.

cabretta Fine, smooth, tight-grained leather made from Brazilian sheepskins used mainly for women's dressy gloves.

calf/calfskin Supple, strong, fine-grained leather from skins of cattle a few days to a few weeks old finished in many ways, or made into PATENT LEATHER (see under TYPES OF LEATHER DEFINED). Used for shoes, handbags, belts, and wallets. Best qualities come from the United States.

capeskin Light, flexible, fine-grained leather made from skin of the South African hair sheep or from other hair sheep. *Der.* Frequently shipped from Capetown, South Africa, hence the name.

carpincho Leather tanned from a water rodent. Often sold as pigskin and used mainly for sport gloves.

cattlehide Heavy leather, usually vegetable-tanned, from cow, bull, and steer hides. Used for sole leather. Also called *cowhide*.

chamois (sha′-mee, or French, shah-mawh′) Originally leather made from an Alpine goat or chamois; now undersplits of oil-dressed and suede-finished sheepskins are correctly called by this name. See ANATOMY OF LEATHER: CHAMOIS TANNING.

chickenskin Leather of unborn calves; light in weight.

cordovan Durable, almost completely non-porous leather, made from the shell of horse-butts used for uppers of fine men's shoes. It is given a characteristic waxy finish in black and reddish-brown colors. *Der.* Named for Cordoba, Spain, where tanning of leather was highly perfected under the Arabs.

cowhide See TYPES OF LEATHER DEFINED: CATTLEHIDE.

crocodile Thick-skinned leather, from a large water reptile, characterized by black markings and a scaly horny surface; very similar to *alligator*.

cross-boarded Leather-industry term for skins processed to make grain more pronounced by folding leather in one direction, pressing with a cork armboard, and rolling; then folding in opposite direction and repeating the process.

crushed leather Leather given a crinkled surface made by hand boarding, by machine boarding, or by embossing to produce an imitation of a boarded finish. See ANATOMY OF LEATHER and TYPES OF LEATHER DEFINED: BOARDED FINISH. Also called *écrasé leather* (eh-kras-zay), a French word for leather crushed to reveal the grain.

deerskin See TYPES OF LEATHER DEFINED: BUCKSKIN.

doeskin **1.** Genuine doeskin is leather made by tanning female or male deerskins by the CHAMOIS PROCESS (see under ANATOMY OF LEATHER) and then buffing it to produce a SUEDED finish (see under ANATOMY OF LEATHER). **2.** Sheepskin or lambskin tanned by CHAMOIS or ALUM process (see under ANATOMY OF LEATHER) and sueded. Should be called *doeskin-finished lambskin*.

écrasé See TYPES OF LEATHER DEFINED: CRUSHED LEATHER.

elkside Misleading term for CATTLEHIDE (see under TYPES OF LEATHER DEFINED) finished to look like elk leather—should be *labeled elk-finished cowhide*.

embossed See under ANATOMY OF LEATHER in category heading.

fancy leather Industry term for leather having a natural grain or a distinctive pattern, e.g., alligator, lizard, and snakeskin. Also includes embossed effects, simulating reptile patterns, or leathers given a decorative finish, e.g., metallic kid.

French antelope lambskin LAMBSKIN (see under TYPES OF LEATHER DEFINED), tanned in France, that has been given a lustrous suede finish to make it look like antelope skin.

French kid Originally KIDSKIN (see under TYPES OF LEATHER DEFINED) imported from France, now refers to any ALUM- or VEGETABLE-TANNED (see ANATOMY OF LEATHER) kidskin that resembles the original.

frog Leather with a distinctive grain and pattern made from the skin of a species of giant frog found in Brazil. Limited in availability and used for women's accessories and trimmings. May be simulated by EMBOSSING (see under ANATOMY OF LEATHER) other leathers and called *frog-grained leathers*.

full grain/full top grain In the leather industry, the side of the skin or hide from which the hair has been removed.

galuchat (ga-lu′-chat) Leather made from tough outer layer of SHARKSKIN (see under TYPES OF LEATHER DEFINED). Used for handbags and novelty items.

ganges Leather embossed to imitate snakeskin.

glacé (gla-say′) Shiny finish applied to kidskins by using a glass roller. Also called *glazed*. *Der.* French, "frozen."

glazé kid/glazed kid KIDSKIN (see under TYPES OF LEATHER DEFINED) given a very shiny surface by means of heavy rollers. Der. French, "shiny."

goatskin Leather made from the skin of the goat. Used for gloves, shoe uppers, and handbags. Also see TYPES OF LEATHER DEFINED: KIDSKIN.

horsehide A durable fine-grained leather from horses and colts. Usually imported and used flesh side up with GRAIN (see under ANATOMY OF LEATHER) used for inside surface of shoe uppers.

Also see TYPES OF LEATHER DEFINED: CORDOVAN LEATHER.

hunting calf See TYPES OF LEATHER DEFINED: REVERSE CALF.

"in the white" Undyed and unfinished tanned leather.

Java lizard Lizard skins with black, white, and gray coloring. Imported from Java in Indonesia, and used for handbags, shoes, and belts.

kangaroo Durable scuff-resistant leather made from kangaroo and wallaby hides. Similar to KIDSKIN (see under TYPES OF LEATHER DEFINED) in appearance and imported mainly from Australia.

kid/kidskin Leather made from young goat skins. Used for women's shoe uppers, handbags, belts, and fine gloves.

kip/kipskin Leather-industry term for pelts of young steers, cows, or horses that weigh between 15 and 25 pounds, as distinguished from skin or hide of older animals.

lambskin Leather made from skin of a young sheep.

lizard Reptile leather with pattern similar to grains of rice. Often named for place of origin in India and Java. Used for shoe uppers, handbags, belts, and ornamental trimmings.

mocha Fine-sueded glove leather made from skins of blackhead or whitehead sheep from Somaliland, Sudan, and Egypt. Used for women's fine gloves and shoes.

Moroccan leather Fancy goatskins with a pebbly GRAIN (see under ANATOMY OF LEATHER), often dyed red. Originally tanned in Morocco and mainly used for handbags and slippers.

nap finish Leather finish that creates a suedelike finish (see ANATOMY OF LEATHER) on the grain side of the leather.

nappa Glove leather from sheepskins or lambskins of domestic New Zealand or South American origin that have been tanned by CHROME, ALUM, or COMBINATION methods (see under ANATOMY OF LEATHER).

nubuck An imitation deerskin made from cattle hide. See TYPES OF LEATHER DEFINED: BUCKSKIN #1.

ostrich Leather with a distinctive rosette pattern caused by removal of plumes from ostrich skins. Used for fine shoes and handbags.

patent leather Leather processed on the grain side to form a bright, hard, brittle surface. Done by degreasing, stretching on frames, coating with paint and linseed oil, then alternately baking in the sun and rubbing with pumice stone. VINYL (see under OTHER MATERIALS USED IN ACCESSORIES: PLASTICS) is used to make imitation patent leather.

peccary Leather processed from the skin of the wild boar of Central and South America. Used mainly for pigskin gloves.

pebbled finish An embossed leather finish similar to tiny cobblestones or pebbles.

Persians Leather industry term for hair-sheepskin leather tanned in India. See TYPES OF LEATHER DEFINED: SHEEPSKIN.

pigskin Leather made from the skin of the pig. It has groups of three tiny holes caused by removing the bristles and giving it a distinctive pattern.

pin seal High-grade skins from hair seal with fine pebbly grain. Imitated widely by embossing patterns on calfskin, cowhide, goatskin, and sheepskin, and then called pin-grain calfskin, etc.

plastic patent Simulated or imitation PATENT LEATHER (see under TYPES OF LEATHER DEFINED: LEATHERS) made from a vinyl compound that is durable and will not split or crack like genuine patent. May have a crushed surface or be embossed with a design, e.g., alligator or snakeskin. Used for shoes and handbags and in lighter weights for jackets, coats, and trimmings. Popular from 1960s on.

python Leather processed from skin of a large nonpoisonous snake with medium-sized scales and distinctive markings. Available in black and white and tan and white. It is sometimes dyed bright red, yellow, blue, and other colors. Used for handbags, shoes, and trimmings.

rawhide Leather in natural pale beige or yellowish color made from CATTLEHIDES (see under TYPES OF LEATHER DEFINED) not actually tanned but dehaired, limed, and stuffed with oil and grease.

reverse calf Calfskin finished with flesh side out, GRAIN side (see under ANATOMY OF LEATHER) inside. Called *hunting calf* in England.

rosette Mark left on ostrich skin when quill is removed.

Russian   Leather tanned with birch bark, which has distinctive odor. Usually finished in brown and originally from Russia. Term now used for any similar brown calfskin.

saddle   Natural tan leather made from vegetable-tanned STEERHIDES or CATTLEHIDES (see under TYPES OF LEATHER DEFINED) and used for tooled-leather handbags, belts, and saddles for horses.

sealskin   Leather made from genuine Alaska fur seal hides. Rare, because the Alaska fur seal is protected by the U.S. government. Also see TYPES OF LEATHER DEFINED: PIN SEAL.

sharkskin   Almost scuff-proof leather made from the skin of certain species of sharks. The "outer armor," called **shagreen**, is removed before the skins are tanned. Used for shoes, belts, handbags, wallets, and cigarette cases.

shearling   Short curly wool skins of sheep or lambs sheared before slaughter and tanned with the wool left on. Used for slippers, gloves, coats, and jackets, with the sueded-flesh side out.

sheepskin   Leather from sheep, characterized by more than average sponginess and stretchability, frequently sueded. Small skins with fine grain are called LAMBSKIN (see under TYPES OF LEATHER DEFINED). Used for shoes, handbags, coats, and jackets. Sheepskin tanned with wool left on is often used leather side out for coats and sport jackets. See TYPES OF LEATHER DEFINED: SHEARLING.

side leather   CATTLEHIDES (see under TYPES OF LEATHER DEFINED) too large to process in one piece, are cut down the center back into two parts—each part is called a **side**. Used for sole leather or shoe uppers and for belts.

snakeskin   Diamond-patterned leather with overlapping scales processed from skin of a number of species of snakes (e.g., diamond-backed rattlesnake, python, cobra, or boa).

sole leather   Heavy stiff leather, usually CATTLE-HIDE (see under TYPES OF LEATHER DEFINED), used for the soles and built-up heels of shoes.

split buckskin/deerskin   See TYPES OF LEATHER DEFINED: BUCKSKIN.

staking   A means of making leather more pliable by passing it over a blunt metal blade.

steerhide   Heavy leather from skins of castrated male cattle, usually used as SOLE LEATHER for shoes or to make SADDLE LEATHER (see under TYPES OF LEATHER DEFINED).

suede   Leather, usually LAMBSKIN, DOESKIN, or splits of CATTLEHIDE (sometimes called REVERSE CALF; see under TYPES OF LEATHER DEFINED) that has been buffed on the flesh side to raise a slight texture. Sometimes buffed on grain side or on both sides of a SPLIT (see under ANATOMY OF LEATHER) to cover small defects.

top grain   Leather-industry term for first SPLIT (see under ANATOMY OF LEATHER) from grain side of leather. Used for shoes and handbags.

undersplit   One of the under layers of leather obtained when leather is SPLIT (see under ANATOMY OF LEATHER).

vici kid   Term used for all GLAZÉ KID (see under TYPES OF LEATHER DEFINED). Formerly trade term for a chrome tanning process.

wallaby   Leather made from the skins of a small species of kangaroo family. Similar to KANGA-ROO LEATHER (see under TYPES OF LEATHER DEFINED) but sometimes finer grained.

FURS

HISTORY AND SIGNIFICANCE OF FUR TO FASHION ACCESSORIES

Furs were probably the first materials used to clothe humans. **Furs** are the skins of animals with the hair attached. Fur is used in accessories to provide warmth, as in headwear and gloves; or for decorative effects, as in collars, trim, or for stoles. Fur has been a status symbol because of its relatively high cost and its luxurious appearance and soft feel. The popularity of individual furs changes with fashion trends. For example, monkey fur was a popular trimming in the 1920s, while red, green, or other furs dyed to unusual colors may be seen in the early 21st c.

The use of fur has been a subject of controversy because some individuals object to the killing of animals for their pelts. These objections intensified when some animals almost became extinct through overhunting. As a result, in 1969, the U.S. Congress passed the **Endangered Species Act,** which banned importation and sale of pelts of some animals. Some individual states have also passed laws restricting the sale of furs from endangered animals. In 1975, a Convention on International Trade in Endangered Species of World Fauna and Flora was established.

Fabrics imitating fur are also available and are used in accessories in the same way as genuine fur.

ANATOMY OF FUR AND FUR PRODUCTION PROCESSES

True furs have two elements: a dense, short undercoat, called **underfur,** and much longer hairs called **guard hairs.** A few commercially used furs, such as Persian lamb, have no guard hairs. Kid and pony have no underfur. The best quality peltry is called a **prime pelt.** Animals must be hunted during the season when the pelt is at its fullest. For most animals, this is during the coldest winter months.

In order to make furs useful in garments, they must be dressed. Dressing consists of cleaning, softening, fleshing (removal of any flesh remaining on the skin), and stretching. The skin is TANNED (see LEATHER: ANATOMY OF LEATHER) to preserve it. Finally, the pelts may be dyed, bleached, or **tipped** (the guard hairs dyed) in order to achieve a uniform color or to produce decorative effects.

Accessory items generally have a less complex construction than fur coats; however, larger items such as fur stoles may require techniques such as **letting out,** in which fur is cut into narrow diagonal strips that are sewn together. It is more likely that accessory items and trim would be cut from a single pelt, or by sewing one pelt to another. This is called the **skin on skin** technique.

TYPES OF FUR DEFINED

Alaskan seal   Soft velvety fur from the genuine Alaska seal. All pelts are sheared and dyed either black or brown and other colors. Sealing is controlled by the U.S. government with pelts coming from the Pribilof Islands, off the coast of Alaska. Used for coats, jackets, hats, and muffs. Durability is high. Expensive because of the limited quantity available. Argentina and Ecuador also protect the species.

antelope Stiff flat hair, similar to calf, in beautiful soft brown color; rarely used for fur as the number of antelopes is very limited.

badger Heavy, warm, durable fur with long silvery gray guard hairs and dense white or tan underfur.

bearskin Pelt of a bear.

beaver Rich velvety brown fur that, when sheared, reveals a wide silvery stripe down the center. Preferred color is blue-brown; sometimes left natural or bleached beige for "blonde beaver." Most beaver is sheared and coarse guard hairs are plucked out.

blending Fur-industry term for lightly applying dye to tips of hairs of furs, such as mink and sable, to improve the coloring.

broadtail lamb Natural, unsheared, flat MOIRÉ PATTERN (see under TYPES OF FUR DEFINED), with silky texture. Colors may be natural brown, grays, or black or possibly dyed.

brush Bushy tail of an animal, usually a fox, used as trimming.

burunduki (bur-oo'-duke-ee) Usually small, lightweight delicate skins with nine alternate stripes of white and black on a yellow or orangish background. Skin obtained from rodent native to Russia similar to American chipmunk. Used for linings and trimmings.

caging Fur-cleaning process, in which furs are revolved in cagelike wire drums that permit the sawdust, used for cleaning, to fall out through the wire mesh.

calf/calfskin Flat, short, stiff-haired fur from young cattle, usually brown spotted with white, also may be black and white, all black, or brown. Used for trimmings, handbags, belts, and shoes.

caracul See TYPES OF FUR DEFINED: KARAKUL.

chinchilla Silky-haired fur with a very delicate skin. Best quality has slate-blue underfur and guard hairs that are white and darker at the tips, center back is gray. This small rodent is native to the Andes Mountains in South America. May also be raised on fur ranches. Mutation colors are now available.

Chinese lamb See TYPES OF FUR DEFINED: KARAKUL.

civet cat Spotted fur characterized by elongated black marks against a dark gray background with a greenish cast. Not widely used. Comes from southern China and the Malay Peninsula. The little spotted skunk of South America is sometimes incorrectly called the civet cat.

coney Synonym for rabbit.

crosses Fur term for small pieces of fur, such as paws and gills, sewn together to make a large piece that is cross-shaped—used particularly on varieties of lamb.

ermine Pure white fur from weasel family with short guard hairs and silky soft underfur. Best quality from the far north—Siberia, in particular. As the animal roams further south, it develops protective coloration of light shades of brown. Traditionally used by royalty since Middle Ages and still used on ceremonial robes of British peerage.

feathering Applying extra dye delicately to guard hairs of fur by means of a feather dipped in dye. Used to improve appearance of the fur.

fisher Color shading from brown to blackish tones with long guard hairs and dense underfur. Used primarily for scarfs and jackets usually in its natural state. Best quality pelts come from Labrador. Very good durability; fairly scarce and expensive.

fitch Moderately priced fur, with yellow underfur and black guard hairs with a silky texture; found in Europe. *White fitch,* another type, is found in Ural Mountains of southern Russia. Used for coats, jackets, and trimmings. Durability is very good; relatively inexpensive. Color ranges from ecru with black markings to orange tones.

fox Fur with long lustrous guard hairs and deep dense underfur. There are four primary types of foxes and many miscellaneous types. Main groups are: *(a) red fox*—includes black, silver, platinum, and *cross fox* (yellowish with a black cross marking) as color phases; *(b) white fox*—with blue fox a color phase; *(c) gray fox;* and *(d) kit fox.* Northern kit fox is protected by Canadian government. Found on every continent except South America, and also raised on fur farms. Used for scarfs, muffs, and trimmings. Other fox furs include black, blue, cross, gray, platinum (also called platina), red, silver, and white.

fun furs Longhaired and unusual furs worked in an interesting manner into garments.

guanaco (gwa-nak'-ko) Reddish-brown fur from the young guanaco or guanaquito found in

Argentina. Inexpensive and not durable, it is used for trimmings, and is the only member of the llama family used for fur.

hare Soft short-haired fur, similar to RABBIT (see TYPES OF FUR DEFINED), but with more tendency to mat. The arctic hare from northern Europe and Asia has a long guard hair and is sometimes used to imitate the Arctic fox. Durability is low but higher than rabbit fur.

Hudson Bay sable See TYPES OF FUR DEFINED: MARTEN.

karakul/caracul (kar′-ah-kul) Lamb pelt with a MOIRÉ appearance (see under TYPES OF FUR DEFINED)—best pelts are the flattest. Majority of skins are white and may be dyed; or may be rusty brown, dark brown, or black. Best quality from Russia. When skins are from China, called *Chinese lamb* or *Mongolian lamb.* Used for hats, scarves, muffs, and trimmings. Durability is moderate.

kidskin Short-haired flat gray fur with wavy pattern, inexpensive fur with low durability. The best pelts come from young goats of India, China, Ethiopia, and South America.

kojah See TYPES OF FUR DEFINED: MINK.

kolinsky Brownish fur with medium-length silky guard hair and slightly yellowish underfur. Used primarily for scarves and trimmings, it is used in imitation of American and Canadian mink. Durability is fair.

krimmer See TYPES OF FUR DEFINED: LAMB.

lamb Many types of lamb are processed for fur, but the three main types are: *Persian lamb, broadtail lamb,* and *karacul lamb.* **Persian lamb** is a curly lustrous fur that is usually black but occasionally brown or white. Dark colors are always dyed to color the white skin. Quality is determined by the tightness of the curl and formation of interesting patterns called "flowers." Popular for coats and trimmings, its durability is high and its is now available in new mutation colors. **Broadtail lamb** has a natural, unsheared, flat MOIRÉ PATTERN (see under TYPES OF FUR DEFINED), with a silky texture. Colors may be natural brown, gray, black, or dyed. **Karakul** (kar′-ah-kul), or **caracul**, lamb pelt has a moiré pattern. The best pelts are the flattest. The majority of skins are white and may be dyed; or may be rusty brown, dark brown, or black.

When skins are from China, karakul is called *Chinese lamb* or *Mongolian lamb.* It is used for hats, scarves, muffs, and trimmings. Durability is moderate. Other lamb variations include *Afghan, Astrakhan, Argentine, Bessarabian, Iranian, Kalgan, Soviet Union, India, China,* and *Southwest Africa.* Crimean lamb is called *crimmer* or *krimmer.* Also see TYPES OF FUR DEFINED: MOUTON-PROCESSED LAMB.

leopard Spotted jungle-cat fur that has no underfur in the best qualities. Better qualities have shorter hair. Good durability; very limited in supply and expensive. No longer permitted by law to be used in United States.

lynx Long silky-haired delicately spotted fur. Colors vary from white, blue gray, pale gray, and brown. Used for trimming. Spain protects the *Spanish lynx.*

lynx cat Differs from lynx, being darker in color with darker spots and shorter guard hairs, similar to the American wildcat. Used extensively for trimmings.

marguay See TYPES OF FUR DEFINED: SPOTTED CAT.

marten Soft rich fur with fairly long guard hair and thick underfur similar to SABLE (see under TYPES OF FUR DEFINED); blue-black or brown colors preferred, but ranges to canary yellow. Important variations include **baum marten,** which has medium-length brown guard hairs and yellow-brown underfur and resembles sable. Fair to good durability; expensive. **Stone marten** fur has brown guard hairs and grayish white underfur that is judged for quality by the contrast of two colors. Both baum marten and stone marten are used primarily for scarves.

mink Fur with silky to coarse guard hairs and dense, soft underfur. Best qualities of the dark pelts are lustrous with the guard hairs giving off a blue reflection. Originally only **wild mink,** its skins procured from animals that run wild in the forest, was available. Zoological name is *Mustela vison,* and animal is from the weasel family. *Vison* is the European name for mink. Since the 1940s, much mink is raised by fur farmers in the United States. **Natural mink** is mink that has not been dyed or colored in any manner. Many color variations are now available due to the development of new strains of **mutation mink,** strains of mink developed scientifically on fur farms by carefully mating the animals. Original wild pelts were brown. From mating the odd animals, many new colors were produced. Also during the 1960s, mink with longer hair was produced through breeding. A trade name for this type was **kojah.** Most mink is used in the natural color and the fur is of good durability. With the growth in popularity of the fur stole during the 1950s, and the production of more pelts by fur farming, mink became available to the masses. **China mink** is a less expensive yellowish mink found in China and dyed to imitate North American colors, and **Jap,** or **Japanese mink,** is also a muddy yellow-colored mink from Japan that is always dyed in imitation of more expensive American mink.

moiré pattern (mwa-ray′)   Fur term for appearance of Persian broadtail and American processed broadtail—flat furs with a wavy surface.

mouton-processed lamb   Woolly fur with a dense pile, made by shearing the merino sheep rather than "hair" sheep. Used for hats. Inexpensive, warm, and durable. Generally dyed brown, frequently water-repellent.

muskrat   Fur with long guard hairs and dense underfur, processed three different ways: *a)* dyed and striped to resemble mink and sable; *b)* sheared and dyed to imitate Alaskan seal and called *Hudson seal-dyed muskrat;* and *c)* left natural and finished to improve the coloring. Best qualities of northern muskrat, which is brown or black, are used for Hudson seal-dyed muskrat and come from the Great Lakes region in the United States. Southern pelts, which vary in color, are used for natural muskrat coats. Durability is moderate to high.

nutria   Fur with a velvety appearance after long guard hairs have been plucked, its color ranges from cinnamon brown to brown with gray stripes. Fur is similar to beaver although not as thick, lustrous, and rich in color. This animal is a water rodent of northern Argentina that is wild or ranch-bred. Used for trimmings. Durability is moderate. Sometimes it is kept in natural state with long guard hairs and short underfur in lustrous brown. When produced on a ranch, it is bluish-beige in color, slightly coarser, and may be dyed.

ocelot   Spotted fur with elongated dark markings against a tan background. The peltries with flatter hair are the best quality and come from Brazil and Mexico. This durable fur is in short supply, relatively expensive.

opossum   Long straight guard hairs and dense underfur, which in the natural color is either black or gray, from a wild animal. Best qualities come from Australia and the United States. Used for trimmings or dyed to imitate other furs such as skunk and fitch, it is moderately priced.

otter   Relatively short-haired fur with silky lustrous guard hair and dense underfur—the most durable fur for the weight and thickness. Preferred color has blue-brown guard hairs and underfur slightly lighter with the base being gray to white in color. Best qualities come from eastern Canada. Some otter is sheared and plucked. Also see TYPES OF FUR DEFINED: SEA OTTER.

paw   Fur term for small pieces of fur from paws of animals.

platina   See TYPES OF FUR DEFINED: FOX.

Persian lamb   Curly lustrous fur that is usually black but occasionally brown or white. Dark colors are always dyed to color the white skin. Quality is determined by the tightness of the "knuckle" curl and formation of interesting pattern called "flowers." Best quality comes from Bokara, Russia, from Karakul sheep. Others come from Afghanistan, Southwest Africa, and Iran. Popular for coats and trimmings. Durability is high. Now available in new mutation colors. Also see TYPES OF FUR DEFINED: LAMB.

pony   Short-haired flat fur with a wavy MOIRÉ (see TYPES OF FUR DEFINED) appearance. Used in natural color, bleached, or dyed pale colors. Best quality comes from Poland and Russia. Durability good, but short bristly fur has a tendency to wear "bald."

rabbit   Soft light fur in a variety of colors used in natural state or can be dyed or processed as follows: *a)* striped to imitate muskrat, *b)* sheared to imitate beaver, and *c)* sheared and stenciled to resemble leopard. Poor durability; inexpensive.

raccoon   Has long, light silver guard hair and dark-brown underfur. Lighter weight peltries from the southern part of the United States are used for coats. The northern United States provides heavy-skinned pelts used primarily for hats and trimmings. **Sheared raccoon** is processed by plucking out guard hairs and shearing to produce a velvety-textured fur similar in appearance to beaver, but not as soft or silky and more cinnamon brown in color with lighter stripes, which is much less expensive than beaver.

Raccoon dog See TYPES OF FUR DEFINED: USSURIAN RACCOON.

sable Luxurious fur with lustrous long silky guard hairs and soft dense fluffy underfur; preferred color, a blue-black-brown. Skins that are light brown in color are tipped, blended, and called *dyed sable*. Used for coats or scarfs, with best quality, called *Russian crown sable*, coming from Siberia. Animal is also found in Canada, China, Korea, and Japan. Durability is good; very expensive. Golden sable in amber tone is less expensive.

seal Fur from seals. That from the **hair seal** is stiff, rather short-haired fur with a natural blue-black or blue-and-black mottled effect that may be dyed various other colors. This fur comes from two varieties of seals, the *harp seal* and the *hooded seal,* whose habitat is the North Atlantic. Baby hair seals are white in color, and used to make sealskin leathers as the fur is slightly woolly. **Fur seal** fur is soft and velvety and comes from the genuine Alaska seal. All pelts are sheared and dyed either black or brown and other colors. Sealing is controlled by the U.S. government with pelts coming from the Pribilof Islands, off the coast of Alaska. Used for hats and muffs. Durability is high. Expensive because of the limited quantity available. Other countries also protect this species.

sea otter Fur with silky guard hairs and silky underfur in a deep blue-black or brown with sprinklings of white hairs. Having exceptionally soft, dense, and luxurious pelts, sea otters were hunted almost to extinction for their fur. Now protected in the United States, these animals can no longer be hunted and their fur cannot be used.

shearing Process used on furs (e.g., beaver, lamb, muskrat, raccoon, and seal) to cut hairs to same length to give them a velvety appearance.

shearling Pelts from "wool" lambs, which have been processed with the hair intact, therefore classifying them as "fur" rather than "leather." Usually sueded on the leatherside.

skunk Black fur with long guard hairs and thick underfur with characteristic white stripe down back. Quality of fur depends on ability of the underfur to remain black rather than take on a brownish or rust-colored appearance. For an all-black fur, peltries have white streaks removed and are dyed to darken the skin. Best qualities are from the Dakotas and Minnesota and also Canada and South America. **Zorina,** a South American skunk, is similar with flatter fur and silky texture.

spotted cat Variety of spotted fur that comes from three main types of South American cat: the *chati cat*, the *marguay* (mar′-gay), and *long-tailed cats*. Markings are more rounded than those of the OCELOT (see under TYPES OF FUR DEFINED); fur is less expensive.

squirrel Very soft gray or brown relatively short fur that takes dye readily and may be made any color or worked into a two-toned pattern. Best qualities come from Europe, Asia, Russia, Poland, Finland, and Canada. Used mainly for trimmings. Low durability; moderately priced.

tanuki See TYPES OF FUR DEFINED: USSURIAN RACCOON.

Ussurian raccoon Longhaired, yellowish brown peltry with shoulder and tail tipped with black, slightly coarse guard hair, and long, dense underfur. May be dyed, sheared, or used in natural state, mainly for collars and trim. Comes from a species of dog that resembles a raccoon in appearance. The Japanese species, known as **tanuki,** has the most silky, fully-furred pelt (but is not the largest). Other qualities come from Manchuria, Korea, Siberia, and parts of Europe. Also called *raccoon dog, Armur raccoon, Chinese raccoon, Jap fox, Jap raccoon.* These names cannot be used when merchandising pelts in the United States. Color is similar to red fox with distinctive cross markings.

vison See TYPES OF FUR DEFINED: MINK.

weasel Soft silky short guard hairs and silky underfur similar in texture to ERMINE (see under TYPES OF FUR DEFINED), a close relative. Color varies with the seasons—winter, white; spring, yellowish; summer, streaked with brown or gray; and brown all year in southern climates.

wolf Longhaired fur with long silky guard hairs and dense underfur. Pale-colored skins are sometimes stenciled to imitate lynx; others are used in natural state or dyed brown, black, or gray. Quality depends on fluffiness and density of underfur that supports the long guard hairs. The best quality comes from the timber wolf of Canada. Used for trimmings and scarves. The red wolf is protected in the United States.

wolverine   Coarse fur with long brown guard hairs and dense gray underfur. Very durable; best qualities found in the Arctic regions, also found in the Rocky Mountains and Siberia. Used for trimming.

zebra   Flat, stiff fur with wide, irregularly shaped black stripes against a light-colored background. Comes from Africa. Calf is sometimes stenciled to imitate zebra.

zorina   See TYPES OF FUR DEFINED: SKUNK.

FEATHERS

USAGE OF FEATHERS IN ACCESSORIES

A **feather** is an individual unit from a bird's plumage that consists of a quill or hollow shaft surrounded by closely arranged parallel barbs. A feather usually tapers from the thicker part of the quill to the far tip. Feathers have been used from earliest times as decorative hair ornaments, necklaces, or body ornaments. They have also been used from the 16th c. on fans or to decorate hats. Contemporary usage of feathers is largely in headwear, in decorative scarves called boas, and for surface ornamentation of hair accessories. They are sometimes used on handbags or jewelry. Excessive use of feathers took a severe toll on bird populations in the late 19th and early 20th c.; therefore, laws were passed in most states that restricted usage of feathers from many species. At present songbird and eagle feathers, as well as those of other wild birds, are not permitted to be used for clothing or accessories in the United States. Those available are generally from birds that can be raised domestically.

ANATOMY OF FEATHERS

A feather is composed of a horny stem, the **quill,** that has a smooth front and a grooved back. The flat portion of the feather is called the **vane** and is composed of many individual, small, parallel filaments called **barbs.** At the base of

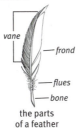

vane
—frond
—flues
—bone
the parts
of a feather

the feather are fluffy, fuzzy filaments called **flues** or **fluff.**

HOW TO BUY FEATHERS

The feathers currently available for purchase include ostrich, rooster (called *coque* or *cock*), peacock, pheasant, goose, turkey, duck, and guinea hen. Feathers can be purchased as individual feathers or in one of the following categories:

loose feathers   Those feathers sold by weight. Generally used in trimming objects, they may be of better quality (**selected**) or of lesser quality (**not-selected**).

pads   Individual feathers fastened with adhesive to a felt pad that can be used in making hats.

strung feathers   Feathers matched for color, quality, and size and strung into a strip with all the feathers facing in one direction.

boa (bow'-ah)   Round, narrow, fluffy long strip of feathers or swansdown. This can be worn as a separate accessory (see ACCESSORIES: SCARVES, SHAWLS, AND HANDKERCHIEFS: TYPES OF SCARVES DEFINED) or used as trimming on headwear or other accessories.

skins   Feathers that are sold attached to the bird's skin.

TYPES OF FEATHERS DEFINED

aigrette feather (ay-gret')   Extremely long, delicate, white feathers with plume at the tip, from the egret, a member of the heron family—a long-legged wading bird that almost became extinct from the demand for these feathers. Popular in the 1920s, it is now illegal in the United States to use these feathers on clothes or accessories. Also spelled *aigret*.

amazon plume   Early term for an ostrich feather. Generally taken from the wing of the bird with the tips of the barbs curled so shaft is concealed.

biot (bee-oh)   Long strip of short, stiff feathers created by stripping the vane from the stem.

bird-of-paradise feather   Long plume brilliantly colored, often golden-orange. Taken from beneath the shoulder or tail of full-grown male birds of paradise. Used on hats or headdresses. Illegal to import into the United States. Introduced on evening wear by Yves Saint Laurent in 1969.

chandelle (shan-del)   Feather BOAS (see HOW TO BUY FEATHERS) of 8 to 11 inches in width that are made from flat turkey feathers.

cock feather   Long curly feathers from the tail of the rooster, often black, blue, and green with iridescent highlights.

cockade   Tuft of feathers used as trim.

coq feather (cok)   French for "cock or chicken feathers."

cosse   Any short, stiff feather.

down   Fluffy soft fibers taken from under the feathers of water fowl, e.g., geese and ducks.

egret feather   See TYPES OF FEATHERS DEFINED: AIGRETTE.

eiderdown (eye-der-down')   Soft fine under feathers from the eider duck. Also called *down*. *Der.* From the feathers of the *eider duck*.

grebe feather   Feathers from a waterfowl, similar to ducks, that are ivory-colored, flecked with brown.

guinea feather (gin'-ee)   Small, flat feathers from the guinea hen that are characterized by black, white, and gray striated markings.

hackle   Commercial term for rooster feathers.

herl   Short, delicate, stiff fronds of peacock feather that have been removed from the stem and are bundled together and used as trimming.

jabiru (jab-ih'-roo)   Soft fuzzy plumage from a storklike South American bird. Feathers are white, pale smoke colored, and black and white.

marabou   Delicate, fluffy, fine feathers from tail and wing of a species of stork made into trimmings that sell by the yard in black, white, and all colors. Because of the expense of these feathers, less-expensive feathers are sometimes substituted.

nagoires (nay-joh-res)   Goose feathers from the shoulder area.

ostrich feather   Long, curly plume feathers from the ostrich, a native African bird. Natural color of the feathers from the female bird is beige barred with white. Most feathers are dyed in colors.

paradise feather   See TYPES OF FEATHERS DEFINED: BIRD-OF-PARADISE FEATHERS.

parried feathers   Those feathers that have had their quills shaved or sanded in order to make them more flexible.

peacock feather   Long, thin, dark feather with brilliantly marked "eye" in greenish blue at the tip, from upper tail of peacock. Individual feathers became a fad among the hippies, carried in the hand, in the late 1960s.

pheasant feather   **1.** Long, stiff tail feather from the domestic game bird, with striated markings of orange, black, and brown. **2.** Small, soft body feathers of the same bird, sometimes used to cover hats or hatbands.

plumage   The mass of feathers that come from the bird's neck and chest area.

plume   A single, large feather. Plumes most often used are from ostriches.

rhea feather (ray'-ah)   Either of two South American *ratite* birds, resembling *African ostrich*, having long draping feathers.

schlappen   Rooster tail feathers that are small, narrow, and pointed.

swan's down   Soft underfeathers of swans. Also spelled *swansdown*. Compare with MARABOU (see under TYPES OF FEATHERS DEFINED).

GEMS, GEM CUTS,
and SETTINGS

HISTORY AND SIGNIFICANCE OF GEMS, GEM CUTS, AND SETTINGS TO FASHION

A **gem** is a crystalline mineral that is rare, beautiful, durable. It must also be portable and suitable for personal adornment. For the most part gems are used in jewelry and are valued for their appearance. In some civilizations certain gems were considered to have supernatural power. Fewer than 100 of more than 2,000 minerals have been used as gems, and only 16 of these are considered important. The demand for individual gems is dictated by current fashion trends. Generally, gems must be cut and polished to bring out their maximum beauty and they are placed in various kinds of settings. Preferences for both gem cuts and settings are also subject to fashion.

ANATOMY OF GEMS

Gems are divided into a number of categories. **Precious stones** is the term applied to a gem that is not only beautiful, durable, and portable, but also rare (e.g., diamonds, rubies, sapphires, and emeralds). **Semiprecious stones** are gems too plentiful to be considered rare (e.g., topaz, garnet, tourmaline, amethyst, and quartz). **Ornamental stones** exist in such large quantities that they are not considered precious or semiprecious gems (e.g., coral and turquoise). **Marine gems** are gems that are found primarily in the sea (e.g., pearls, amber, and

coral). Gems are also classified as **transparent, semi-transparent,** or **opaque.**

The popularity of using gems in jewelry has led to attempts to imitate genuine gems. **Simulated gems** are copies of precious gems made of **paste,** a highly reflective transparent type of flint glass that is faceted or molded. Gems are also made from other inexpensive materials. Simulated gems should not be confused with **synthetic gems,** which are manufactured in a laboratory and have the same physical and chemical properties as genuine gems. Virtually all types of gems can be manufactured, including synthetic diamonds, emeralds, and sapphires. These gems are used in watches and sold for use in fine jewelry.

Three marine gems used as gemstones include **amber,** an amorphous fossil resin exuded from prehistoric trees that is found in deposits along the southern coast of the Baltic Sea. Poland, Germany, Rumania, Sicily, and Myanmar are the major producers. Amber exists in colors ranging from clear to brownish red and is translucent. The most popular color is a "clear" yellow. **Red coral** is a translucent substance made up of calcareous skeletons secreted by tiny marine animals found in tropical seas. Coral is used for necklaces, rosaries, and bracelets and may be cut into beads. **Genuine pearls** are secured from oysters in which a grain of sand irritates the oyster, causing it to secrete a deposit over the grain, forming the pearl. Very expensive and rare, pearls must be matched in size and color if they are to be used in luxury jewelry. They range from translucent to opaque. In color they are most often white or faintly yellowish or bluish, but they may be pink, yellow, purple, red, green, blue, brown, or black. Genuine pearls also include:

a) **baroque pearls,** which are irregular in shape;

b) **freshwater pearls** of chalk-white color found in mussels in freshwater streams in the United States and not as lustrous as Oriental pearls;

c) **Oriental pearls,** the most beautiful and expensive natural pearls from Japan, the Pacific Islands, the Persian Gulf, Australia, Venezuela, and Panama;

d) **seed pearls,** tiny irregularly-shaped real pearls, formerly used in necklaces, and now used primarily for embroidery on sweaters or wedding dresses.

Cultured pearls are secured by artificially implanting oysters with a tiny round piece of mother-of-pearl, placing oysters in cages, and lowering them into the ocean. Pearls are formed around the irritant. Pearls formed this way do not have many layers of coating, and can only be distinguished from genuine pearl by x-ray. **Simulated pearls** are not gems, but plastic or glass beads coated with a solution called "pearl essence" made from an adhesive combined with fish scales giving an iridescent luster.

Gems are also classified by what is known as a **crystalline structure,** with atoms arranged in a definite pattern. **Cryptocrystalline** gems have a very fine crystalline structure only visible with x-rays. **Amorphous** gems do not have a crystalline structure. The diamond, ruby, and amethyst are crystalline; semi-precious or ornamental gems, such as turquoise and opal, are amorphous.

Only a qualified gemologist can determine accurately the name of a gem. This is done by testing the gem for hardness, specific gravity, light reflection, and crystalline structure. The **Mohs scale** is used to rate the degree of hardness of precious gems. The diamond, the hardest gem, has a hardness of 10 and will scratch any gems that rate below it. A set of minerals used to test gems was invented by Friedrich Mohs and is as follows:

Mineral	Hardness
Talc	1
Gypsum	2
Calcite	3
Fluorite	4
Apatite	5
Orthoclass (feldspar)	6
Quartz	7
Topaz	8
Sapphire	9
Diamond	10

The unit of weight used for gemstones is the **carat.** In actual weight 1 carat equals 200 milligrams (0.200 grams). Fractions of a carat are divided into 10 points. Thus, a 1½ c. stone would be 1.5, or 1 carat and 5 points. So as not to be confused with KARAT (see under OTHER MATERIALS USED IN ACCESSORIES: GOLD), which is related to the quality of gold, the abbreviation used is "c." **Grain** is the measure used to determine the weight of pearls and sometimes diamonds, and one grain is equal to 50 milligrams or ¼ carat. This measure is not the same as the troy grain, a traditional European weight measurement.

TYPES OF GEMS DEFINED

agate Variety of CHALCEDONY quartz (see under TYPES OF GEMS DEFINED) consisting of bands of color arranged in curved or wavy parallel bands and called *banded agate* or in widening circular rings and called *eye agate.* Also with fern or foggy effect called *moss agate* or *mocha stone.*

alexandrite Transparent or translucent variety of the mineral CHRYSOBERYL (see under TYPES OF GEMS DEFINED), which is one color in daylight and another color under artificial light. May appear emerald green in daylight and columbine-red at night. Found in Russia in 1833 on the same day Czar Alexander II celebrated his attainment to majority and thus named after him.

almandite garnet Transparent to opaque semi-precious garnet in deep red, violet red, brownish red to almost black. Includes the CARBUNCLE (see under TYPES OF GEMS DEFINED).

amethyst Transparent purple or violet-colored quartz of the crystalline variety. Rated as a semi-precious stone because it exists in large quantities. Best qualities are a clear even color in the darker tones. The finest qualities come from

Uruguay, Ural Mountains, and Brazil. Other sources include Sri Lanka, Japan, South America, and Mexico.

Arizona ruby See TYPES OF GEMS DEFINED: RUBY.

asterism Ability of a gemstone to project a star-shaped pattern as in RUBIES and SAPPHIRES (see under TYPES OF GEMS DEFINED). Produced synthetically in trademarked Linde Star® and Hope® sapphires.

andradite garnet Transparent to opaque GARNETS (see under TYPES OF GEMS DEFINED) called by various names: **topazolite**, yellow and transparent; **demantoid**, grass-green and transparent, also known erroneously as *olivine* and as *Ural emerald*; **melanite**, black opaque garnets formerly used for mourning jewelry.

aquamarine Transparent variety of BERYL (see under TYPES OF GEMS DEFINED) from which the emerald comes. Has the same crystalline structure and hardness, but color is aqua rather than green. Comes from Ural Mountains, Brazil, and Madagascar. One large aquamarine found in Minas Gerais, Brazil, weighed 243 pounds.

balas ruby See TYPES OF GEMS DEFINED: SPINEL.

banded agate See TYPES OF GEMS DEFINED: AGATE.

beryl Mineral from which the EMERALD (see under TYPES OF GEMS DEFINED) is obtained.

birthstone Precious or semiprecious stone assigned to the month of birth, often worn in a ring. Although the breastplate of Jewish high priests (worn first by Aaron) contained 12 stones, and there were in ancient times 12 stones for the signs of the Zodiac, the custom of a birthstone for each month is comparatively recent. Became popular among the Hebrews in Poland in the 18th c., reaching its greatest popularity in the 20th c. Popular birthstones are: January—garnet; February—amethyst; March—aquamarine, bloodstone; April—diamond, white sapphire; May—emerald; June—alexandrite, moonstone, pearl; July—ruby; August—peridot, sardonyx; September—sapphire; October—opal, tourmaline; November—citrine (yellow quartz), topaz; December—lapis lazuli, turquoise, zircon.

bloodstone Opaque variety of the mineral quartz characterized by red spots on a dark green background. The early church frequently used it to engrave sacred objects, the red spots simulating the blood of Christ. Found in India and Siberia. Also called *heliotrope.*

Borazon® Trademark for General Electric's industrial artificial diamonds. First made in 1957, now tons are produced yearly. More suitable than natural diamonds for some industrial purposes.

Brazilian emerald Misleading term for a green TOURMALINE (see under TYPES OF GEMS DEFINED) used as a gemstone.

Brazilian peridot Misleading term for a yellow-green TOURMALINE (see under TYPES OF GEMS DEFINED) used as a gemstone.

Brazilian sapphire Misleading term for a blue TOURMALINE (see under TYPES OF GEMS DEFINED) used as a gemstone.

cairngorm Popular stone in Scotland. See TYPES OF GEMS DEFINED: SMOKY QUARTZ.

canary diamond Fancy diamond in a definite yellow color. As differentiated from diamonds that have a yellow tinge, genuine yellow diamonds are rare and expensive.

Cape May diamond Misleading term for rock crystal from Cape May, New Jersey.

cape ruby Gem from the GARNET (see under TYPES OF GEMS DEFINED) group, ruby red to black in color and found in deposits with diamonds in Africa. No relationship to genuine ruby.

carbuncle Variety of ALMANDITE GARNET (see under TYPES OF GEMS DEFINED) that varies from deep red and violet-red to brownish red and black. Transparent red varieties are used for gems. Before scientific testing, often believed to be a RUBY or SPINEL (see under TYPES OF GEMS DEFINED).

carnelian Transparent to translucent reddish variety of CHALCEDONY (see under TYPES OF GEMS DEFINED) that may be pale red, deep clear red, brownish red, or yellow green. Also called *sard. Der.* Latin, "flesh-colored."

cat's eye 1. Variety of opalescent greenish CHRYSOBERYL, that is CHATOYANT when cut CABOCHON style (see under ANATOMY OF GEM CUTS). Light seems to fluctuate lengthwise across the stone as it is turned under the light. Also called *cymophane* and *oriental cat's eye.*

2. Variety of QUARTZ (see under TYPES OF GEMS DEFINED), also chatoyant, which is grayish, brownish, or green in color. Not as valuable as #1.

chalcedony   (kal-say-doe'-nee) Transparent to translucent varieties of QUARTZ known by different names for each color. Red is called CARNELIAN, apple green called CHRYSOPRASE, dark green with red spots is called BLOODSTONE or HELIOTROPE, black-and-white banded is called ONYX, and brown banded with white called SARDONYX. See under TYPES OF GEMS DEFINED.

chlorspinel   See TYPES OF GEMS DEFINED: SPINEL.

chrysoberyl   A mineral with a hardness of 8.5 from which the following gems are obtained ALEXANDRITE, ORIENTAL CAT'S EYE, and CHRYSOLITE (see under TYPES OF GEMS DEFINED).

chrysolite   See under TYPES OF GEMS DEFINED: PERIDOT.

chrysoprase   Apple-green variety of CHALCEDONY quartz (see under TYPES OF GEMS DEFINED), which comes from California, Oregon, and Silesia.

citrine   (sit-reen') Yellow crystalline quartz that resembles TOPAZ (see under TYPES OF GEMS DEFINED) in color and transparency, sometimes erroneously sold as topaz. Comes from Brazil.

corundum   Extremely hard mineral rating 9 on MOHS SCALE (see under ANATOMY OF GEMS), which produces the precious gems RUBY and SAPPHIRE (see under TYPES OF GEMS DEFINED). Also comes in other colors, but these are not so valuable and are called *fancy sapphires*. All red corundum gems are called rubies.

cross stone   See TYPES OF GEMS DEFINED: FAIRY STONE.

crystal   **1.** Genuine rock crystal, a mineral. See TYPES OF GEMS DEFINED: QUARTZ. **2.** Beads or simulated gems of faceted glass resembling rock crystal.

cubic zirconia   Synthetic stone made to imitate the diamond.

cymophane   See TYPES OF GEMS DEFINED: CAT'S EYE.

diamond   Transparent variety of nearly pure carbon. This is the hardest mineral known and very brilliant when faceted. Colorless stones are most generally known, but diamonds also come in yellow, brown, green, red, and blue. Diamonds are graded according to color, cut, weight, clarity, and brilliance. Originally found only in India, now many come from Brazil and South Africa, with 95% coming from the latter.

emerald   Precious gem from the mineral BERYL (see under TYPES OF GEMS DEFINED). Hardness is 7½ to 8. Best stones are transparent to translucent green, and large stones of clear color are rare, thus making them very valuable. Comes from Colombia and Brazil, also found in Ural Mountains and Australia.

eye agate   See TYPES OF GEMS DEFINED: AGATE.

fairy stone   Mineral frequently found in the shape of a cross caused by twin crystals. Usually reddish brown in color and translucent to opaque. Used for crosses for the clergy or for curiosity items. Also known as *staurolite* and *cross stone*.

fancy diamond   Any diamond with a distinctive color and high degree of transparency. May be yellow or brown, with green, red, or blue, the latter three being the most rare.

fancy sapphires   See TYPES OF GEMS DEFINED: CORUNDUM.

feldspar   A transparent to opaque mineral with vitreous to pearly luster and a hardness of 6½. Various colors of gem varieties are called by the following names: opalescent, called *moonstone*, comes from Switzerland, Elba, and Sri Lanka; green, called *amazon stone*, comes from the Urals and Pennsylvania; blue, called *Labradorite*, comes from Labrador; yellow, called *orthoclase*, comes from Madagascar; and reddish, called *sunstone* or *aventurine*, comes from Norway and Siberia.

fire opal   Semitransparent to transparent variety of opal that is yellow, orange, or red in color. May show a play of color.

garnet   Gems with a hardness of 6½ to 7½ that exist in too large a quantity to be considered precious gems. Exists in all colors except blue and ranges from transparent to opaque. Varieties include ANDRADITE and ALMANDITE (see under TYPES OF GEMS DEFINED).

golden beryl   Yellow transparent variety of the mineral BERYL (see under TYPES OF GEMS DEFINED). It is semiprecious.

goshenite   Colorless transparent variety of the mineral BERYL (see under TYPES OF GEMS DEFINED).

harlequin opal (har-lay'-kin) White opal that displays uniform patches of colors resembling a mosaic.

helidor Yellow transparent variety of the mineral BERYL (see under TYPES OF GEMS DEFINED) from southwest Africa.

heliotrope See TYPES OF GEMS DEFINED: BLOOD-STONE.

hematite Iron mineral that is opaque black, or black with red streaks and metallic luster. Comes from England, Norway, Sweden, and Lake Superior region.

Herkimer diamond Misleading term for ROCK CRYSTAL (see under TYPES OF GEMS DEFINED).

Hope Star® Trademark for a synthetic STAR SAPPHIRE (see under TYPES OF GEMS DEFINED).

hyacinth Name used for clear transparent ZIRCONS (see under TYPES OF GEMS DEFINED) of yellow, orange, red, and brown varieties. Also called *jacinth.*

imitation gems Reproductions of fine gemstones in colored glass or other inexpensive material as distinguished from man-made SYNTHETIC GEMS (see under TYPES OF GEMS DEFINED). The latter, although man-made, are chemically identical to gems occurring in nature.

jacinth See TYPES OF GEMS DEFINED: HYACINTH.

jade Includes two minerals of similar appearance, **nephrite** and **jadeite**. The former is the most common variety with a hardness of 6 to 6½, and color variations from white to leaf green. Often found in China, Turkestan, Siberia, and Alaska. Jadeite is lustrous, transparent to opaque, and more rare with a hardness of 6½ to 7. Color is white or greenish white to emerald green, translucent to opaque, and found in upper Burma, Yunnan in southern China, Tibet, Mexico, and South America. In 1965, boulders weighing as much as 10,000 pounds containing gem-quality jade (nephrite) were found in Alaska. Popular in China for centuries either carved into objects or used for jewelry.

jargon See TYPES OF GEMS DEFINED: ZIRCON.

jasper Form of opaque QUARTZ (see under TYPES OF GEMS DEFINED) available in brown, dark green, grayish blue, red, or yellow colors.

jet An opaque mineral made largely of carbon, a variety of lignite or coal, which polishes easily.

Comes from England, Spain, France, and the United States. Black varieties of QUARTZ, OBSIDIAN (see under TYPES OF GEMS DEFINED), and glass also masquerade as this mineral. All were used for pins, earrings, and beads in mourning jewelry during Victorian era.

Lake George diamond Misleading term for ROCK CRYSTAL (see under TYPES OF GEMS DEFINED).

lapis lazuli Translucent to opaque mineral in tones of blue, deep blue, azure blue, Berlin blue, and greenish blue. It is a mixture of lazurite and other minerals. Comes from Afghanistan, Siberia, and Chile. In contemporary times, used for beads, brooches, pendants, and cuff links.

Linde Star® Trademark for a synthetic gem that imitates the star sapphire.

malachite Ornamental opaque stone that exists in too large a quantity and is too soft to be a precious or semiprecious gem, mainly from Ural Mountains. May have irregular rings of various tones or be banded. Primary color is green—from emerald green to grass green.

marcasite (mar-ka'-sight) Mineral with a metallic luster having the same composition as iron pyrite, but with different crystals. Cut material sold as marcasite is usually pyrite.

mauve diamond (mowv) Fancy diamond of a purplish hue.

melanite See TYPES OF GEMS DEFINED: ANDRADITE GARNET.

mocha stone SEE TYPES OF GEMS DEFINED: AGATE.

moonstone Opalescent gem variety of FELDSPAR (see under TYPES OF GEMS DEFINED), which is cut CABOCHON style (see under ANATOMY OF GEM CUTS).

morganite Transparent pink to rose variety of the mineral BERYL (see under TYPES OF GEMS DEFINED). *Der.* Named after J.P. Morgan, financier and collector of gems.

moss agate See TYPES OF GEMS DEFINED: AGATE.

nephrite See TYPES OF GEM DEFINED: JADE.

obsidian Volcanic glass rather than a mineral. Usually black in color, but also comes in red, brown, and greenish black. Attractive colors are cut as gems. Comes from Mexico, Greece, California, and Wyoming.

off-color diamond Trade term used in America for a diamond with a tinge of an undesirable color, particularly yellow or brown, which is easily discernible.

olivine The gemologists' term for PERIDOT (see under TYPES OF GEMS DEFINED).

onyx Variety of CHALCEDONY quartz (see under TYPES OF GEMS DEFINED), which consists of parallel straight bands of black and white. Used for cameos and stones for rings. A ring popular for many years is composed of a large onyx with small DIAMOND (see under TYPES OF GEMS DEFINED) mounted on it.

opal Transparent to opaque gem, which is AMORPHOUS (see under ANATOMY OF GEMS) and has a pleasing play of color, or opalescence, when cut CABOCHON (see under ANATOMY OF GEM CUTS). Comes in many colors including the valuable dark gray, blue, and black colors called *black opal*. Also see TYPES OF GEMS DEFINED: FIRE OPAL and HARLEQUIN OPAL.

oriental cat's eye See TYPES OF GEMS DEFINED: CAT'S EYE.

peridot (pehr′-ee-dot) Transparent gem that is bottle green to olive green in color and comes from Myanmar, Ceylon, and Brazil. Also called *chrysolite*. Called OLIVINE (see under TYPES OF GEMS DEFINED) by mineralogists.

quartz Mineral used for gems that exists in both crystalline transparent varieties, and CRYPTOCRYSTALLINE (see under ANATOMY OF GEM CUTS) TRANSPARENT or OPAQUE varieties (see under ANATOMY OF GEM CUTS). CRYSTALLINE (see under ANATOMY OF GEM CUTS) varieties include *rock crystal, amethyst, rose quartz, smoky quartz, citrine, tiger's eye,* and *cat's eye.* Cryptocrystalline quartz appears to the unaided eye to be amorphous, but revealed as crystalline under the microscope. Usually regarded as chalcedony although various colors go by different names (e.g., *carnelian* or *sard, chrysoprase, bloodstone* or *heliotrope, agate, onyx, sardonyx, jasper.*)

rhinestone A colorless transparent artificial gem made of glass or PASTE (see under ANATOMY OF GEMS), usually cut like a diamond, and used widely for costume jewelry and buttons. *Der.* Originally made in Strasbourg, France, on the Rhine River.

rock crystal Clear transparent crystalline variety of the mineral QUARTZ (see under TYPES OF GEMS DEFINED). Exists in such large quantities

that it is inexpensive. May be carved for beads. May also be imitated by glass poured into molds to make beads.

rose quartz Transparent crystalline variety of QUARTZ (see under TYPES OF GEMS DEFINED) in rose-pink color.

rubicelle See TYPES OF GEMS DEFINED: SPINEL.

ruby Transparent precious gem that comes from the mineral CORUNDUM. Pigeon's blood red is the preferred color. Some stones have an ASTERISM and are called STAR RUBIES. Best quality comes from Burma. The terms *cape ruby* and *Arizona ruby* are misleading and refer to GARNETS. The term *balas ruby* is misleading and refers to a SPINEL (see cross references under TYPES OF GEMS DEFINED).

sapphire All-precious transparent CORUNDUM (see under TYPES OF GEMS DEFINED) mineral of a color other than red. Preferred color is cornflower blue and called "Kashmir blue." Other sapphires may be white, pink, or yellow. May also be asterated and then called a STAR SAPPHIRE (see under TYPES OF GEMS DEFINED). Rates next to the DIAMOND (see under TYPES OF GEMS DEFINED) in hardness.

sapphirine See TYPES OF GEMS DEFINED: SPINEL.

sard See TYPES OF GEMS DEFINED: CARNELIAN.

sardonyx Variety of CHALCEDONY quartz that is composed of banded layers of sard or CARNELIAN, and layers of white (see under TYPES OF GEMS DEFINED).

simulated gems Term applied to copies of precious gems made of PASTE, or other inexpensive materials. See under ANATOMY OF GEMS. Sometimes confused with SYNTHETIC GEMS, which are man-made but chemically identical to natural gems.

smoky quartz Transparent variety of *crystalline quartz* in smoky yellow to dark brown. The national gem of Scotland. Also called *cairngorm*. Sometimes mistaken for TOPAZ (see under TYPES OF GEMS DEFINED).

spinel Transparent to opaque semiprecious mineral that closely resembles the ruby. Softer and lighter in weight than a ruby with hardness of 8 on MOHS SCALE (see under ANATOMY OF GEMS). Preferred color is deep ruby-red; comes in a great variety of other colors including violet and purple. Misleading terms for the above include:

balas ruby, rubicelle, almandine, sapphirine, and *chlorspinel.* Spinels should be identified by color name. A large red stone on the English Crown, called the Black Prince's ruby, was later proved to be a spinel.

star ruby   Genuine ruby from corundum mineral which shows a five- or six-pointed star or ASTERISM when cut CABOCHON style (see under TYPES OF GEMS DEFINED).

star sapphire   Genuine sapphire from CORUNDUM (see under TYPES OF GEMS DEFINED) mineral that shows a five- or six-pointed star or ASTERISM (see under TYPES OF GEMS DEFINED) when cut CABOCHON (see under ANATOMY OF GEM CUTS). Color varies from blue to gray and transparent to translucent. The 116-carat Midnight Star Sapphire and the 563-carat Star of India, the largest star sapphire in the world, were recovered after a jewel robbery at the Museum of Natural History in New York City in 1965.

staurolite   See TYPES OF GEMS DEFINED: FAIRY STONE.

synthetic gem   Gem manufactured in a laboratory having the same physical and chemical properties as genuine gems. Virtually all types of gems can be manufactured, including synthetic diamonds, emeralds, and sapphires. These gems are used in watches and sold for fine jewelry when mounted in necklaces, bracelets, and rings.

tanzanite   First discovered in the foothills of Mount Kilimanjaro in Tanzania, Africa. In 1968 was confirmed to be blue zoisite by gemologists—the first ever found. Name was changed by Tiffany's of New York to tanzanite, from place where it was found. Not a precious stone, but beautiful when cut. Changes color when held in light to a blue, richer than a sapphire; purple, similar to amethyst; and pinkish salmon brown. One gem found was 2,500 carats and when cut weighed 360 carats.

tiger's eye   Semiprecious variety of QUARTZ (see under TYPES OF GEMS DEFINED) is CHATOYANT when cut CABOCHON (see under ANATOMY OF GEM CUTS). Yellowish-brown, bluish, or red in color. Found in South Africa.

topaz   Transparent gem of which the most precious is wine-yellow in color. Other colors include colorless, yellowish brown, gray, pale tints of green, blue, lavender, and red. With a hardness of 8, only the DIAMOND, RUBY, SAPPHIRE, and CHRYSOBERYL are harder; the EMERALD and SPINEL are of equal hardness. (See cross references under TYPES OF GEMS DEFINED.) Found in Europe, South America, Sri Lanka, Japan, Mexico, Utah, Colorado, and Maine.

topazolite   See TYPES OF GEMS DEFINED: ANDRADITE GARNET.

tourmaline   Transparent semiprecious mineral that comes in many colors: achroite, colorless; rubellite, rose-red; siberite, violet; indicolite, dark blue, green, blue, and yellowish green. Sometimes erroneously called *Brazilian emerald, Brazilian peridot* (pehr'-ee-dot), *Brazilian sapphire,* and *peridot of Ceylon.*

turquoise   Opaque amorphous ornamental stone that comes in sky blue, greenish blue, or apple green. Used for jewelry, but exists in too large a quantity to be rare. Popular for jewelry made by Native Americans of Arizona and Mexico; usually set in silver for bracelets, necklaces, pins, and earrings.

Ural emerald   See TYPES OF GEMS DEFINED: ANDRADITE GARNET.

zircon   Transparent gem with a luster approaching the DIAMOND (see under TYPES OF GEMS DEFINED) when brilliant cut is used. White colorless stones resembling diamonds are sometimes referred to as *matura diamonds,* a misleading term. Yellow, orange, red, and brown zircons are called *hyacinth* or *jacinth;* all other colors, including colorless gray and smoky, are called *jargons,* while blue are called *blue zircon.* An 103-carat zircon is in The Smithsonian Institution in Washington, D.C.

ANATOMY OF GEM CUTS

Various methods are used to cut gemstones that are mounted into gold and other metals in order to create jewelry. The basic steps in cutting precious gems such as diamonds are these:

1. **marking,** if the stone is large enough to be split into several parts, its crystalline structure is evaluated to determine how it will split best. The next step is to mark where it will be split.

2. **cleaving,** a groove is cut, a wedge inserted in the groove, and the wedge struck to split the stone along the cleavage.

3. **sawing,** cutting the stone with a special saw.

4. **girdling,** rounding the stone into a cone shape.

5. **faceting,** placing the main **facet,** a small plane cut in a gemstone, to enhance its ability to reflect light—the more facets, the more brilliance.

In describing cut gems, the following terms are often used.

bevel Slanted cut on gemstone, to give light reflection, especially on square-cut gemstones.

chip **1.** A small or an irregularly shaped cut diamond. **2.** A break on the edge of a larger diamond.

cleavage Ability of gemstone to break along the crystalline structure lines; especially important when cutting valuable diamonds.

crown Upper portion of a brilliant-cut faceted stone (e.g., a diamond). Also called *bezel.*

doublet Jewelry term for two pieces of glass or gems cemented together to form one large stone.

false doublet Stone made from two pieces cemented at the GIRDLE (see under ANATOMY OF GEM CUTS), in which a genuine stone makes up the crown or top, and a cheaper stone or glass is used for the PAVILION or bottom part (see under ANATOMY OF GEM CUTS).

Preferences for cuts is subject to current fashions in gems. One of the popular cuts is the **brilliant cut,** a faceted cut used particularly for diamonds and transparent gems. There can be 58, 64, 72, or 80 facets. It usually appears with a flat surface on top, called the **table,** sloping outwardly to the **girdle** or widest point, and tapered to a point at the bottom where a small facet called the **culet** (kue´-lit) is cut. In jewelry industry terminology the lower portion below the girdle of a brilliant cut gem is called the **base** or **pavilion.** When mounted, only about one third of the gem is visible. The number of facets and the precision in cutting increase the brilliancy of the stone. Brilliant cut stones may be made in various shapes: round; oval; **marquise** (mar-keez´), which is an

brilliant gem cut top

brilliant gem cut side

marquise cut top

marquise cut side

oval with pointed ends; **pear cut** with one pointed end and one rounded end that is shaped somewhat like a pear and is used particularly for large diamonds; and **heart-shaped cut** in the shape of a heart and used for large diamonds. The **old mine cut** was a type of brilliant cut in the 19th c. that retained much of original stone and had a larger culet and smaller table when compared to modern cuts. The **cushion cut** is a variation of the brilliant cut that is square shaped with the corners cut off and rounded at the widest part of the stone or girdle. It is used particularly for large diamonds and transparent stones. **Melee** (may-lay´) is a collective term for small, brilliant-cut diamonds usually .20 to .25 carats.

pear gem cut

heart gem cut

Other popular gem cuts include:

baguette cut (ba-get´) Small stones cut in oblong shape with FACETS (see under ANATOMY OF GEM CUTS). Usually placed horizontally along the side of a larger center diamond. *Der.* French, "rod."

baguette gem cut top

cabochon cut (ka-bow-shown´) **1.** Type of cut used for gemstones that involves rounding off the top of the stone so that it is higher in the center and slopes to the rim. Used particularly for STAR RUBIES and SAPPHIRES (see under TYPES OF GEMS DEFINED). **2.** A **high cabochon** cut is a stone with a flat base and a higher elongated top. Also called a *tallow top cut.*

cabochon gem cut top

cabochon gem cut side

cameo cut A raised design carved out of a stone (e.g., onyx or banded sardonyx), which has more than one layer. The foreground color is carved away, leaving a white design exposed on a colored surface, usually of black or orange. Also see JEWELRY: OTHER TYPES OF JEWELRY DEFINED: WEDGEWOOD® CAMEO in alphabetical listing.

high cabochon

lentil shaped cabochon

chatoyancy (sha-toy´-an-see) Optical properties in certain gems produced when stone is cut. As stone is turned, a single streak of light reflects from needlelike crystals arranged parallel to one another. See TYPES OF GEMS DEFINED: CAT'S EYE or TIGER'S EYE. *Der.* French, *chatoyer*, "to change luster," as a cat's eye.

cushion cut Variation of the BRILLIANT CUT (see under ANATOMY OF GEM CUTS).

emerald cut A type of STEP CUT (see under ANATOMY OF GEM CUTS) with all four square corners cut off diagonally. Used particularly for emeralds and large diamonds. Also see ANATOMY OF GEM CUTS: CUSHION CUT.

emerald gem cut top

intaglio/intaglio cut (in-tal′-yo) Method of cutting gems by engraving design into the surface. Compare with CAMEO carving (see under ANATOMY OF GEM CUTS).

oval cut Variation of the BRILLIANT CUT (see under ANATOMY OF GEM CUTS) made in oval shape.

oval gem cut

pavilion Jewelry industry term for lower portion below the GIRDLE of a BRILLIANT-CUT gem (see under ANATOMY OF GEM CUTS). Also called the *base*.

rose cut top

rose cut Simple faceted cut, used for inexpensive gems.

rose cut side

square cut See ANATOMY OF GEM CUTS: EMERALD CUT.

step cut Rectangular stone cut with facets that are oblong and placed in horizontal positions in steps or rows, both above and below the girdle, or widest part of the stone.

table See ANATOMY OF GEM CUTS: BRILLIANT CUT.

tallow top cut See ANATOMY OF GEM CUTS: CABOCHON #2.

ANATOMY OF GEM SETTINGS

Stones are mounted so that they can be placed into an article of jewelry. The **collet** is the rim of the metal device into which the gem is set and, depending on the shape of the gem, may be round, oval, rectangular, or square. If the gem is irregularly shaped, the collet follows the shape of the gem. Metals used for genuine jewelry are usually silver, platinum, or 14k or 18k gold. COSTUME JEWELRY (see JEWELRY) uses any type of metal, sometimes gold washed or gold-plated. The stone rests on a sort of ledge under the upper part of the collet, then the upper edge is pounded down around the gem to hold it in place. **Coronet settings** have edges that are shaped into toothlike structures that are pounded down to hold the gem in place.

The following are the most widely used settings.

channel setting Grooves of metal used to hold stones. Also called *flush setting*.

channel setting

fishtail setting Series of scallops (like fish scales) holding stone in place.

flush setting See ANATOMY OF GEM SETTINGS: CHANNEL SETTING.

paste setting Stone is glued in place; method used for inexpensive stones.

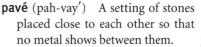
fishtail setting

pavé (pah-vay′) A setting of stones placed close to each other so that no metal shows between them.

pronged setting Stone held in place by narrow projecting pieces of metal.

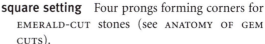
pronged setting

square setting Four prongs forming corners for EMERALD-CUT stones (see ANATOMY OF GEM CUTS).

Tiffany setting High-pronged setting for solitaire stone introduced by Tiffany & Co., New York jewelers, in 1870s, and often imitated. In 1971 Tiffany introduced a modernized version of its famous setting.

COMPONENTS OF ACCESSORIES: GEMS, GEM CUTS, AND SETTINGS

STRAW *and* STRAWLIKE MATERIALS

MATERIALS FROM WHICH STRAW IS MADE

Straw is a vegetable substance or a synthetic imitation. Natural straw comes from dried stems of such grains as barley, oats, rye, and wheat, from stems and stalks of other plants, from leaves, and from bark. Some types of straw are of

straw bag

such fine quality that they are identified by the name of the locality where they are obtained. For example, **leghorn straw** is a fine, smooth braid plaited with thirteen strands of straw that is made from the upper part of wheat stalks grown near Livorno (called Leghorn in English), a town in Tuscany, Italy. **Milan** (mih-lan´) **straw** is made from the lower part of a type of wheat stalk, called *pedal straw,* grown near the city of Milan in Italy. It is plaited, using seven strands in each braid. A **Panama hat** is made of fine, expensive straw obtained from the leaves of the *jipijapa* plant.

One of the important uses for straw is in headwear. Straw may be woven into bodies of hats, a difficult process often done by people who live where the straw is grown. The body is shaped through **blocking,** a process of putting the hat on a wooden form in the shape of the hat, steaming and then drying. Alternatively, straw may be made into narrow "straw braid" that is stitched together in a circular manner. Straw can also be used in handbags, particularly the basket type; in footwear; belts; and as trim.

Imitations of natural straw can be made from a variety of manufactured materials such as cellophane, rayon, nylon, polypropylene, and various plastics.

TYPES OF TRUE AND SYNTHETIC STRAW DEFINED

abaca   Fiber from the leaf stems of the abaca plant that are coarse, creamy white to brown in color, strong and durable. Used to make hats. Referred to as *Manilla hemp,* though it is not a true hemp.

baku   **1.** A fine, lightweight, expensive straw with a dull finish that is woven in the Shandung province (Shantung) of China. This fiber is also obtained from the buri palm in Sri Lanka and along the Malabar coast. **2.** A coarser straw from Taiwan, also used for millinery.

balibuntal   A very light fiber, obtained from unopened palm leaf stems in the Philippines, that is used in better grades of straw hat braid.

cabuya plant   Plant from Ecuador that is similar to the North American century plant. Fibers are removed from its leaves and used to make handbags.

cellophane   Generic name, once a trademark, for thin transparent film made of cellulose acetate. It is used in ribbon-sized strips to cover paper fibers imitating straw or used alone as synthetic straw for hats, handbags, etc.

corn husks The dried outer covering of ears of corn that are sometimes woven into handbags and hats.

jute See TEXTILES IN ACCESSORIES: NATURAL FIBERS DEFINED.

natural straw Straw made from any vegetable plant or tree grown in the soil, e.g, bark, coconut fibers, grass, hemp, or palm tree fibers.

panama See MATERIALS FROM WHICH STRAW IS MADE and TYPES OF STRAW DEFINED: TOQUILLA.

raffia (raf'-ee-uh) Fiber from species of Madagascar palm used for making hats, bags, and fabrics.

rice straw Fibers obtained from the stems of rice plants.

rush straw The stems of some aquatic plants that are round. They are dried and used in making headwear and handbags.

sisal Finely woven smooth straw with a linen finish made from Philippine sisal hemp.

toquilla Fibrous veins from the leaves of the toquilla palm tree of Equador. Used to make PANAMA HATS (see under HEADWEAR, VEILS, AND HAIR ACCESSORIES: TYPES OF HEADWEAR DEFINED: HATS AND BONNETS).

tuscan A straw obtained from the tops of bleached wheat stems from the region of Tuscany in Italy. Often woven into lacelike patterns.

CLOSURES

HISTORY AND USAGE OF CLOSURES IN FASHION ACCESSORIES

A **closure** is a device used to close or fasten garments or accessories (synonyms: *closing, fastener*). As long as individuals have worn clothing, they have required some means of closing areas of the items they have worn. These closures may be purely functional, but often they have a decorative purpose as well. In antiquity, straight pins and other types of pins, somewhat like contemporary safety pins, were used. The Greeks and Romans used buttons and loops, that fastened around the buttons. A **button** is a small round disklike device that is usually made with holes punched in the center or a shank on the back through which thread is passed in order to fasten it to the garment. To close an area, the button is attached to one side of an opening and slips through a hole or loop on the opposite side.

Northern Europeans used pins or brooches to fasten garments. Although buttons were introduced in the 13th c. as trim, they did not become functional until the 14th c. when buttonholes were developed. By the 16th c., buttons of all types were in use. The earliest buttons were made of bone, wood, and metal. As technology for their manufacture was refined, materials such as pewter, ceramics, glass, brass, cut steel, shell, and plastic were added. By the 20th c., buttons were more utilitarian than decorative. By the end of the 20th c., other closures were being used in many areas where buttons were formerly placed. In accessories today they are used to close footwear, gloves, and handbags.

Another fastener is the **buckle.** This is a decorative or functional clasp that is made of similar materials to those listed for buttons. A buckle usually consists of a rectangular or curved rim, often with one or more movable tongues, or it may be a clip device fixed to the end of a strap that is used to fasten two ends of a belt, to close a shoe, or to fasten a strap. Buckles were used in Greece and Rome to fasten belts, and in Northern European regions as part of military equipment. Gold buckles remain from the 7th c. Elaborate and costly, buckled belts were worn as status symbols by knights in the late Middle Ages. Highly decorative shoe buckles fastened shoes for the upper classes in the 17th and 18th c. At present ornate, purely decorative, buckles are found only on women's shoes. Those on men's shoes are generally both functional and simple. Buckles appear on accessories such as belts, handbags, and shoes.

Hook and eye closings use a small metal hook on one side of an opening and either an embroidered loop or a small metal loop on the other side. Little used in accessories, these closures occasionally are found as fasteners on collars and cuffs. The **snap closure,** a round metal fastener, is made in two pieces. One piece is sewn to one part of an opening and the other to the opposite side. One side has a raised center prong that fits into a recessed center area on the second piece. A **gripper closure** is very similar and consists of a metal fastener in the shape of a large snap that is clamped onto either side of an opening by a machine, rather than being sewn. Such closures appear occasionally on footwear, belts, handbags, and gloves.

A **laced closing** is a leather thong or cord laced through small metal or embroidered eyelets. Before the development of buttons, this was a popular method of fastening garments in the Middle Ages. From the 18th c. and on, it became the most common method of fastening shoes. Belts sometimes close by lacing.

Although the name **zipper** was coined and registered as a trademark by B.F. Goodrich Co. in 1925, the forerunner of this device was invented in 1891 by Witcomb B. Judson. He called it a *clasp locker.* Gideon Sundback improved the design. He manufactured *Hookless Fasteners* for use on corsets, gloves, sleeping bags, money belts, and tobacco pouches. Goodrich used zippers in what he called "Zipper boots." By the 1930s zippers were so widely used in garments ranging from handbags to men's trousers that "zipper" became a generic term applied to any toothed, slide fastener. This device consists of parallel rows of metal or nylon teeth on adjacent edges of an opening, that are interlocked by a sliding tab. The zipper teeth may be covered by fabric tape and almost invisible or can be made in various lengths and weights for use on handbags, luggage, and footwear. Large-sized zippers are called **industrial zippers.**

Velcro® is the trademark for a tape woven with minute nylon hooks that mesh with loops on opposite tape. Used on footwear, handbags, luggage, and belts, this closure was first used by astronauts. The generic term for this type of closure is *hook and loop.*

TYPES OF CLOSURES DEFINED

abalone button (ah-bah-low-nee′) Type of pearl button made from shell of a mollusk, called an ear shell or sea-ear, found off Pacific coast of the United States.

belt buckle Any ornamental or functional device, usually plastic or metal, used to fasten a belt.

blazer button Distinctive brass or gold-plated brass button with a monogram, a coat-of-arms, or a crest embossed or engraved on top. Usually sold by the set, which includes three large and four small sleeve buttons. The name derives from their use on blazers.

blind eyelet Shoe-industry term for metal eyelet concealed in the inner surface of leather while the outside layer has a punched hole through which the shoestring is pulled.

bound buttonhole Buttonhole with edges finished with separate strips of fabric or leather binding.

bound buttonhole

brass button Gilt button made of brass or of other metals or plastic gilded to simulate brass.

buckle See HISTORY AND USAGE OF CLOSURES IN FASHION ACCESSORIES.

button See HISTORY AND USAGE OF CLOSURES IN FASHION ACCESSORIES.

buttonhole Opening for button to go through in order to secure the garment. Generally classified as either a BOUND or a WORKED buttonhole (see under TYPES OF CLOSURES DEFINED). The use of buttonholes dates from about the 15th c.

button hooks See TYPES OF CLOSURES DEFINED: SPEED LACING.

chain closure Laced closing using a metal chain instead of a lacer.

cinch buckle/cinch closure See TYPES OF CLOSURES DEFINED: RING BUCKLE.

clip closure Metal fastener with a spring-backed device on one side of the garment and a ring, eyelet, or slotted fastener on the other side.

covered button Ball or disk-type button covered with fabric either matching or contrasting with garment.

covered zipper Zipper made with fabric tape covering teeth so that teeth do not show when zipper is closed.

crocheted button Shank-type buttons made by crocheting over a disk, a ball, or a barrel-shaped object. Sometimes used on crocheted accessories such as handbags.

cut-steel buckle Popular buckle made of polished steel with jewel-like facets. Sometimes used on silk or moiré afternoon or evening shoes and on belts.

D-ring closure **1.** See TYPES OF CLOSURES DEFINED: RING BUCKLE. **2.** Closings on footwear that are D-shaped through which shoe laces are threaded.

frog Ornamental fastener using cording or braid through which a soft ball made of cording or a button is pulled. Also called *olivettes.*

frog

galosh closure Closing with a metal hook on one side that clips into a metal fastener with several slots in order to adjust the degree of tightness. *Der.* Similar to closings for galoshes in the early 20th c.

glitter button   Any type of button set with rhinestones or imitation gems. Also see TYPES OF CLOSURES DEFINED: RHINESTONE BUTTON.

glove button   Tiny buttons, usually round and often pearlized, used to button long gloves.

gold button   Any type of gold-colored button, formerly solid gold or plated.

gripper closure   Metal fastener in the shape of a large snap that is clamped onto the base material.

hook and eye   See HISTORY AND USAGE OF CLOSURES IN FASHION ACCESSORIES.

hook and loop closure   See CLOSURES: VELCRO®.

industrial zipper   See TYPES OF CLOSURES DEFINED: ZIPPER.

laced closing   See HISTORY AND USAGE OF CLOSURES IN FASHION ACCESSORIES.

lacing studs   See TYPES OF CLOSURES DEFINED: SPEED LACING.

latch buckle   Round, square, or oblong metal plates attached to each end of a belt and closed over one another. A swivel from one end of the belt slips through a slot in the other end and turns to fasten.

loop and button   Closing with a series of corded loops on one side and covered or round buttons on the other side. Sometimes used on gloves.

machine-made buttonhole   Buttonhole made on a sewing machine with a zig-zag stitch or by a special attachment.

mother-of-pearl button   Button made from nacre, the inside shell of the oyster.

pearl button   Classic button for almost any use, originally made from shells. Sometimes called "ocean pearl" until development of plastic in the 1930s, after which imitation pearl buttons were widely used. Also see TYPES OF CLOSURES DEFINED: MOTHER-OF-PEARL BUTTON.

piped buttonhole   Buttonhole similar to BOUND BUTTONHOLE (see under TYPES OF CLOSURES DEFINED) in which piping, a folded piece of bias binding, is used around the opening.

poker chip button   Extra-large round, flat button with a shank on the back. *Der.* From size and shape of a poker chip.

rhinestone button   Any button set with stones made of glass or PASTE (see under GEMS, GEM CUTS, AND SETTINGS: ANATOMY OF GEMS) which simulates a diamond.

ring buckle   Two rings on one end of belt through which the opposite belt end threads—first through both, then back through one—and pulls tight. When rings are made in the shape of a "D," called a **D-ring buckle**. Also called *cinch buckle* or *cinch closing*. Borrowed from fastenings on horse bridles and saddle straps and used mainly on belts.

shank button   Button with metal or plastic loop on the back.

shoe buckle   Buckles worn on the shoe were very popular in the 17th and 18th c. At first they functioned to close the shoe; however, they gradually became a purely decorative element. The style has been revived periodically in the 19th and 20th c. when they were limited to women's shoes; however, the style has been revived more recently for both men's and women's shoes.

slide fastener   See TYPES OF CLOSURES DEFINED: ZIPPER.

snap closure   See HISTORY AND USAGE OF CLOSURES IN FASHION ACCESSORIES.

speed lacing   Closing on boot consisting of metal hooks replacing eyelets for upper part of lacing. Used particularly on ice skates, ski boots, and hiking boots. Also called *button hooks* or *lacing studs.*

stud   Small ornamental closure used since the mid-18th c. that is separate from the garment. It consists of a broader section, a short post, and a smaller buttonlike end that is inserted through an eyelet to fasten a shirt front, a neckband, or cuffs. Also called *collar button.*

tailored buttonhole   See TYPES OF CLOSURES DEFINED: WORKED BUTTONHOLE.

toggle closure   Rod-shaped button usually of wood attached by rope loop on one side of an accessory and pulled through similar loop on opposite side.

toggle closing on coat

Velcro®   See HISTORY AND USAGE OF CLOSURES IN FASHION ACCESSORIES.

wooden button Made of wood in all sizes and shapes—may be in ball shape with shank on back or diskshaped.

worked buttonhole Buttonhole made by covering the raw edges of a slit in the fabric with hand or machine stitches. In hand-worked buttonholes, first the slit is made, then the raw edges are covered by embroidering them with a buttonhole stitch. Machine-made worked buttonholes are stitched first, then cut open. A stitch similar to the buttonhole stitch is made by the sewing machine. The shapes of worked buttonholes may vary as follows: **barred** or **rectangular buttonhole,**

barred buttonhole

a worked buttonhole with straight bar, called a bar tack, embroidered across the ends; **oval buttonhole,** a worked buttonhole with fan-shaped arrangement of stitches at both ends; **tailored buttonhole,** a worked

oval buttonhole

tailored buttonhole

buttonhole with a bar tack at one end and a fan-shaped arrangement of stitches at the other end; **keyhole buttonhole,** a worked buttonhole with a bar tack at one end and an area of much enlarged fan-shaped stitches at the other, so as to allow a place for the button shank to rest.

zipper See HISTORY AND USAGE OF CLOSURES IN FASHION ACCESSORIES.

COMPONENTS OF ACCESSORIES: CLOSURES

EMBROIDERIES *and* SEWING STITCHES

ROLE AND FUNCTION OF EMBROIDERIES AND SEWING STITCHES IN ACCESSORIES

Embroidery is fancy needlework or trimming using colored yarn, embroidery floss (a soft-twisted thread), soft cotton, silk, or metallic thread. It may be done

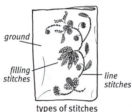

ground

filling stitches

line stitches

types of stitches

by hand or on sewing machines or mechanized machines for mass production. For example, one such machine, the **Schiffli machine,** can embroider the entire width of fabric at one time in either elaborate or simple designs. Both eyelet and quilted designs may be made in many colors simultaneously. Among the accessories that are most likely to use embroidery for decoration are handbags, shawls, scarves, and handkerchiefs. Occasionally the fabrics used to cover shoes or hats may also be embroidered. Some of the more common types of embroidery that may be used on accessories are defined below and illustrated.

In primitive times, straws or grasses were used to embroider with bone needles. Gold embroidery was first made by Assyrians and later copied by Egyptians, Greeks, and Romans. Each country in Europe developed its own type of embroidery. For accessories embroidery generally serves a purely decorative function. Fine types of hand embroidery are most likely to be used on handkerchiefs. Some handbags may be ornamented with NEEDLEPOINT (see TYPES OF EMBROIDERY DEFINED) or similar decorative techniques.

Sewing stitches can sometimes be used to decorate an item, but they more often serve a utilitarian function. Occasionally they are both functional and decorative. Sewing can be done by hand or by machine and frequently serves to hold several sections of an accessory together. Examples in-clude sewing the sole of a shoe to the upper section, stitching the parts of gloves together, or sewing together pieces of a handbag. Sewing stitches may be used to finish the edges of such items as scarves or handkerchiefs.

TYPES OF EMBROIDERY DEFINED

Appenzell embroidery (ap-en′-tsell) Fine Swiss DRAWN WORK (see under TYPES OF EMBROIDERY DEFINED) used chiefly on handkerchiefs and fine muslin, a cottage industry in Switzerland. *Der.* Named for town in Switzerland where it originated.

appliqué (ap-plee-kay) Surface pattern made by cutting out fabric or lace designs and attaching them to another fabric or lace by means of embroidery or stitching.

Arrasene embroidery (ar-a′-seen) Embroidery with simple stitches to create a velvetlike effect that is made by using Arrasene thread, made of silk or wool, which resembles CHENILLE (see under TEXTILES IN ACCESSORIES: TYPES OF YARNS DEFINED) Introduced in the 1880s. *Der.* Named for town of Arras, France.

arrowhead stitch

arrowhead stitch/arrowhead Embroidery consisting of two stitches

60

slanted to form an arrow, used singly or filled in with the satin stitch. Often used as reinforcement or decorative element, where it is called an **arrowhead.**

Assisi embroidery (ahs-si´-si)   Cross-stitch embroidery in which the design image is outlined and the background is worked solidly in cross stitch. Originated in the Assisi area of northern Italy. See TYPES OF EMBROIDERY DEFINED: CROSS-STITCH.

backstitch embroidery   Outline embroidery similar to HOLBEIN work (see under TYPES OF EMBROIDERY DEFINED), but single-faced instead of double.

bargello stitch (bar-gel´-low)   Stitch worked vertically on canvas or scrim over a given number of threads to form a zigzag pattern. Visual impact results from color usage and stitch length variations. Also called *flame* and *Florentine stitch.*

bargello stitch

bar tack   Embroidery detail used either to reinforce an area, such as the end of a buttonhole, or as a decorative device. Made by taking several parallel stitches of the same size, then passing another thread around the parallel threads on the surface of the fabric. This latter thread is attached to the fabric only at the ends.

basket stitch   Embroidery stitch resembling series of overlapped cross-stitches used to fill in backgrounds.

basket-weave stitch   NEEDLEPOINT stitch (see under TYPES OF EMBROIDERY DEFINED) in which a series of diagonal stitches is most often used to fill background.

beading   **1.** Embroidery in which beads of various kinds are sewn onto blouses, dresses, handbags, wedding dresses, sweaters, or blouses. **2.** Lines of small embroidered eyelets as seen in WHITEWORK embroidery (see under TYPES OF EMBROIDERY DEFINED).

Beauvais embroidery (bo-vay´)   Tapestrylike embroidery done in many colors. *Der.* Named after city in France where it originated.

Berlin woolwork   Allover type of NEEDLEPOINT embroidery done on canvas, primarily using the CROSS-STITCH (see under TYPES OF EMBROIDERY DEFINED). *Der.* Name dates from 1820 when

Berlin wool was used. Also called *canvas* or *cushion style* embroidery.

blackwork   Embroidery originally done in black silk on white linen, fashionable from 16th to 17th c. Sometimes worked in an allover continuous scroll design and used to decorate collars, cuffs, smocks, and handkerchiefs. In modern times, the technique has evolved to geometric pattern stitching executed on an even-weave textile. When reversible, called HOLBEIN WORK (see under TYPES OF EMBROIDERY DEFINED) Also called *Spanish blackwork.*

blackwork

blanket stitch   Embroidery stitch that looks like a series of connected Us. Originally used to finish edges of binding on blankets, now used for decorative effect. Also called *purl stitch* or *open buttonhole stitch.*

blanket stitch or open buttonhole stitch

bonnaz (bo-nahz´)   Machine embroidery, sometimes worked on canvas-based cloth, with all types of designs possible as the operator can make the machine go in any direction. Used on sweaters, dresses, hats, gloves, and handbags. *Der.* Named after J. Bonnaz, a French inventor.

Breton work   Peasant embroidery in colored silk and metallic threads made in floral and geometric designs, largely done in CHAIN STITCH (see under TYPES OF EMBROIDERY DEFINED). Also called *Brittany work. Der.* Originated in Brittany.

brick stitch/brickwork   BLANKET STITCH (see under TYPES OF EMBROIDERY DEFINED) used on flat fabric in continuous rows resembling a brick wall. Also called *long and short stitch, featherwork, Irish stitch, tapestry shading stitch.*

brocade embroidery   Embroidery made by needlework done over the designs of brocade fabric.

broderie anglaise   See TYPES OF EMBROIDERY DEFINED: MADEIRA EMBROIDERY.

bullion embroidery (bull-yawn´)   Embroidery done with fine gold wire, also embroidery done with gold or silver threads, or cords, originating with the Phrygians (a region of what is now central Turkey) in ancient times.

bundle stitch or sheaf stitch

bundle   Embroidery stitch resembling a small bow knot. Made by taking 3 or 4 long loose stitches side by side, then placing a small stitch across at the center, drawing them together. Also called *sheaf stitch*.

buttonhole stitch Embroidery stitch similar to BLANKET STITCH (see under TYPES OF EMBROIDERY DEFINED) worked close together with an extra purl at the edge. Used for WORKED BUTTONHOLE (see under CLOSURES: TYPES OF CLOSURES DEFINED). The basic stitch for NEEDLEPOINT LACE (see under LACES AND BRAIDS: ANATOMY OF LACE) and the most commonly used stitch for edging design areas in cutwork. Also called *close stitch*.

Byzantine stitch Slanting embroidery stitch, similar to SATIN STITCH (see TYPES OF EMBROIDERY DEFINED), worked on canvas as a background filler over 3 or 4 vertical and horizontal threads in diagonal pattern.

cable stitch Embroidery stitch, similar to chain stitch, with extra stitch connecting the links. See TYPES OF EMBROIDERY DEFINED: CHAIN STITCH.

canvas embroidery See TYPES OF EMBROIDERY DEFINED: BERLIN WOOL WORK and NEEDLEPOINT.

cashmere work Rich, varicolored embroidery, frequently inlaid APPLIQUÉ (see under TYPES OF EMBROIDERY DEFINED) done in India, with complicated needlework covering almost entire surface, used for shawls.

catch stitch Loose stitch, like a series of Xs crossed near their top. Also called *cat stitch*.

catch stitch

chain stitch Embroidery stitch, making connected loops that form a chain on the front.

chain-stitched embroidery Machine embroidery worked in different designs using a chain stitch.

chenille embroidery (shen-neel′) Originated in France, this embroidery uses fine CHENILLE yarn (see under TEXTILES IN ACCESSORIES: TYPES OF YARNS DEFINED) with flat stitches producing a soft, velvetlike pattern.

chain stitch

Chinese embroidery Single- or double-faced embroidery that usually covers an entire robe or gown with motifs of cherry blossoms, birds, butterflies, and dragons. Done in satin, chain, French knots, feather, and other stitches with silk, gold, or silver threads in an elaborate and intricate design. Originally floss and metal threads were worked over a painted design.

close stitch See TYPES OF EMBROIDERY DEFINED: BUTTONHOLE STITCH.

continental stitch Diagonal stitch used on canvas and worked over 2 threads used to make the pattern or to fill in needlepoint backgrounds. Also called *tent stitch*. Shown at EMBROIDERIES AND SEWING STITCHES: NEEDLEPOINT.

couched embroidery/couching Decorative embroidery made by laying a long piece of yarn or embroidery floss flat while tiny stitches are worked around it at intervals to fasten it tightly.

couching

counted cross-stitch embroidery Embroidery done on an even-weave textile, using CROSS-STITCH (see under TYPES OF EMBROIDERY DEFINED) and usually worked with embroidery floss. Design is usually executed following a graph pattern.

counted thread embroidery A category of embroidery. For specific types, see TYPES OF EMBROIDERY DEFINED, COUNTED CROSS-STITCH, BLACKWORK, ASSISI EMBROIDERY, NEEDLEPOINT, and DARNING.

crewel work Embroidery made with heavy, colored, crewel yarns, usually of loosely twisted two-ply worsted, on a linen fabric or ground. Motifs are filled in with many types of stitches.

cross-stitch Decorative stitch that forms an X worked in various colored yarns on a plain background.

cross-stitch

cutwork (*opus scissum*) (oh′-puss siss′-um) Embroidery made by embroidering the edges of a design with BUTTONHOLE STITCH (see under TYPES OF EMBROIDERY DEFINED) and cutting out the background fabric around the designs. BARS OR BRIDES (see under LACES AND BRAIDS: ANATOMY OF LACE) are frequently used to connect the larger cut-out areas.

cutwork

darning Vertical stitches woven through horizontal stitches in a one-to-one checkerboard pattern to resemble plain-woven cloth. Used for mending holes or as an embroidery stitch to fill in backgrounds.

diagonal stitch Embroidery stitch worked diagonally over double threads of canvas with stitches varying in lengths.

double-running stitch A basic BLACKWORK stitch (see under TYPES OF EMBROIDERY DEFINED) that is a tiny running stitch, worked and then reversed, so that new stitches fill spaces and make a pattern similar to machine stitch. Also called *line stitch, square stitch, stroke stitch, two-sided stitch, Holbein stitch,* and *Italian stitch.*

drawn fabric work Various embroidery stitches are executed with a fine thread and pulled tightly on canvas or an even-weave textile, thereby compressing the yarns of the textile together to produce an open lacelike appearance. Also known as *pulled fabric work* or *pulled thread embroidery.*

drawn thread work *(opus tiratum)* (oh′-puss tir-ah′-tuhm) Open lace-like-appearing design resulting from withdrawing yarns from an even woven textile. The remaining yarns are bundled together, stitched over, or folded back on each other to create pattern. Also called *withdrawn thread work* or *withdrawn fabric embroidery.*

drawn thread work

eyelet embroidery Holes punched out and embroidery worked around the hole, by hand or on a SCHIFFLI MACHINE (see under ROLE AND FUNCTION OF EMBROIDERIES AND SEWING STITCHES IN ACCESSORIES). Also see TYPES OF EMBROIDERY DEFINED: MADEIRA EMBROIDERY.

fagoting **1.** Stitch, similar to single FEATHER STITCH (see under TYPES OF EMBROIDERY DEFINED), used to join two edges of fabric together in decorative openwork effect.

fagoting #1

2. Openwork embroidery done by drawing out horizontal threads of a fabric, then tying the vertical threads in groups to produce open spaces. **3.** Method of joining two fabric edges together by means of embroidery stitches to produce a lacelike effect. Fagoting is part of a group of techniques known as INSERTIONS (see under TYPES OF EMBROIDERY DEFINED).

feather stitch Decorative stitch that looks like a double row of Vs, branching out first to one side then

feather stitch

to the other in a continuous line that is a line stitch based on a buttonhole or chain-stitch variation. See TYPES OF EMBROIDERY DEFINED: BUTTONHOLE STITCH and CHAIN STITCH.

filling stitch Any type of embroidery stitch used to fill in a design, which may be outlined if desired. Also used to refer to couched-grid stitches that are used to fill in a design (see TYPES OF EMBROIDERY DEFINED: COUCHED EMBROIDERY).

fishbone stitch Embroidery stitch resembling the backbone of fish made with a long diagonal stitch crossed at one end with a small diagonal stitch worked in the opposite direction. Stitches usually branch out from a center line. Similar to FEATHER STITCH (see under TYPES OF EMBROIDERY DEFINED), but worked closer together.

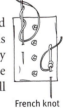
fishbone stitch

flame embroidery See TYPES OF EMBROIDERY DEFINED: FLORENTINE EMBROIDERY.

flame stitch See TYPES OF EMBROIDERY DEFINED: BARGELLO STITCH.

Florentine embroidery Embroidery done on canvas in zigzag patterns and in shaded colors. Also called *flame embroidery,* from the effect it achieved, or *Hungarian point embroidery.*

Florentine stitch See TYPES OF EMBROIDERY DEFINED: BARGELLO STITCH.

free motion machine embroidery Creation of machine embroidery by using decorative thread and dropping the device in the sewing machine that moves the fabric. The embroiderer creates abstract or realistic designs by moving the fabric in various directions.

French knot Decorative stitch used for embroidery. Embroidery floss is looped around the needle, usually 2 times, needle is pulled through the material, forming a small nub or ball of yarn on the surface.
French knot

gros point (groh pwanh) See TYPES OF EMBROIDERY DEFINED: PETIT POINT.

hardanger embroidery (hard-ahn′-ger) Open form of needlework made in diamond or square patterns on even-weave cotton or linen cloth. The material is stitched with satin stitch type squares called kosters blocks. This technique is native to the Hardanger region of western Norway.

Hedebo (head-day′-bow)   Danish form of WHITE-WORK that incorporates CUTWORK (see under TYPES OF EMBROIDERY DEFINED) and NEEDLE-POINT LACE (see LACES AND BRAIDS: ANATOMY OF LACE).

hemstitch   **1.** Ornamental stitch made by drawing out several parallel threads, then fastening together groups of vertical threads at regular intervals making hourglass shapes. Used as borders on blouses, handkerchiefs, etc. **2.** Machine hemstitching is done with a special attachment on sewing machines that gives the same effect as above. When cut through the middle, each edge forms a PICOT edge (see TYPES OF EMBROIDERY DEFINED: PICOT STITCHING).

hemstitch #1

hemstitching   Embroidery in which several parallel yarns are removed from the fabric and fine stitches used to catch a group of three or four cross threads at regular intervals giving an even openwork arrangement. This type of embroidery, done at the edge of the hem, holds and decorates at the same time.

herringbone stitch   Name of the CATCH STITCH (see TYPES OF EMBROIDERY DEFINED), when used for embroidery work. Also called *Russian stitch, Russian cross-stitch,* and *witch stitch.*

Holbein work (hole′-bine)   Delicate, reversible, outline embroidery done in double-running stitch, using exact geometrical or conventional designs that is part of the embroidery technique called BLACKWORK (see under TYPES OF EMBROIDERY DEFINED). Popular for trimming in the 16th c. *Der.* Named after the painter Hans Holbein (1465–1524) because design was so frequently shown on his paintings. Also called *Rumanian embroidery.*

honeycomb stitch   Machine or hand zigzag stitch used for smocking, mending, overcasting, as well as attaching elastic, stretch lace, and blanket binding. Looks like 3 rows of diamond-shaped stitches.

Indian embroidery   Oriental embroidery done by East Indian natives on cloth. May use small glass mirrors decoratively stitched to the fabric.

insertions   Open, straight-line areas on fabric created either by joining two

lace insertion

lengths of fabric with lace-type stitching, or by withdrawing threads from fabric and either HEMSTITCHING (see under TYPES OF EMBROIDERY DEFINED) across or drawing ribbon through the voids.

Japanese embroidery   Elaborate embroidery worked with colored silk or metallic threads in satin stitch, forming an intricate design or scene. Also includes padded and shaded embroidery.

laid stitch   Embroidery stitch made by first placing yarn or floss on area and then working small stitches over it to hold it in place. Similar to filling stitches used in CREWEL WORK (see under TYPES OF EMBROIDERY DEFINED).

lazy daisy stitch   Single CHAIN STITCH (see under TYPES OF EMBROIDERY DEFINED) used in embroidery with extra stitch added at outer edge to hold loop in place to form a petal. Also called *detached chain stitch.*

lazy daisy stitch

liquid embroidery   Not actually embroidery, but color applied to fabric with ballpoint-shaped paint tubes in special colors. Paint is squeezed from the tube to outline designs on a cloth. Creates a permanent and washable design resembling colored-thread embroidery. When seen at a distance, gives the general effect of embroidery.

Madeira embroidery (ma-deer′-a)   Eyelet embroidery cut or punched and then overcast. Made with openings arranged in floral or conventional designs on fine lawn or linen. Also called *broderie anglaise* (brod-e′-ree onh-glase′), *Ayrshire, English, Moravian work,* or *Swiss embroidery. Der.* From Island of Madeira, where work was originally done by nuns using very pale blue thread on a white ground.

metal thread embroidery   Embroidery stitched in gold, silver, copper, or other metal and metallic threads. Often combined with silk thread embroidery and utilized in Oriental embroidery, clerical embroidery, and military emblems and badges.

needle tapestry work   Embroidery worked in variety of stitches on canvas to resemble woven tapestries.

needlepoint   Allover wool embroidery worked on open canvas or scrim with yarn in a variety of stitches. Used for

needlepoint

household articles, fashion items, and decorative art. Regular-sized stitches called *gros point,* small stitches called PETIT POINT (see under TYPES OF EMBROIDERY DEFINED). Also called *canvas work.*

needleweaving Figure-eight stitching around the remaining lengthwise yarns of a textile after the crosswise yarns have been withdrawn. The grouping of the stitched threads can form lacelike patterns. Also called *Swedish weaving, Swedish darning.*

openwork Embroidery made by drawing, cutting, punching, or pulling aside threads of fabric to form open spaces in the design. For various forms of openwork, see TYPES OF EMBROIDERY DEFINED: DRAWN FABRIC WORK, HARDANGER, and MADEIRA WORK.

oriental couching Series of long straight stitches placed side by side, with each stitch intersected in the center by a short diagonal stitch. Also called *Rumanian stitch, janina stitch, figure stitch,* and *antique couching.*

outline stitch Variation of STEM STITCH (see under TYPES OF EMBROIDERY DEFINED). Used to outline stems, leaves, and other motifs in embroidery.

padding stitch Running stitch sometimes used in rows to provide a base for embroidery stitches, e.g., SATIN STITCH (see under TYPES OF EMBROIDERY DEFINED), worked on top.

petit point Canvas embroidery worked from right to left, over single threads, through large meshes. The same stitch worked over double threads is called **gros point.**

picot stitching Stitch used in lacemaking that forms loops of thread extending from the edges.

punch/punched work Embroidery of openwork type made by pulling certain threads aside with a needle or stiletto and securing them with embroidery stitches. Also called *Rhodes work.*

purl stitch **1.** See TYPES OF EMBROIDERY DEFINED: BLANKET STITCH. **2.** Double purl stitch is used in making buttonholes and is formed by throwing thread over the needle as it crosses.

raised embroidery/raised work Embroidery done in the SATIN STITCH OVER PADDING STITCHES

scallop

(see under TYPES OF EMBROIDERY DEFINED) to give a raised effect in the design. Used for monograms, scallops, etc.

rococo embroidery (row-cok'-oh) Type of embroidery made with very narrow ribbon, often called *China ribbon embroidery* or *silk ribbon embroidery.*

saddle stitch Running stitch made in contrasting or heavy thread. Frequently used for trim on coats, sport dresses, and gloves.

satin stitch Embroidery stitch with straight, usually long, stitches worked very close together either vertically or slanted to fill in a large area (e.g., leaf or flower).

satin stitch

seed embroidery Type of German embroidery done with seeds for floral motifs and CHENILLE YARN (see under TEXTILES IN ACCESSORIES: TYPES OF YARN DEFINED) for stems and leaves, formerly used for handbags.

seed stitch Embroidery stitch consisting of tiny individual back stitches, worked at random to fill background.

shadow embroidery/shadow work Embroidery worked with a CATCH STITCH (see under TYPES OF EMBROIDERY DEFINED) on the wrong side of transparent fabric.

smocking Decorative needlework used to hold gathered cloth together. The stitches catch alternate folds in elaborate honeycombed designs.

Spanish embroidery **1.** Muslin worked with HERRINGBONE filling stitches. **2.** Lacelike embroidery made on muslin or cambric with braid and closely placed BUTTONHOLE stitches. (See cross-references under TYPES OF EMBROIDERY DEFINED.) Also called *Sicilian embroidery.*

stem stitch **1.** Embroidery stitch with overcast stitches placed close together making a rounded, raised, ropelike effect. **2.** Outline stitch used in CREWEL WORK (see under TYPES OF EMBROIDERY DEFINED).

tambour work (tam-boor') Embroidery worked with a hooked needle and a stitch on a double drum-shaped frame. The stitch is similar to the CHAIN STITCH (see under TYPES OF EMBROIDERY DEFINED).

tapestry stitch Short vertical stitches used in canvas work to imitate tapestry fabric.

venetian ladder work Outline embroidery done with two parallel lines of buttonhole stitches connected with CROSS-STITCHES (see under

TYPES OF EMBROIDERY DEFINED) at intervals in ladder-style. Used mainly for border work in conventional designs.

whitework Embroidery executed in white thread on a white textile.

TYPES OF SEWING STITCHES DEFINED

back stitch Stitch used for hand sewing to prevent seam from ripping out. Each stitch goes back over the space left by previous stitch, giving the appearance of a machine stitch.

back stitch

backstitch Sewing term for reversing stitch on sewing machine. Used to secure threads at the beginning and ending of seams.

baste *v.* To stitch fabrics together either by hand or using a large machine so as to hold them in place temporarily prior to sewing final seams. After stitching, bastings are removed.

basting *n.* Loose running stitches, often alternating long and short, used to hold sections of garment together before machine stitching.

blind stitch See TYPES OF SEWING STITCHES DEFINED: SLIP STITCH.

buttonhole stitch See TYPES OF EMBROIDERY DEFINED: BUTTONHOLE STITCH.

chain stitch Machine stitch made by a commercial sewing machine done with a single thread, forming a chain on the back, used for hems and shoes—easy to remove.

cross-stitch X-shaped stitch used to attach a hem or facing. One half of the stitch catches the hem or facing and the other half the base fabric.

gathering Drawing up fullness along several threads in a row of stitching. Also see TYPES OF SEWING STITCHES DEFINED: SHIRRING.

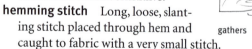
gathers

hemming stitch Long, loose, slanting stitch placed through hem and caught to fabric with a very small stitch.

lock stitch Machine stitch done with one thread coming across the top of the machine around the tension and through the needle. Other thread comes from a bobbin on the underside of the machine.

overcasting **1.** By hand: diagonal edging stitch that always enters the fabric from the same side and goes around raw edge to keep it from fraying. **2.** By machine: a similar finish for raw edges made by a special sewing-machine attachment or a serger.

overcasting #1

running stitch Very tiny even stitches placed close together and used for seams, tucking, gathering, and quilting. Stitches and spaces between them should be equal in length.

shirring Three or more rows of gathers (see GATHERING under TYPES OF SEWING STITCHES DEFINED) made by small running stitches in parallel lines. Used to produce decorative control of fullness in selected areas, such as at tops of gloves. Also called *gauging.* May be made by using a large stitch on the sewing machine and then pulling the bobbin thread to form gathers or by using elastic thread on the bobbin.

shirring

slip stitch Small, almost invisible stitches with connecting thread hidden under fabric. Used to join an edge to a single layer (e.g., a hem or facing). Also called *blind stitch, blind hemming, invisible hemming.*

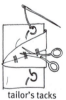
slip stitch

tack To sew together lightly with invisible stitches or to join by sewing loosely at just one point.

tailor's tack Large stitch taken through two thicknesses of fabric with a loop left between the layers. The layers are cut apart, leaving tufts in each piece to be used for guide marks in clothing construction. Also called *mark stitch.*

tailor's tacks

top-stitch Machine stitching showing on the right side of the garment.

whip stitch Short overcast stitch used on rolled or raw edges.

zigzag stitch Sewing machine stitch giving a saw-toothed effect used to connect two flat pieces of fabric together. Also used on edges of fabric to eliminate fraying.

OTHER DECORATIVE MATERIALS USED *to* ORNAMENT ACCESSORIES

BEADS

A **bead** is a piece of glass, plastic, wood, crystal, gem, or other material bored through the center and strung on leather, cord, thread, or chain and used as jewelry. Other uses are for embroidery or ornamentation of a surface. Beads may be round, cylindrical, square, disc-shaped, pendant-shaped, oblong, etc. The earliest archeological evidence of beads dates to a Neanderthal archeological site in France thought to be in use from c. 38,000 B.C. The beads found there are made from grooved animal teeth and bones and were probably worn as pendants. Other prehistoric sites have yielded beads that were first made from natural materials but later showed evidence of being worked into different shapes and forms. Throughout recorded history, beads have been used in jewelry and to decorate apparel. They have been made from materials ranging from wood to metals and precious stones. Many are made of glass.

If used as ornamentation, beads must be applied to a surface. If the surface is hard, they can be cemented in place. They can be attached to fabrics by stitching through a hole in the bead. More often, beads are strung onto thread and the thread carrying the beads is sewn, or COUCHED, to the fabric. A technique called TAMBOUR embroidery can also be used with strung beads. A special tambour hook creates a CHAIN STITCH on the back of the fabric from the thread on which the beads are strung. (See under EMBROIDERIES AND SEWING STITCHES: TYPES OF EMBROIDERY DEFINED.) Beads can even be woven into fabric by using yarn on which beads have been strung as part of the woven structure, usually in the crosswise direction.

In contemporary accessories, beads are most likely to be used in jewelry or as decoration on fabrics that are made into footwear, handbags, scarves, and shawls. Beads can be made into almost any shape or color. Glass beads may be **transparent** or clear; **opaque** and transmit no light, or **greasy**, which means that they permit the passage of light but cannot be seen through. **Opal glass** allows the passage of light but is milky in appearance and translucent, somewhat like the OPAL gemstone (see GEMS, GEM CUTS, AND SETTINGS: TYPES OF GEMS DEFINED). Glass with a striated or layered appearance is known as **satin glass.** Glass beads with an inner white core are called **whitehearts.** Glass beads may be lined with silver or a reflective material, gold or gilt, or various colors. Dozens of effects may be possible with the creative use of beads.

SOME TYPES OF BEADS DEFINED

American Indian beads   Tiny opaque beads of various colors used to make necklaces and belts. Also used for embroidery on moccasins, headbands, belts, and other Native American clothes.

aurora borealis crystal (aw-ror'-ah bore-ee'-al-is) Glass beads coated with solution causing them to reflect rainbow colors.

Austrian crystal Lead crystal made with 32% lead oxide, that is faceted and polished to give full spectrum light reflection in sunlight or artificial light. Usually colorless but may be coated on back to reflect a color, e.g., red or blue (or both colors if coated on both sides). Made in village of Innsbruck, Austria.

baroque pearls See GEMS, GEM CUTS, AND SETTINGS: ANATOMY OF GEMS.

cut-steel beads Tiny faceted steel or other metal beads, similar in appearance to MARCASITE (see under GEMS, GEM CUTS, AND SETTINGS: TYPES OF GEMS DEFINED), popular in last half of the 19th and early 20th c.

gold beads **1.** Beads of 14k to 18k gold sometimes purchased one at a time and added to a necklace chain. **2.** Beads plated with gold. **3.** Beads in costume jewelry that have a gold-colored finish.

rondella (rohn-del'-ah) Small, round, metal disk that is placed between beads. It may be plain or ornamented with stones.

SPANGLES

Spangles are small, thin, decorative, sparkling pieces used to ornament fabric. They are usually made of metal or plastic and have a hole through which thread can pass. Spangles can be made in many shapes, in a wide range of colors, and in iridescent reflective effects. When a spangle is small and round with a hole in the center, it is usually called a **sequin**. A **paillette** is usually larger than a sequin and has a hole closer to its edge. When used on accessories, these ornaments are most likely to be found on evening handbags, shawls, and scarves, although they can be applied to any fabric surface. Often bead ornamentation is combined with spangles.

ARTIFICIAL FLOWERS

An artificial flower is made from ribbon, fabric, paper, or plastic in imitation of a real flower. Flowers can range from very precise imitations of real blooms to stylized versions. They are most commonly found as a decorative element on headwear, but can also be used on footwear and handbags, or may be utilized as an ornament that can be pinned to a garment or on an accessory such as a scarf.

SHELLS

A **shell** is the hard outer covering of a soft-bodied mollusk. Shells often have very distinctive shapes and colors, which is why they are used as an element of jewelry. They can be strung together on cords or chains to make necklaces or bracelets. They may also be cut into pieces to make buttons, beads, or other ornaments, or they may be worked into cameos (see GEMS, GEM CUTS, AND SETTINGS: ANATOMY OF GEM CUTS: CAMEO CUT).

SEEDS

A **seed** is the part of a plant that, if planted, has the potential to become a new plant. Some seeds, when dry, have an attractive appearance and are used occasionally to make jewelry or in decorations on the surface of accessories.

TORTOISE SHELL

Tortoise shell is an attractive, brown, speckled material, obtained from the shell of the hawksbill turtle, which was prized for its attractive appearance. Its widespread use as a decorative material in such objects as hair ornaments, eyeglass frames, jewelry, and other trimmings caused the turtle to be hunted to near extinction, so use of the natural material has been banned. Very good imitations of genuine tortoise shell are now made of plastic and used in similar applications.

IVORY

Ivory is a hard material that makes up the tusks of various animals. These include elephants, hippopotami, walruses, whales, warthogs, and boars.

Although the mammoth is now extinct, mammoth ivory is obtained from the remaining fossilized tusks that are found in the Arctic. The preferred source of ivory for many years was elephants, both African and Asiatic. Ivory from elephants is now in scarce supply because of overhunting and international restrictions on trade in ivory and in objects made from ivory. As a result the horns and teeth of many animals are also called ivory. For example, "elk ivory" is from the antlers of elk, and some nuts are used to produce "vegetable ivory."

Import of elephant ivory to the United States is severely restricted. Only antique ivory that is more than 100 years old and for which the buyer has documentation proving its age can be brought into the country. Ivory from other species is also restricted, so any person considering bringing items of "ivory" into the United States should consult the U.S. Fish and Wildlife Service for clarification of rules governing imports.

Ivory is generally white or various shades of off-white or tan. This material can be carved and shaped easily, is durable, and can be polished to a high luster. It has long been popular for use in jewelry and buttons. Good imitations of ivory can be made out of plastic resins and bone.

OTHER MATERIALS
USED *in* ACCESSORIES

A variety of materials are integral to the structure of the accessory item. These include metal, synthetic resins, plastics, and wood. Some have been used for thousands of years. Others are the result of technological innovation. Accessory designers use both natural and synthetic materials in the soles of shoes, in frames for handbags, as umbrella handles, in closures, and in countless other ways.

METALS

Precious and baser metals have a number of qualities that make them useful in the fabrication of accessories. They can be good conductors of electricity and heat; are capable of being worked easily; are capable of being stretched into a thin wire or flattened into a very thin sheet; and have a high light reflection. Metal may be found in ores mixed with other substances, but a few kinds (gold, copper, silver, and platinum) can be found in their free state. This probably accounts for the early use of some of these materials by prehistoric people. Metals may be used in their pure state, but with advances in the science of metallurgy, they are more likely to be combined with other substances to increase their hardness or durability. Metals may also be **plated** (applied as a coating on a base material). This decreases the cost of an article while maintaining an attractive surface. Metal links can be formed and joined together to form a flat flexible material called **mesh.**

The most common metals used in accessories are listed below.

GOLD

A yellow-colored precious metal with a high luster, **gold** has maintained its value as a result of its beauty, because it does not corrode, and because it can be worked with ease. Gold has been so widely accepted for its ornamental value that many other baser metals are colored in its imitation. In its pure state, gold is too soft to be durable. It is usually made into alloys called *karat gold* and used for *plating,* or gold-washed jewelry items. **Karat** is a measure of the quality or fineness of gold, especially that used in jewelry. Gold of 24K is 100 percent gold with no alloys added; however, gold of this quality is too soft for jewelry. An **alloy** is a metal that, when mixed with a second metal, improves certain qualities. When alloys are added to gold, the resultant products are labeled as 12K, 14K, or 18K gold meaning that 12/24, 14/24, or 18/24 of the metal is gold. The remainder is the alloy. The letter K is used as an abbreviation.

Mixing it with other metals can alter the color of gold. The higher the gold content, the more yellow the gold will be. **Yellow gold** alloyed with gold, silver, and copper is the most frequently used type of gold.

These other color variations are:

blue gold alloyed with iron or arsenic—about 25 percent alloy.

gray gold alloyed with iron—15 to 20 percent alloy.

70

green gold 14 or higher karat gold alloyed with silver, copper, zinc, or cadmium—15 to 40 percent alloy.

red or pink gold alloyed with copper and, sometimes, silver.

white gold alloyed with a high percent of silver, but does not tarnish.

Gold is used for making jewelry. It may also be used in watch bands or for ornamenting other accessories. When used ornamentally, except for the most exclusive items, gold-colored ornaments are likely to be either plated or imitations.

SILVER

Silver is a whitish-gray precious metal with high luster. Used in jewelry and other decorative accessories since at least 4,000 B.C., silver, like gold, has maintained its appeal. Alloys can make silver harder, tougher, and easier to fuse. **Sterling silver** is made of 92.5 percent silver and 7.5 percent of another metal. Much of the silver used in jewelry is 80 percent silver and 20 percent copper. Silver will tarnish when exposed to sulfur and hydrogen sulfide in the atmosphere.

Like gold, silver may be plated or may be imitated by using other baser metals with similar coloring. Silver is commonly found in jewelry, watch bands, and other ornaments for accessories.

PLATINUM

Platinum is a silvery-colored precious metal with high luster. Obtaining platinum requires extensive refining of platinum-bearing ores. These processes were only developed in the 18th and 19th c., and it was only about 1900 that jewelers began to use platinum in expensive jewelry. The complexity and high cost of obtaining the metal limits its use in jewelry.

COPPER

A reddish, easily worked metal that is found in the free state, **copper** has been used since prehistoric times for ornaments and tools. Several alloys of copper are also used for ornaments. Jewelers value

bronze, an alloy of copper with tin or other elements, because it takes a high polish and it can be cast into interesting forms. **Brass** is an alloy of copper and zinc and can be produced in varying colors and takes a high polish.

OTHER METALS

nickel silver A silver gray metal, which contains no silver but is largely composed of copper alloyed with nickel and zinc. Its surface is very similar in appearance to sterling silver and the metal takes a high polish.

chrome/chromium A steel gray metal, or alloy with the metal, that resists tarnishing and corrosion. Most often used to plate a base metal. Chrome-plated materials are often found in handbag frames and clasps. They may be used in costume jewelry, and in other places where their durability and luster is important.

steel A strong metal consisting of iron combined with various alloys. **Stainless steel** is an alloy of iron with chromium that is highly resistant to rust and corrosion. Steel is the metal most likely to be found in the structure of accessories. For example, the ribs and shaft of umbrellas are usually made of steel. Frames and closures for handbags may be steel. Occasionally it is used by craftpersons for making jewelry.

iridium (ih-rid′-ee-em) Metal frequently alloyed with platinum to make a more durable metal for use in jewelry.

rhodium White-colored metal of the platinum group used for plating jewelry.

PLASTICS

Plastic is a nonmetallic material, usually produced from organic compounds, that is capable of being shaped, extended, molded, or extruded into pliable sheets, films, or other structures. Plastics may be either **thermoplastic,** capable of being remolded by heat after formation or **thermosetting,** unable to be reformed once it is formed into a particular shape. Both types of plastic may be used in accessories. For example, plastic films such as polyvinyl chloride (PVC), often called **vinyl,** and polyurethane (PU) might be used in creating leatherlike materials or waterproof linings in handbags. Thermosetting plastics include materials such as LUCITE (see below) that are used in heels of shoes, in handbags, and jewelry. Many of the lenses in eyeglasses are now made from plastic rather than glass.

Because plastic is a manufactured material, various types of plastic often are identified by trademarks registered by particular companies. Some of the most commonly found trademarked plastics include:

bakelite   Rigid plastic patented in 1909 that can be brightly colored and worked into different shapes. It was used in costume jewelry in the 1930s. Bakelite jewelry has become highly collectible and is frequently imitated. Contemporary jewelry that imitates this rigid plastic is made from modern plastics.

Lucite®   Trademark for transparent acrylic plastic used for handbags, sandals, shoe heels, and jewelry.

RUBBER AND SYNTHETIC RUBBER

Rubber is a natural material derived from the sap of certain tropical trees. It is very elastic. As a result of shortages of rubber and because of its deterioration when exposed to certain atmospheric conditions, scientists developed a wide variety of synthetic materials with similar properties that are called **synthetic rubber.** These materials might also be considered types of PLASTICS (see OTHER MATERIALS USED IN ACCESSORIES).

One of the most common uses of these materials is in footwear, especially for soles and waterproof overshoes. The following are the materials most likely to be used for such products:

micro-cellular rubber (MCR)   Rubber that has had air incorporated into it, making it lighter and better for cushioning. Also known as *blown rubber.*

resin rubber   Synthetic material used predominantly in dress shoes for women, men, and children.

ethel vinyl acetate (EVA)   Synthetic material that has a similar appearance to MICRO-CELLULAR RUBBER (see under RUBBER AND SYNTHETIC RUBBER) and that can be molded for footwear soles.

polyurethane (PU)   Exceptionally durable, widely used, synthetic soling material.

polyvinyl chloride (PVC)   A resin that is easily molded for footwear soles.

Another use for rubber and synthetic rubbers is as elastic thread or yarn in areas where stretch is required, such as hosiery.

GLASS

Glass is created from combining certain minerals called silicates and other chemical substances to form a hard, brittle material that is usually translucent or transparent. It can be colored in the manufacturing process. Glass is most commonly used in accessories as a decorative element. Jewelry is often made of clear or colored glass. Other common uses are as buttons, as clasps on handbags, and as umbrella handles. In eyewear (see ACCESSORIES: EYEWEAR), glass, as well as plastic, can be used to make the lenses, and can be shaped to correct visual deficiencies.

WOOD

Wood, the hard material found under the bark of trees, is utilized in accessories as a decorative element that may also be part of the functional elements. For example, wood is sometimes used to make the frame of a handbag, the handle of an umbrella, or a heel of footwear. Many woods have attractive grain markings and can be used effectively in jewelry or to make buttons for closures. In some of these uses, wood is painted in various colors.

ACCESSORIES

BELTS

HISTORY AND SIGNIFICANCE OF BELTS TO FASHION

Belts serve both decorative and practical functions. They may be used to shape a garment so it fits the body at, above, or below the anatomical waistline. They may also keep skirts or trousers in place. They may provide a decorative accent. Sometimes they are worn over one shoulder in military fashion. In the past and in poetic writings, a belt could also be called a *girdle.* Belts in classical antiquity were mostly of the sash type used to bring loose-fitting garments close to the body at various places. In the Middle Ages, as fitted garments were made, belts became important and a man's or woman's wealth could be determined by the richness of his or her linked, elaborately jeweled belt. Contemporary belts are influenced by fashions. They take on more or less importance depending on the cut of dresses, skirts, and trousers and can range from simple unobtrusive leather belts in dark colors to elaborately ornamented accessories that provide a focal point for a design.

ANATOMY AND COMPONENTS OF A BELT

Belts encompass the body and, therefore, with a few exceptions, are generally long and narrow in shape. They may range from a simple length of fabric, leather, or other material that ties around the body to a complex structure of leather, straw, fabric, metal, or combinations of these materials. Belt closures may be ornamental as well as functional. A typical simple contemporary belt intended for wearing around the waist would consist of a strip of leather or fabric that is several inches longer than the waist measurement with closures or fasteners at each end. If the closure is a buckle with a tongue, the belt will have several holes, placed at the opposite end from the buckle, through which the belt tongue will go. Having several holes makes it possible to adjust the belt fit.

A variation of the typical long, narrow belt is a **contour belt.** Such belts are curved so that they conform to the body shape. Often they are wider in the front or the back, and various versions have been fashionable periodically.

TYPES OF BELTS DEFINED

American Indian belt Leather belt decorated with woven American Indian beadwork in bright colors and motifs.

bandoleer Wide belt having loops to hold cartridges with one or two straps extending over shoulders. Also spelled *bandolier.*

bikini chain belt Fine gold chain worn with bikini or hip-hugger pants. Introduced in late 1960s.

braided belt Belt made by plaiting narrow strips of leather, vinyl, elastic, thong, or fabric that may buckle or tie.

cartridge belt Webbed or leather belt, worn by armed forces and law enforcement officers, with individual spaces for ammunition. The belt may have an attached holster for a gun. This style without a holster but with a

cartridge belt

row of fake bullet cartridges was adopted as a fashion fad.

chain belt Belt made of various sizes of chain. May be a single chain or a series of chains looped to medallions or imitation jewels at intervals.

chain belt

cinch belt Wide belt worn pulled tight, usually of elastic or fabric, either laced or clasped in front, popular in 1940s and 1950s.

cincture (sink'-cher) Synonym for *belt. Der.* Latin, *cinctur,* "a girdle."

cinch belt

contour belt Any belt that is curved so that it conforms to the body's shape. It may be wider in the front or the back, and various versions have been fashionable periodically.

contour belt

corselet belt Wide belt, sometimes enclosing the rib cage, frequently laced up front in a manner similar to peasant's bodice.

cowboy belt Wide leather belt, sometimes with tooled designs, worn at top of hipbone by frontier cowboy to hold gun holster. Adapted for women's and men's sportswear.

cummerbund Wide fabric belt, sometimes pleated lengthwise, that is fastened in back. Worn with men's semiformal dinner suit, also worn by women. Copied from wrapped cloth belts worn in Eastern European countries. *Der. kamarband,* "loin-band."

cummerbund

D-ring belt A narrow belt closed by pulling the end through two D-shaped rings.

gaucho belt (gow'-cho) Belt made of medallions of leather and metal joined with chain; introduced in late 1960s. *Der.* Spanish, "cowboy" of South America.

Greek belt Long narrow sash that crosses over chest and winds around waist, a fashion innovation of the 1960s copied from sash worn in ancient Greece. Also called *cross-girdling.*

half belt Belt that does not extend around the entire waistline. It may be used in the back only. One such belt is the **martingale belt,** a half belt worn on back of a garment above or below normal waistline. *Der.* Part of horse's harness designed to hold head down.

kidney belt Extremely wide belt, similar to a POLO BELT (see under TYPES OF BELTS DEFINED), worn when motorcycling to prevent injury.

martingale belt See TYPES OF BELTS DEFINED: HALF BELT.

mesh belt Belt made of extremely small metal links fastened together to form a flexible fabriclike band.

money belt Belt worn under or over clothing when traveling, with hidden zippered compartment for money.

money belt

monk's belt Fashion term for a belt of cincture-type made of rope, braided rayon, or nylon with tassels on the ends.

obi-styled sash Sash that is approximately 4″ to 5″ wide at the center and tapers to 1″ to 1½″ at the ends. It is worn wrapped around the waist twice and tied, with the ends hanging down the front. The tapered ends may be of contrasting colors or fabrics. Although it is a single piece of fabric, it gives the appearance of a double sash. Adapted in 1980s from the **obi,** which is a sash approximately 15″ wide and 4 to 6 yards long, worn by Japanese men, women, and children on top of a kimono. It is folded lengthwise with the fold toward the hem, wrapped twice around the waist, and tied in a flat butterfly bow in back. Style of tying and design of fabric vary according to age and sex. Sometimes spelled *obe.*

polo belt Wide leather belt covering the rib cage; it fastens in front with three small buckles on narrow leather straps. Originally worn by polo players for protection. Also see TYPES OF BELTS DEFINED: KIDNEY BELT.

safari belt Wide belt with attached flap pockets in front.

Sam Browne belt Belt around waist with extension strap over right shoulder, worn by U.S. Army officers, guards, and some policemen. Also called *shoulder belt. Der.* From British general, Sir Samuel Browne, who, having lost his left arm, couldn't support his sword without this special belt.

sash Any belt of soft material that loops over and ties in a knot or bow rather than buckling.

sash

self-covered belt Any belt cut out of the same fabric as the garment, usually stiffened with a liner. Available in kits for the home sewer. If tied, it is called a *self sash.*

self sash   See TYPES OF BELTS DEFINED: SELF-COVERED BELT.

serpentine belt   Belt made in wavy design, zigzagging around the body.

shoulder belt   See TYPES OF BELTS DEFINED: SAM BROWNE BELT.

skirt-belt   Belt with attached peplum (a wide ruffle extending below the waist) that forms a short skirt. Introduced in late 1960s to wear over jumpsuits, body stockings, and pants.

spaghetti sash   A sash made of a long narrow piece of fabric, with cording inserted as filler to give a rounded effect, sometimes knotted at the ends.

surcingle belt   A webbed belt woven in plain or striped fabric fastened with a metal buckle through which a harness leather tab is pulled. Sometimes has a zippered pocket for money. *Der.* From the girth that fastens a horse's saddle or blanket.

thong belt   1. Wide leather belt with eyelets at each end through which a piece of rawhide is laced. 2. Belt made of braided rawhide.

tooled leather belt   1. Handmade leather belt of various widths embossed with various motifs. May be purchased in kits. 2. Belts imitating the above, stamped out by machine, sometimes imported from Mexico and Central America. 3. Belts from India in intricate designs that are inked in various colors.

webbed belt   Belt of heavy canvas webbing, usually wide and fastened with a clip buckle, worn by military. Adapted for casual wear by men and women in various widths and colors from 1960 on.

weight belt   1. Belt of nylon webbing fitted with approximately twelve pound weights. Used for scuba diving and underwater swimming. Extra weights may be added. 2. Wide leather-textured vinyl or fabric belt with eight to ten pound weights worn under or over clothing as a reducing aid or figure improver.

EYEWEAR

HISTORY AND SIGNIFICANCE OF EYEWEAR TO FASHION

Accessories worn over the eyes to improve vision or to protect the eyes from the glare of the sun are called **eyewear.** The most common form of eyewear is called **eyeglasses** or **glasses.** Glasses were first introduced in Italy in the late 13th c. where they were an indication of wisdom, as few people could read. Experimentation with devices to hold the glass in place and to keep eyeglasses (also called *spectacles*) in place continued until 1730 when Edward Scarlett, a British optician, invented rigid sidepieces that rested on the top of the ears. During the 17th c., colored lenses were introduced for protection from the sun. Eyeglasses were available in clear glass and also in glass tinted blue or green.

Benjamin Franklin invented bifocal lenses in the 18th c. Trifocals were patented in 1827. **Bifocals** consist of lenses divided in two parts, one to correct for nearsightedness and one to correct for farsightedness. **Trifocals** have three sections. The lowest section is for reading; the middle section for intermediate vision, for drawing, playing the piano, or playing cards; the uppermost section for seeing at a distance.

Other vision aids were also used, for example, the **monocle,** a man's single eyeglass used for one eye that was held in place by the cheek and forehead muscles. When not in use, it was suspended on a ribbon around the neck. Although it was developed in the 1700s, its greatest popularity was in the 1800s. The **pince-nez** (pahns-nay´) was an eyeglass without ear pieces that was kept in place by a spring gripping the bridge of the nose. The word derived

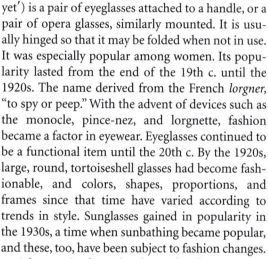

monocle

pince-nez

from the French, "nose-pincher." A **lorgnette** (lorn-yet´) is a pair of eyeglasses attached to a handle, or a pair of opera glasses, similarly mounted. It is usually hinged so that it may be folded when not in use. It was especially popular among women. Its popularity lasted from the end of the 19th c. until the 1920s. The name derived from the French *lorgner,* "to spy or peep." With the advent of devices such as the monocle, pince-nez, and lorgnette, fashion became a factor in eyewear. Eyeglasses continued to be a functional item until the 20th c. By the 1920s, large, round, tortoiseshell glasses had become fashionable, and colors, shapes, proportions, and frames since that time have varied according to trends in style. Sunglasses gained in popularity in the 1930s, a time when sunbathing became popular, and these, too, have been subject to fashion changes.

Advances in the technology of making eyewear and in medical care of the eyes have resulted in still more variations in eyewear. These advances include:

antireflective coating A coating applied to lenses so that reflection of light from the lens is eliminated, thereby improving vision, reducing eye fatigue, and making the eyes more visible.

color-graded glasses Tinted glasses with the lens color varying from light at the bottom to dark at the top. Designed for use in a car; maps can be read through the clear section at bottom.

Photochrome® lens A lens that darkens as the light increases and vice versa. These lenses were an innovation of the 1980s.

Polaroid® glasses Trademark for special sunglasses with lenses that polarize light, especially effective in cutting down glare and protecting the eyes from ultraviolet light.

progressive lens A lens that gradually adds focal power across its surface so that the same lens permits distant, intermediate, and close viewing. No lines are visible at the point where the focus changes.

ANATOMY OF THE EYEGLASS

Conventional eyeglasses are made with plastic or glass lenses that fit into metal or plastic frames with **temples;** shafts attached to each side and curved at the distant ends to fit over the ears.

diagram of eyeglasses

STYLES OF EYEGLASSES DEFINED

aviator's glasses Sunglasses with lenses wider at sides of face and sloping toward nose. Made in imitation of goggles worn by early airplane pilots. Also called *flyboy glasses. Der.* From style worn by aviator pilots.

Ben Franklin glasses Small elliptical, octagonal, or oblong lenses with delicate metal frames, worn perched on the middle of the nose. A fad started in 1965 imitating the glasses seen in paintings of Benjamin Franklin, U.S. statesman. Also called *granny glasses.*

Ben Franklin glasses

bug-eyed glasses Bulging convex sunglasses shaped like the eyes of an insect. Some glasses are made of a solid piece of plastic shaped to head and face. Unusual colors such as red are sometimes used to give a psychedelic appearance to viewer. An innovation of the late 1960s.

butterfly glasses Large rimless sunglasses with lenses made in the shape of a butterfly's wings, a fashion of the late 1960s.

clip-on sunglasses Sunglasses without frames made with a clip at the center or on either side that allows them to attach over the top of prescription glasses. Some, called **flip-up glasses,** have hinges that permit them to flip up.

Courréges glasses Sunglasses, introduced by Andrè Courréges in 1966, made of a strip of opaque plastic that circles the face extending to the ears. A tinted horizontal sliver of glass or plastic runs through the center of the plastic. Copied widely, they became known by the name of the French couturier who originated the style.

eyeglass case See HANDBAGS AND RELATED ACCESSORIES: TYPES OF RELATED ACCESSORIES DEFINED.

eyeglass chain/eyeglass cord Chain or cord that has loops that slip over the temples of glasses so that when glasses are not being used, they can be worn around the neck. May be plain or decorated with crystals, pearls, beads, and the like.

flip-down glasses Ben Franklin-type glasses with separate hinged lenses that pull down so that eyeshadow or mascara can be applied. Also used for inserting contact lenses.

flip up glasses See STYLES OF EYEGLASSES DEFINED: CLIP-ON SUNGLASSES.

flyboy glasses See STYLES OF EYEGLASSES DEFINED: AVIATOR'S GLASSES.

folding glasses Glasses with both folding bridge and temples that condense to a 3″ size for easy carrying.

goggles Protective glasses, usually with impact resistant lenses in wide frames wrapped around temples, held on by strap around head and worn by auto racers, skiers, etc. Goggles for underwater swimming are watertight.

goggles

granny glasses See STYLES OF EYEGLASSES DEFINED: BEN FRANKLIN GLASSES.

half-glasses Glasses for reading with shallow lenses, allowing wearer to look over top for distance viewing.

half-glasses

harlequin glasses (har′-lee-kwin) Glasses with diamond-shaped lenses. Eyeglasses slanting up to corner peaks.

horn rims/horn-rimmed glasses Eyeglasses with heavy frames of dark horn, or mottled brown plastic imitating horn.

instant sunglasses Lightweight, impact-resistant, shaped plastic that is placed behind regular glasses when outdoors.

Lennon specs Sunglasses with circular metal-rimmed lenses and thin metal temples. *Der.* John Lennon, member of the English rock group, The Beatles, made this style popular. Originally English workmen's sunglasses.

lifestyle eyewear   Used in retailing eyeglasses to describe frame and lens selections that emphasize personal image and/or specific use such as computer, sports, career, and evening eyewear.

louvre sunglasses   (loo′-vra) Molded plastic sunglasses made with tilted slats similar to Venetian blinds. Introduced from France in mid-1980s.

owl glasses   Extra-large sunglasses with very wide heavy rims that give the look of a surprised owl.

rimless glasses   Lenses attached to metal nose piece and ear pieces but not outlined by a frame. Popular from 1930s to 1940s, and revived in 1960s and after.

safety glasses   Glasses made of impact-resistant lenses and safety frames worn by industrial workers. Also called GOGGLES (see under STYLES OF EYEGLASSES DEFINED).

shades   Slang for sunglasses.

specs   Slang for eyeglasses; a shortened form of spectacles.

sunglasses   Eyeglasses with dark-colored lenses to protect eyes from the sun's glare invented about 1885. They became popular after being worn by movie stars in Hollywood in 1930s and 1940s, and a prevalent fashion from 1960s and after in various shapes and sizes. Some made with mirrored lenses.

temple   Shaft attached to side of glasses, curved at one end to fit over the ear. Also called *bow*.

tortoiseshell glasses   Glasses with frames made to imitate tortoise shell, which is an attractive, brown, speckled material, obtained from the shell of the hawksbill turtle. The turtle has been hunted to near-extinction, and the use of the natural material has been banned. Heavy tortoise shell frames became popular in the 1930s, 1940s, and 1950s, replacing metal frames and rimless glasses worn earlier.

wraparound glasses   Sunglasses made of a molded piece of plastic shaped like a headband that is cut out for insertion of the lenses. Similar to COURRÈGES GLASSES (see under STYLES OF EYEGLASSES DEFINED) but with a wider viewing area .

Footwear may be of the slip-on variety or closed with lacers or buckles. When the lacers end in tassels, they are known as **tassel-ties.** In the early 1980s Velcro® was introduced for closings. For detailed discussion of closures, see CLOSURES in the COMPONENTS OF ACCESSORIES section of this book.

FOOTWEAR MANUFACTURE

The basic steps in constructing most footwear are: A pattern is created that consists of all the pieces of the UPPER (see under ANATOMY OF SOME FOOTWEAR TYPES) part of the footwear. A mechanical or manual cutter uses this pattern to cut out each piece of the footwear. Next these pieces are stitched together. The upper is placed over a plastic or wooden form called the **last,** which is the size and shape of the foot. A **combination last** has a heel that is narrower than the toe. Next, the SOLE must be attached to the upper. Usually an insole is attached to the last, and the upper is attached to the INSOLE. The rest of the sole may be nailed, stitched, glued, or joined by heat to the upper (see cross references under ANATOMY OF SOME FOOTWEAR TYPES).

Specialized footwear, such as ski boots or some winter or protective footwear, may be created by other methods in which the material used to make it is injected into a mold. The material used for such footwear is usually rubber or synthetic plastics or resins.

Soles can be made from these materials: LEATHER, SOLID OR FOAM RUBBER, SYNTHETIC RUBBER, POLYVINYL CHLORIDE, ETHYLENE VINYL ACETATE, and POLYURETHANE. See LEATHER and OTHER MATERIALS USED IN ACCESSORIES: RUBBER and PLASTICS for a discussion of these materials.

Different manufacturing techniques have developed. Among the best known of these are:

Blake See FOOTWEAR MANUFACTURE: MCKAY METHOD.

Littleway shoe construction Process of shoe construction or manufacturing that uses a staple to attach the INSOLE to the UPPER. The OUTSOLE may be sewed on with a lockstitch or cemented to the insole. See cross references under ANATOMY OF SOME FOOTWEAR TYPES.

McKay shoe construction Shoe manufacturing process in which the UPPER is pulled around the last and fastened to the INSOLE by means of tacks. The OUTSOLE may be attached by stitching or by cementing. (Invented by Lyman Blake in 1861.) See cross references under ANATOMY OF SOME FOOTWEAR TYPES.

stitchdown shoe construction Manufacturing process for shoes that involves turning of the shoe UPPER to the outside rather than around and under the last. The OUTSOLE is stitched to the extended edge around the shoe. This simple, flexible low-cost shoe construction, used formerly for infants' shoes, is now used for all types of shoes. Sometimes they are made with two soles and called **double stitchdown.** When made with three soles, they are called **triple stitchdown** (see cross references under ANATOMY OF SOME FOOTWEAR TYPES).

turned shoe construction Lightweight shoe, usually in PUMP style (see under FOOTWEAR STYLES DEFINED: SHOES), constructed by stitching sole to upper inside out then "turning" to right side with seams on inside.

veldtschoen construction Method of making shoes in which the UPPER (see ANATOMY OF SOME FOOTWEAR TYPES) is turned out at the bottom edge, cemented, and stitched to the sole.

TYPES OF HEELS DEFINED

Heels may be flat, medium, or high and measured in **eighths** of an inch, e.g., a ⅛ heel is 2″ high, a ⅛ heel is ½″ high. The inside edge of a heel is called the **breast** of the heel. An extra replaceable piece on bottom is called the **heel lift.** Heels may be made of wood, plastic, Lucite, or metal. They come in a variety of heights and shapes as follows:

baby Louis heel SEE TYPES OF HEELS DEFINED: LOUIS HEEL.

ball heel Spherical heel made of wood or Lucite.

ball heel

bell-bottom heel See TYPES OF HEELS DEFINED: LOUIS HEEL.

block heel See TYPES OF HEELS DEFINED: CUBAN HEEL.

boulevard heel Sturdy high heel, similar to a CUBAN HEEL (see under TYPES OF HEELS DEFINED), that is tapered at sides

boulevard heel

and back, has straight front, and a flange where heel joins with sole.

breasted heel Any heel made with a curved section where it attaches to the sole of the shoe at the SHANK (see under ANATOMY OF SOME FOOTWEAR TYPES).

built-up heel See TYPES OF HEELS DEFINED: STACKED HEEL.

chunky heel High or medium heel that has exaggerated width.

columnar heel High circular-styled heel graduating from wide width at sole of shoe to small base.

common-sense heels Low heel used on children's or infants' shoe made by increasing size of OUTSOLE at heel. See ANATOMY OF SOME FOOTWEAR TYPES.

Continental heel High narrow heel made straight in front with square corners at base and slight curve at back. Has a slight edge that extends forward where it joins the sole. Exaggeratedly high and narrow version is called a SPIKE HEEL (see under TYPES OF HEELS DEFINED).

corkies See TYPES OF HEELS DEFINED: WEDGE HEEL.

covered heel Heel of wood or plastic covered with leather or another plastic.

cuban heel Medium to high, broad heel with slight curve in back, popular in 1930s and 1940s. The **block heel** is a similar straight heel, but set further back and approximately the same width at top and base.

cube heel Square-backed heel made of leather or Lucite.

draped heel Heel on woman's shoe with leather or fabric from COUNTER (see under ANATOMY OF SOME FOOTWEAR TYPES) arranged in folds over the back.

Dutch boy heel Low heel with medium-sized base, its back slants slightly and the inside edge is slanted toward front, where it joins the edge.

elevator heel Man's heel worn to make him appear taller. Inside of shoe is built up at the heel, making the outside of shoe appear lower than it is. Attached heel lift is higher than average.

flange heel Heel that flares or angles to make a wider base.

flat heel Broad low heel originally used on children's shoes, now popular on

women's shoes. Shoes with this heel are called *flats* or *flatties*.

flat/flatties See TYPES OF HEELS DEFINED: FLAT HEEL.

floating pedestal wedge Medium broad heel, similar to a wedge, but cut out under the arch, making it wider at the base of the heel and slanting toward the sole.

French heel High heel that curves inward at back then flares slightly outward at base.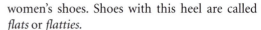

heel lift Replaceable piece on the bottom of a heel.

hooded heel Heel slanting into SHANK of shoe, usually covered in one piece with UPPER. See under ANATOMY OF SOME FOOTWEAR TYPES.

ice cube heel Low, square-cut heel of clear Lucite® introduced in 1970. *Der.* The shape and size of an ice cube.

Italian heel Shoe heel worn from 1770s, on which curves inward at back, similar to LOUIS HEEL (see under TYPES OF HEELS DEFINED). Also has a wedge-shaped extension at top of heel extending under the sole nearly to ball of foot.

Louis heel Heel of medium height curved sharply inward around sides and back, then flared slightly at base, similar to heels worn in Louis XV period. Low version is called **baby Louis heel;** and a **bell-bottom heel** is an exaggerated version with a chunky medium heel, curved inward and then flaring at the bottom.

military heel Medium to low heel with a broad base. Slants slightly in back and usually has an attached rubber lift. Used on comfort shoes and walking shoes for women.

museum heel Medium-height heel with front and back curving inward and then outward to make a flared base. Also called *shepherdess heel.*

pinafore heel Flat leather or rubber heel made in one piece with the sole curved under the arch of the shoe. Made in the same manner that rubber heels and soles are joined on SADDLE OXFORDS (see under FOOTWEAR STYLES DEFINED: SHOES).

pyramid heel Medium-high heel with squared base flaring toward the sole— like an inverted pyramid.

sculptured heel Broad medium-high heel made with a see-through center, introduced in 1960s.

Similar to some freeform pieces of sculpture. Used on wooden clogs in late 1970s.

set-back heel Heel with straight back joined to the sole as far back as possible.

set-back heel

set-under heel Heel with outside edge curving forward under heel.

set-under heel

shepherdess heel See TYPES OF HEELS DEFINED: MUSEUM HEEL.

Spanish heel High heel with a curve similar to a FRENCH HEEL (see under TYPES OF HEELS DEFINED) but has a straight inside edge.

spike heel High curved slender heel with tiny base; usually 3″ to 3½″ high. Also see TYPES OF HEELS DEFINED: CONTINENTAL HEEL.

spring heel Low broad heel with extra layer of leather inserted between heel and sole. Used primarily on children's shoes.

stiletto heel (stil-et′-tow) Set-back heel that ends in a tiny rounded base, usually fitted with a metal tip. As the walking surface is small, there is an enormous amount of weight on the heel. Used mainly from 1950s until mid-1960s and revived in the 1990s.

stacked heel Heel built up of horizontal layers of leather. Also called *built-up heel.*

wedge heel Slanted heel made in one piece with the sole of the shoe. Comes in low, medium, and high heights. Introduced in 1930s. Some heels are cut in one piece with a slight platform sole and are usually covered with jute, fabric, urethane, or leather. Some are made of cork and called *corkies.*

wedge heel

TYPES OF TOES DEFINED

toe Front portion of the shoe covering the toes. Fashion fluctuates between the extremes in wide or narrow toes and in their shape. Names given to various toe shapes include:

bulldog toe Bulbous toe popular on a man's buttoned ankle-high shoe before World War I. Similar to KNOB TOE (see under TYPES OF TOES DEFINED).

Charlie Chaplin toe Wide round toe used on a MARY JANE shoe (see under TYPES OF FOOTWEAR DEFINED: SHOES). Featured by Courrèges in his spring 1967 collection.

crescent toe Narrow-toed shoe ending with a curved rather than a NEEDLE TOE (see under TYPES OF TOES DEFINED).

double-needle toe SEE TYPES OF TOES DEFINED: NEEDLE TOE.

knob toe Bulbous toe introduced in the early 1970s. Similar to BULLDOG TOE (see under TYPES OF TOES DEFINED).

needle toe Long narrow extremely pointed toe. Narrower and more pointed variations are called *double-needle* and *triple-needle toes.* Also see TYPES OF FOOTWEAR DEFINED: SHOES: WINKLE PICKERS.

oval toe Woman's shoe toe, narrower than a round toe but not an extreme point.

platypus toe Squared-off tip of toe shaped like a duck's bill. *Der.* Named for animal with snout shaped in this manner.

safety toe Steel toe box inserted between shoe upper and lining. Used on shoes worn for protection by workmen in industrial plants.

slant/slanted toe Rather wide toe that slants diagonally toward the little toe.

taj toe Tiny pointed and turned-up oriental-type toe used on a shoe.

triple-needle toe See TYPES OF TOES DEFINED: NEEDLE TOE.

walled toe Deep toe cap with vertical edge at least ³⁄₄″ high.

OTHER COMPONENTS OF FOOTWEAR DEFINED

A.T.P./Achilles tendon protector (a-kil′-ees) Padding placed at the back of the heel collar of some athletic shoes to protect the Achilles tendon. Also called *heel horn.*

ankle-strap shoe/sandal Shoe, frequently of the sandal-type, having a strap attached at the top of the heel and going around the ankle. Shown at D'ORSAY PUMP (see under FOOTWEAR STYLES DEFINED: SHOES). Frequently made with PLATFORM SOLE (see under OTHER COMPONENTS OF FOOTWEAR DEFINED). Very popular in the 1930s and 1940s, revived in late 1960s, and very popular in 1980s and after.

arch cushion Pad for support of the arch of the foot. Also called *cookie.*

backstay Reinforcement of the vertical seam at the back of a shoe with a narrow piece of leather.

ballet laces (bal′-lay) Wide satin ribbons used as lacings for ballet slippers, crisscrossing at intervals around ankle and calf and tied in a bow. Worn in 1870s on bathing slippers and during World War I with high-heeled pumps. Reintroduced in 1980s after which they appeared on ballet-inspired shoes with high heels as well as flat shoes.

bumper Rubber strip attached across the front of the toe in some athletic footwear.

calk Device on the heel or sole, of a shoe or boot to prevent slipping or give longer wear; may be a metal plate with sharp points.

cleats Projections attached to soles of sport shoes, made of plastic, wood, rubber, or metal. Used particularly on football, golf, and baseball shoes to prevent slipping.

closed seam Shoe seam, similar to a simple fabric seam, stitched on the inside and edges pressed back. Usually used for joining the shoe at center back.

collar See OTHER COMPONENTS OF FOOTWEAR DEFINED: QUARTER.

Colonial tongue Stiffened shoe TONGUE that extends up from VAMP (see under ANATOMY OF SOME FOOTWEAR TYPES) of COLONIAL SHOE (see under FOOTWEAR STYLES DEFINED: SHOES) and is frequently trimmed with ornamental buckle.

cookie See OTHER COMPONENTS OF FOOTWEAR DEFINED: ARCH CUSHION.

crampons Iron plates with spikes on the bottom that fasten onto shoes or boots so as to facilitate walking or climbing on ice.

creepers Small plates of metal set with spikes fastened over soles of shoes by straps. Worn when walking on ice and snow to prevent slipping.

cushion sole Cork, felt, or foam rubber used under the INSOLE (see under ANATOMY OF SOME FOOTWEAR TYPES) of shoe as shock absorber when walking.

cutouts Shoe-industry term for tiny patterns shaped like diamonds, teardrops, squares, and other shapes cut out of the upper part of shoe to give open-air effect.

doubler Extra layer of soft fabric placed between the leather and the lining of a shoe to make leather look plumper.

Dutchman Triangular wedge placed between INSOLE and OUTSOLE (see under ANATOMY OF SOME FOOTWEAR TYPES) of shoe to improve posture of wearer. Also used between layers of a built-up heel to adjust heel pitch.

edge Shoe-industry term for part of shoe that is visible around outside of front of shoe sole—may be rounded, beveled, or square.

eyestay Section of footwear that reinforces the holes used for lacing.

foxing 1. Extra fancy-cut piece of leather sewed on at the top of the back seam of the shoe for reinforcement and decoration. 2. Strip of rubber fastened to the upper and the shoe that goes all around the shoe.

French seam Shoe seam that starts with a simple or closed seam, restitched on either side on the outside. Used for closing back of shoe.

fringed tongue Shoe TONGUE (see under FOOTWEAR STYLES DEFINED) finished with saw-toothed edge at top.

heel horn See OTHER COMPONENTS OF FOOTWEAR DEFINED: A.T.P.

inlay Shoe-industry term for piece of leather or fabric placed underneath a cut-out layer of leather and stitched into place for a decorative effect.

instep The inside arch area of the shoe.

lug sole Shoe or boot sole with rubber ridges or cleats to provide additional traction.

medallion In the shoe-industry, an ornamental pattern punched in leather in center of man's WING-TIP OXFORD (see under FOOTWEAR STYLES DEFINED: SHOES).

overlay A piece of leather or other material stitched on shoe in decorative manner. Usually made of a contrasting color or a textured leather such as lizard or snakeskin.

perforations Small holes punched through leather of shoe to achieve decorative effect. Used particularly for SPECTATOR PUMPS and BROGUES (see under STYLES OF FOOTWEAR DEFINED: SHOES). Also called *perfs* in shoe trade slang.

perfs See OTHER COMPONENTS OF FOOTWEAR DEFINED: PERFORATIONS.

pinking Saw-toothed trimming on edges of leather used in contrasting color on extra pieces applied to toes and heels of SPECTATOR SHOES (see under STYLES OF FOOTWEAR DEFINED: SHOES) for a decorative effect.

platform sole Midsole of shoe, often made of cork or sponge rubber, raising the foot off of the ground on a platform varying in height from ¼″ to 3″.

quarter Back portion of shoe upper covering the sides and back of the foot. In athletic footwear the top line of the quarter, called the **collar**, is sometimes padded.

rand A leather strip placed between the shoe upper and the sole.

saddle Extra piece of leather sewed over instep of a shoe, usually of contrasting color or texture (e.g., black or brown on white shoes).

saddle seam Hand or machine-stitched seam used on shoes when two raw edges of leather stand up on outside, as on the top of a MOCCASIN (see under STYLES OF FOOTWEAR DEFINED: SHOES).

sock lining Sole-shaped piece of leather or fabric covering shoe insole.

throat The open area at the top of the VAMP (see under ANATOMY OF SOME FOOTWEAR TYPES) where it ends at the INSTEP of the foot (see under OTHER COMPONENTS OF FOOTWEAR DEFINED). May be cut in various shapes.

toe spring The distance between the flat surface on which a shoe stands and the toe end of the shoe.

topline The opening in the shoe around the ankle.

waist The narrow part of footwear between the toe and heel.

welt Narrow piece of leather stitched to shoe upper, lining, and insole before being attached to outsole with seam concealed. A method of shoe construction that permits shoe to be resoled.

wing-tip Decorative leather cap sewn to toe of shoe. Sometimes curved with center point and perforated in patterns.

FOOTWEAR STYLES DEFINED

SHOES

baby doll shoe Low-heeled shoe with wide rounded toes similar to MARY JANE SHOE (see under FOOTWEAR STYLES DEFINED: SHOES),

sometimes with straps over instep. *Der.* Term used to refer to clothing and accessories used for children's dolls and infants' clothes in the early part of the 20th c.

bal/Balmoral (bahl-mor′-al) Basic style of OXFORD with the TONGUE cut in a separate piece from the VAMP of the shoe and joined with stitching across the vamp. (See under ANATOMY OF SOME FOOTWEAR TYPES.) *Der.* First worn at Balmoral Castle in Scotland in early 1850s.

bal/balmoral shoe

ballerina shoe **1.** Soft low kid shoe with thin sole and flat heel, sometimes made with drawstring throat. Inspired by shoe worn by ballet dancers. Also see FOOTWEAR STYLES DEFINED: SLIPPERS: BALLET SLIPPER. **2.** Plain, low-cut pump made with flat or wedge heel and a crepe or man-made sole, introduced in 1980s.

ballerina shoe

Bass Weejun® Trademark of G.H. Bass & Co. for a high-quality moccasin-type loafer with tasseled bow in front using the same type last since 1936. Originally copied from a Norwegian-type moccasin. *Der.* Word from shortened form of Norwegian-Injun.

blucher (bloo′-cher or bloo′-ker) Basic OXFORD type with the TONGUE and VAMP cut in one piece. See FOOTWEAR STYLES DEFINED: SHOES and ANATOMY OF SOME FOOTWEAR TYPES. *Der.* Named after Field Marshal Gebhard Leberecht von Blucher, Prussian commander at battle of Waterloo, 1815, who devised this type of shoe for army wear in 1810.

blucher

blucher bal (bloo′-cher or bloo′-ker) Modified BLUCHER oxford (see under FOOTWEAR STYLES DEFINED: SHOES) with VAMP stitched over QUARTER at sides, but not stitched over TONGUE (see cross-references under ANATOMY OF SOME FOOTWEAR TYPES).

bracelet-tie shoe Woman's ankle-strap shoe with loop extending on rim in center back to hold the strap.

brogan Ankle-length work shoe made of leather and fastened to foot by side flaps either buckled or tied over short TONGUE (see under ANATOMY OF SOME FOOTWEAR TYPES).

brogue Heavy walking shoe, a type of OXFORD (see under FOOTWEAR STYLES DEFINED:

brogue 1916

SHOES), originally made for men, that usually has a wing tip decorated with heavy PERFORA-TIONS and PINKINGS (see under OTHER COMPO-NENTS OF FOOTWEAR DEFINED). Frequently worn for golf but also for city wear. *Der.* From coarse heelless shoe of untanned hide, with hair left on, worn by men in Ireland in 1790.

buck oxford   A BLUCHER-type oxford (see under FOOTWEAR STYLES DEFINED: SHOES) made with sueded split-leather upper. Typically has a red cushion-crepe rubber sole. When made of white leather, called **white bucks.**

Buster Brown®   Comic strip character drawn by R. F. Outcault in the early 20th c. whose haircut, collars, suit, and shoes were widely copied for children's wear. The name became a trademark for children's shoes and is currently a trademark for a wide variety of products.

cack   Heelless shoe with soft leather sole, made for infants in sizes one to five.

chain loafer   See FOOTWEAR STYLES DEFINED: SHOES: LOAFER.

Chinese shoe   Fabric flat-heeled crepe-soled shoe of MARY JANE type (see under FOOTWEAR STYLES DEFINED: SHOES) made with one strap and rounded toe in many colors, sometimes with embroidery. The national shoe of China, which was imported by the United States and sold first at Oriental stores and later at other stores in late 1970s and thereafter.

chunky shoe   Shoes of all types made in exaggeratedly heavy shapes with bulbous toes and massive heels, often with very thick PLATFORM SOLES (see under OTHER COMPONENTS OF FOOTWEAR DEFINED).

chunky shoe

clog   A backless shoe or shoe with low-cut back supported by a substantial SOLE. Clogs were orig-inally made with wooden soles, but are currently available with soles and UPPERS made from many different materials. See cross references under ANATOMY OF SOME FOOTWEAR TYPES.

colonial shoe   Medium-heeled slip-on shoe with stiffened TONGUE standing up over INSTEP (see under ANATOMY OF SOME FOOTWEAR TYPES), frequently decorated with large orna-mental buckle. Worn in the 17th and 18th c. in the United States and revived often.

court shoe   **1.** See FOOTWEAR STYLES DEFINED: ATHLETIC SHOES AND OTHER FOOTWEAR FOR SPORTS: TENNIS SHOE. **2.** British term for PUMP (see under FOOTWEAR STYLES DEFINED: SHOES).

creedmore   Anklehigh shoe with buckled strap over instep.

crepe-soled shoe   Shoe made with crepe rubber SOLE and HEEL (see under ANATOMY OF SOME FOOTWEAR TYPES). Originally worn for sports-wear, they were so comfortable that they were adopted for everyday wear particularly by men and school children, and then became fashion-able for women after the 1970s.

discotheque shoe   A sole with a small heel, fas-tened to the foot by means of a few narrow straps. Popular for dancing at discotheques in the mid- and late 1960s. *Der.* French *disc,* "record," and *-otheque,* "library."

d'Orsay pump/d'Orsay slipper   PUMP with closed heel and toe, cut down to the sole at the sides leaving shank bare (see under FOOTWEAR STYLES DEFINED: SHOES). Often made with high heel. *Der.* Named for *Count d'Orsay,* a French society leader of the 19th c.

d'Orsay pump with ankle strap

dress shoe   **1.** Man's or woman's shoe worn for formal occasions, general wear, and business. Does not include sport shoes or CREPE-SOLED SHOES (see under FOOTWEAR STYLES DEFINED: SHOES). **2.** Girl's shoes worn for special occa-sions, not for school or sportswear.

Duck shoe®   Trademarked OXFORD or SLIP-ON style shoe usually made in two colors (e.g., brown with tan, navy with yellow) of manufactured waterproof materials with chain-tread rubber soles (see cross references under FOOTWEAR STYLES DEFINED: SHOES). Also called *rubber moccasin.*

dyeable shoe   Shoe made of white fabric such as satin, faille, or silk that may be dyed to match a dress. They are worn primarily for evening par-ties or weddings.

Elevator shoe   Trademark, now expired, for a man's shoe with a wedge inserted inside toward the heel to make the man appear taller. Usually made to order.

espadrille (ess-pa´-dril)   **1.** Rope-soled shoe with canvas upper. Some versions tied on with long shoelaces threaded through top of shoe, crossed, and tied around the ankle. Originally worn for

espadrille #1

bathing shoe and later for sportswear. **2.** Restyled in 1980s as an OXFORD, or PUMP (see under FOOTWEAR STYLES DEFINED: SHOES) cut high and straight across instep with medium-high WEDGE HEEL (see under TYPES OF HEELS DEFINED) covered with jute, made with crepe sole, and no lacers. *Der.* French, shoe made of canvas with cord sole.

evening shoe/evening slipper Delicate shoe worn with evening clothes. Women's styles include pumps or sandals in gold, silver, or metallic kid, or luxurious fabrics; men's style is usually a patent-leather pump or slipper.

gillie/ghillie (gil′-ee) **1.** Laced shoe, usually without a tongue, with rounded lacer pulling through leather loops and fastened around the ankle. Worn with Scottish kilt, therefore also called *kiltie* (see FOOTWEAR STYLES DEFINED: SHOES: KILTIE OXFORD). *Der.* Popularized by Edward VIII and sometimes called *Prince of Wales shoe.* **2.** Many adaptations of this style, particularly for women's shoes, include some styles with high heels. *Der.* Scottish, *gille,* "an attendant or personal servant to a Highland chieftain."

Gucci® loafer See FOOTWEAR STYLES DEFINED: SHOES: LOAFER.

gumshoe Colloquial term for sneaker or rubber overshoe. From this comes the slang term meaning a detective or private investigator, alluding to the quiet tread of SNEAKERS (see under ATHLETIC SHOES AND OTHER FOOTWEAR FOR SPORTS), which is useful in confidential work.

Harlow pump SABOT-STRAP pump (see under FOOTWEAR STYLES DEFINED: SHOES) with high CHUNKY HEEL (see under TYPES OF HEELS DEFINED) popular in early 1970s. *Der.* Named after shoes worn by Jean Harlow, Hollywood actress of the 1920s and 1930s.

high button shoe Shoe that comes to the ankle or above and closes with a row of small shoe buttons or shoe laces.

Hush Puppies® Trade name initially used for casual OXFORD OR SLIP-ON SHOES (see under FOOTWEAR STYLES DEFINED: SHOES) with sueded leather uppers and crepe soles. Popular for men, women, and children. The trademark has now been extended to other shoe styles.

Indian moccasin See FOOTWEAR STYLES DEFINED: SHOES: MOCCASIN.

jazz oxford Flat-heeled OXFORD (see under FOOTWEAR STYLES DEFINED: SHOES) made with VAMP line curved and stitched extending downward to arch. (See under ANATOMY OF SOME FOOTWEAR TYPES.) The remainder of shoe is cut in one piece with front lacing.

jellies/jelly beans Molded footwear of soft plastic or rubber made in many styles, e.g., wedgies, multistrapped sandals, flat-heeled thongs, high-heeled pumps, and booties. Some have cut-out "portholes" or lattice strips, and are worn with bright-colored contrasting socks. All are made in a great variety of bright colors. Originally introduced for children. The style was basically a practical fisherman's sandal made of soft plastic. *Der.* Named for soft translucent look of jelly in jelly-bean colors.

kiltie flat A low-heeled shoe with a fringed TONGUE and shoelace tied over top in a bow usually made with crepe SOLE (see under ANATOMY OF SOME FOOTWEAR TYPES).

kiltie oxford Heeled, laced shoe with a shawl or fringed tongue projecting over front of shoe through which laces may be tied. Adopted from Scottish type shoes.

kiltie oxford with wing tip toe

landlady shoe See FOOTWEAR STYLES DEFINED: SHOES: WOOLWORTH® SHOE.

loafer Slip-on shoe of moccasin-type construction with a slotted strap stitched to the VAMP (see under ANATOMY OF SOME FOOTWEAR TYPES). Introduced first for wear by college girls in the 1940s, now a classic worn by adults and children. Variations include **chain loafer,** trimmed with metal links or hardware trim over the instep. A classic shoe since the 1960s. A variant of the chain loafer is the **Gucci® loafer** (goo′chee), the most popular of the fine shoes sold by the Italian firm Gucci since the early 1960s in United States. It has a distinctive gold-metal harness decoration across vamp. Man's shoe has low heel, woman's shoe, a medium heel. The **penny loafer** has a slot in the strap across each vamp into which a coin is sometimes inserted. Pennies were originally inserted, but dimes and quarters are now more generally used. Originally in brown but featured in colors in the 1980s and after. The **tassel-top loafer** has a leather tassle on instep.

penny loafer

mamma shoe Retail store and trade name for shoes worn by older women that stress comfort rather than style. Usually made in an oxford style with medium-high broad heel.

mary jane/Mary Jane® **1.** Low-heeled slipper made of patent leather with blunt toe and single *mary jane #1* strap over the INSTEP (see under ANATOMY OF SOME FOOTWEAR TYPES) that buttons or buckles at center or side. First used as a trademarked shoe for children in 1927, the style has remained popular ever since although currently the trademark is applied to a wide variety of apparel. **2.** In 1980s, a FLATTIE or WEDGIE (see under FOOTWEAR STYLES DEFINED: SHOES) in pump style with buckled strap coming high over the instep. *Der.* Named for shoes worn by character Mary Jane in comic strip Buster Brown drawn by R. F. Outcault in early 1900s. Compare with FOOTWEAR STYLES DEFINED: SHOES: BABY DOLL SHOE.

Miranda pump Platform pump with high, heavy, flared heel. *Der.* Named after Carmen Miranda, a popular movie star of the late 1930s and 1940s.

moccasin Heelless shoe in which the sole is made of leather and comes up to form the QUARTER and part of the VAMP (see under ANATOMY OF SOME FOOTWEAR TYPES). A tonguelike curved piece is hand-stitched to complete the vamp. Thong is threaded around the collar of *moccasin* the slipper and ties on the instep. Frequently is fleece-lined. May have fringe, beadwork, or tassel trim. Sometimes called *Indian moccasin* because this footwear was worn originally by Native Americans.

moccasin-type shoe Shoe construction based on the MOCCASIN (see under FOOTWEAR STYLES DEFINED: SHOES), in which the UPPER starts under the SOLE of the foot and forms the QUARTER with the toe stitched to an oval VAMP (see under ANATOMY OF SOME FOOTWEAR TYPES). Hard soles, sometimes of rubber, are added to produce a more durable shoe than the soft Indian moccasin.

monk shoe Closed shoe with wide, buckled strap over tongue at instep rather than lacings. *monk shoe* Popular for women in 1940s and for men during World War II when this style was favored by U.S. Army Air Corps officers. Revived from time to time.

monster shoe Clumsy bulky shoe with wide bulbous toe and large clunky heel.

mousers Women's leather stocking-pants reaching to the waist with attached chunky-type shoes made of shiny wet-look leather. Introduced by Mary Quant, British designer, in 1969.

mule High-heeled slipper or shoe with VAMP (see under ANATOMY OF SOME FOOTWEAR TYPES) but *mule* no back, often made of fancy leathers and fabrics. Name has been used since 16th c.

open-back shoe See FOOTWEAR STYLES DEFINED: SHOES: SLINGBACK SHOE.

open shank shoe Woman's shoe with closed toe and heel portions but open on sides down to sole; sometimes with side straps connecting VAMP and QUARTER (see under ANATOMY OF SOME FOOTWEAR TYPES). Also see FOOTWEAR STYLES DEFINED: SHOES: D'ORSAY PUMP.

open-toed shoe Women's shoe with the toe section cut out.

opera pump Plain, undecorated woman's PUMP (see under FOOTWEAR STYLES DEFINED: SHOES) with medium to high heel. Upper is cut from a single piece of leather or fabric. Introduced in 1920s and a basic style since then.

overshoe Waterproof fabric or rubber shoe worn over other shoes in inclement weather. Also called RUBBERS. See FOOTWEAR STYLES DEFINED: SHOES and BOOTS: ARCTICS, GALOSH, and RAIN BOOTS.

oxford **1.** Originally a shoeman's term to differentiate low-cut shoes from boots. Now a basic style of low shoe usually fastened with shoe laces, but may be closed with buckles, Velcro®, or other type of fasteners. Shown in ANATOMY OF SOME FOOWEAR TYPES. **2.** A half-boot. *Der.* Named for Oxford University where the style was a half boot introduced in England about 1640 and worn by university students.

penny loafer See FOOTWEAR STYLES DEFINED: SHOES: LOAFER.

platform shoe Shoe with thick mid-sole, usually made of cork and covered so that the wearer appears taller. Popular for women in 1940s and revived by Paris *platform shoe* designer Yves Saint Laurent in 1960s. Worn by men in 1970s. Revived periodically.

plug/plugged oxford Low, laced shoe cut with VAMP and QUARTERS (see under ANATOMY OF SOME FOOTWEAR TYPES) in one piece and a separate lace stay, e.g., SADDLE OXFORDS (see under FOOTWEAR STYLES DEFINED: SHOES).

pre-walkers Infant's shoe with very soft soles worn before child begins to walk.

Prince of Wales shoe See FOOTWEAR STYLES DEFINED: SHOES: GILLIE.

pump Slip-on shoe with low-cut, rounded, or V-shaped THROAT, a heel that may be of any height and may be covered with the same material as the UPPER. (See under ANATOMY OF SOME FOOTWEAR TYPES.) Toes vary from rounded to pointed depending on the current style. Sometimes made with open toe and/or open heel in SLINGBACK style (see under FOOTWEAR STYLES DEFINED: SHOES). A classic style for women for day or evening since 1920s.

rubbers Waterproof lightweight shoes that pull on over regular shoes in inclement weather. Also called OVERSHOES. See FOOTWEAR STYLES DEFINED: SHOES: STORM RUBBERS, and TOE RUBBERS.

rubber shoe/rubber moccasin See DUCK SHOE® under FOOTWEAR STYLES DEFINED: SHOES.

Ruby Keeler shoe Low-heeled pump tied across instep with ribbon bow similar to tap shoes. *Der.* Named after tap dancer Ruby Keeler, popular star of 1930s films, who made a stage comeback on Broadway in 1971 in a revival of the 1917 musical *No, No, Nanette.*

sabot (sa-bo′) **1.** Shoe carved from one piece of wood, worn by peasants in France, Belgium, Spain, and Portugal. Also worn with Dutch national costume. **2.** CLOG shoe (see under FOOTWEAR STYLES DEFINED: SHOES) with thick wood SOLE and open HEEL, made with closed leather VAMP or leather bands across INSTEP (see under ANATOMY OF SOME FOOTWEAR TYPES).

sabot-strap shoe Woman's shoe with a wide strap across instep usually buckling to one side. May be used on a SPECTATOR PUMP shoe (see under FOOTWEAR STYLES DEFINED: SHOES).

saddle oxford/saddle shoe Sport or school shoe traditionally made of white buck calf with a

saddle oxford

brown or black leather "saddle" shaped section over the middle of the shoe. Usually made with rubber soles, it has been a basic style since the 1920s, very popular in the 1940s, and still worn. Now made in various colors.

safety shoe Work shoe with a heavy metal reinforced toe, or another protective feature, worn by industrial workers.

Scholl's® exercise shoe A trademark for a wooden sandal with a sole shaped to fit the foot and with special carving underneath the ball of the foot for gripping the foot when walking; made with only one wide strap over front of foot, buckled to adjust the size, and having an outer sole of ridged rubber. Action of foot on carved sole when walking provides healthful exercise. Introduced in late 1960s, and still worn.

shell See FOOTWEAR STYLES DEFINED: SHOES: SKIMMER.

shower shoe Plain heel-less PUMP (see under FOOTWEAR STYLES DEFINED: SHOES) with upper of fishnet and sole of rubber or crepe. Worn at home, in the shower, or at the beach.

side-gore shoe Slip-on shoe, usually with high vamp, that has triangular insertions of elastic at sides.

side-laced oxford Oxford, laced at side front rather than center front, made with low wedge heel, reinforced counter, side perforations near sole for ventilation, and cushioned arch support.

skimmer Very low-cut women's PUMP (see under FOOTWEAR STYLES DEFINED: SHOES) with shallow sides set on low or flat heels, usually made of very soft leather. Also called *shell.*

slingback shoe Any shoe with an open back and a strap around the heel of the foot to hold it in place. May be made in pump or sandal style.
slingback shoe

sling pump See FOOTWEAR STYLES DEFINED: SHOES: SLINGBACK SHOE.

slip-on shoe Any shoe which stays on the foot without using straps or fasteners, e.g., a PUMP, LOAFER, or MOCCASIN (see under FOOTWEAR STYLES DEFINED: SHOES). Also called a *step-in shoe.*

Space® shoe Trademarked name for side-laced leather orthopedic shoes, with extra moving space for each toe, custom-made over casts of the wearer's feet. Made with thick crepe soles and low wedge heels for comfort.

spectator pump Two-toned pump frequently made in contrasting colors of black, navy, red, or brown on white. Extra sewed-on toe and heel pieces of another color sometimes have PERFORATIONS and are PINKED at edges. See under OTHER COMPONENTS OF FOOTWEAR DEFINED.

spectator pump

Sperry Topsiders® Trademark for shoes with a specially designed rubber sole that provides good traction on a wet boat deck; often made in LOAFER or SNEAKER style with canvas upper (see under FOOTWEAR STYLES DEFINED: SHOES and ATHLETIC SHOES AND OTHER FOOTWEAR FOR SPORTS). This type of shoe is often referred to simply as a **topsider**. The trademark now applies to a wide variety of footwear.

step-in shoe See FOOTWEAR STYLES DEFINED: SHOES: SLIP-ON SHOE.

stocking shoe Shoe covered with knitted fabric and attached to a long stocking. Introduced in late 1960s by shoe designer Beth Levine.

storm rubbers Waterproof overshoes with rounded flap coming up over the instep.

tango shoe A woman's shoe that is cut high in the back with an ankle strap that buckles or ties.

tap shoe Any shoe worn by a tap dancer. Made with metal plates at tip of toe and back edge of heel to increase sound when dancing. Men's style is usually a patent-leather PUMP or OXFORD (see under FOOTWEAR STYLES DEFINED: SHOES); women's is usually a low-heeled patent-leather pump with ribbon tie at instep. Also see FOOTWEAR STYLES DEFINED: SHOES: RUBY KEELER SHOE.

tassel-top loafer See FOOTWEAR STYLES DEFINED: SHOES: LOAFER.

T-strap shoe/sandal Shoe made with a strap coming up from the VAMP to join second strap across the INSTEP, forming a **T**. May have high or low HEEL with open or closed SHANK. Popular since 1920s. See cross references under ANATOMY OF SOME FOOTWEAR TYPES.

t-strap shoe
1928

toe rubbers Overshoes, worn by women, that fit over the toes and have either a strap around the heel or snap together over the instep.

topsider See FOOTWEAR STYLES DEFINED: SHOES: SPERRY TOPSIDER®.

tuxedo pump Low-heeled pump with rounded toe usually made of patent leather with grosgrain trim around the COLLAR of the shoe and a broad flat grosgrain bow on the VAMP (see under ANATOMY OF SOME FOOTWEAR TYPES).

walkers Ankle-high, laced shoe, usually made of white leather, with manufactured or leather soles. Worn by children when first learning to walk.

walking shoe Any comfortable shoe with a relatively low heel, sometimes made with a cushion or crepe sole, worn more for comfort than style.

wedgies Shoes with WEDGE HEELS (see under TYPES OF HEELS DEFINED) completely joined to soles under arches, made in all styles and heel heights. Originally made with high wedge, now also made with low and medium-sized wedges.

white bucks See FOOTWEAR STYLES DEFINED: SHOES: BUCK OXFORD.

wing-tip oxford Laced shoe decorated at toe with wing-shaped overlay perforations, sometimes trimmed with perforations.

winkle pickers British slang for exaggeratedly pointed shoes. *Der.* From suggestion that the pointed toes can dig out snails or periwinkles, from the sand. Shown at FOOTWEAR STYLES DEFINED: BOOTS: BEATLE BOOT.

Woolworth® shoe Shoe that was sold in millions by Woolworth® stores. Made of cotton canvas, in sandal style, in red, navy, paisley, black, or white. This shoe has been entered in the permanent collection in the Metropolitan Museum of Art Costume Collection. Also called *landlady shoe*.

BOOTS

after-ski boot See FOOTWEAR STYLES DEFINED: BOOTS: APRÈS-SKI BOOT.

all-weather boot Calf-high boot made with fleece-lined upper attached to molded waterproof rubber sole with low heel.

ankle boot See FOOTWEAR STYLES DEFINED: BOOTS: DEMI-BOOT, GEORGE, and PANTS BOOT.

après-ski boot (app-reh skee) Bulky insulated boot, often calf-length and may be made of long-haired shaggy fur, worn for warmth after skiing. *Der.* French, "after ski." Also called *after-ski boots*.

arctics **1.** Waterproof rubber boot worn over regular shoes, usually with zipper closing. **2.** See FOOTWEAR STYLES DEFINED: BOOTS: GALOSH.

Beatle boot Ankle-high boot with pointed toe and side gores of elastic styled for men. Prob-

Beatle boot with winkle-picker toe
1964

ably the first fashionable ankle-high shoe to be worn by men for general wear in place of oxfords since World War I period. *Der.* Introduced in the 1960s by the Beatles, an avant-garde rock-music group from Liverpool, England. Also called *Chelsea boot.*

body boot See FOOTWEAR STYLES DEFINED: BOOTS: STOCKING BOOT.

Chelsea boot See FOOTWEAR STYLES DEFINED: BOOTS: BEATLE BOOT.

chest-high boot See FOOTWEAR STYLES DEFINED: BOOTS: WADERS.

chukka boot (chuh′-ka) Men's and boys' ankle-high boot laced through two sets of eyelets, made of splits of unlined sueded cowhide. Has thick crepe-rubber sole. Originally worn by polo players and adopted for general wear in 1950s. *Der.* From *chukka,* a period in polo games. A **desert boot,** introduced in 1960s, differs from a chukka boot in that it is usually lined and has a rubber sole. **Floats,** also introduced in early 1960s, have thick crepe soles and a thick pile lining, but are otherwise like chukka and desert boots.

city boots Women's boots of a more tailored or dressy style that are suitable for wear with business or more formal daytime dress.

combat boot Ankle-high laced boot worn by U.S. armed forces made of special retanned leather designed to be waterproof. Adopted as fashionable footwear in the 1980s and 1990s.

Courrèges boot (Koor′-rej) White calf-length low-heeled fashion boot introduced by French designer André Courrèges in fall of 1963 for wear with miniskirts.

cowboy boot High-heeled dip-top calf-high boot of highly ornate tooled or appliquéd leather, often two tone. First worn by cowboys of the western United States, now adapted for

cowboy boot

women and children. Also called *dip-top boot* and *western boot.*

demi-boot Short boot reaching just to the ankle. Also called *half-boot.*

desert boot See FOOTWEAR STYLES DEFINED: BOOTS: CHUKKA BOOTS.

dip-top boot See FOOTWEAR STYLES DEFINED: BOOTS: COWBOY BOOT.

Doc Martens Laceup boots with air pocket soles to ease pressure on the feet. The boots, first marketed in 1959, were adopted by skinheads and punks in the 1960s and 1970s and subsequently became widely popular among young people.

engineer's boot Man's 12″ high, straight-sided boot with low heel and leather strap buckled across the INSTEP (see under ANATOMY OF SOME FOOTWEAR TYPES). Also has buckle and strap over elastic gore set in the top.

fishing boot See FOOTWEAR STYLES DEFINED: BOOTS: HIP BOOT and WADERS.

floats See FOOTWEAR STYLES DEFINED: BOOTS: CHUKKA BOOT.

Frye® boot Boot of WELLINGTON TYPE (see under FOOTWEAR STYLES DEFINED: BOOTS), first manufactured in 1863 for Union soldiers. A registered trademark of John A. Frye Co. and now produced in a variety of boot styles.

galosh Waterproof ankle-high boot worn over the shoe, fastened with a snap, buckle, or zipper. Rubber galoshes were patented in 1842. Also called *arctics.*

George boot Ankle-high boot made with one-buckle fastening similar to JODHPUR BOOT (see under FOOTWEAR STYLES DEFINED: BOOTS). Widely accepted for general wear by men in late 1960s.

go-go boot Calf-length white boot, similar to COURRÈGES BOOT (see under FOOTWEAR STYLES DEFINED: BOOTS). *Der.* Named because worn by go-go dancers.

granny boot Women's boots laced up the front in imitation of high-topped shoes of 19th c.

half-boot See FOOTWEAR STYLES DEFINED: BOOTS: DEMI-BOOT.

hiking boot Above-the-ankle boot with padded collar and soft leather lining. Uppers are made of various materials

hiking boot

including leather, GORE-TEX®, or MANUFACTURED FIBER FABRIC (see TEXTILES IN ACCESSORIES: DIFFERENT TYPES OF FABRIC STRUCTURES:

MULTICOMPONENT FABRICS, and FIBERS AND YARNS: THE BUILDING BLOCKS OF FABRICS). Laced up front through riveted D-RINGS with SPEED LACING (see CLOSURES: TYPES OF CLOSURES DEFINED) at top. Usually has a cushioned INSOLE and padded QUARTER and TONGUE. HEEL and lug-type OUTSOLE are made of Vibram® (a durable synthetic rubber blend) welded to UPPER (see cross references under ANATOMY OF SOME FOOTWEAR TYPES). Also called *hikers* and *mountain climbing boot.*

hip boot   Thigh-length rubber fishing boot with straps at sides to fasten to belt at waist. Usually insulated and made with a cushioned innersole, steel shank, semi-hard toe cap, and cleated sole. Also see FOOTWEAR STYLES DEFINED: BOOTS: WADERS.

hobnailed boot   Boot with a sole into which short nails with large heads have been set. The nailheads serve to prevent wear on the soles.

insulated boot   Any boot with a lining for protection against cold, rain, snow, and bad weather. May be lined with fur, acrylic pile, wool, or foam-bonded fabric.

jodhpur boot (jod'-poor)   Ankle-high boot fastened with one buckle on the side, worn for horseback riding and for general wear. Similar to GEORGE BOOT (see under FOOTWEAR STYLES DEFINED: BOOTS). *Der* Named for Jodhpur, a city in India.

jungle boot   Combat boot used by U.S. Army in Vietnam. Made with heavy steel SHANK (see under ANATOMY OF SOME FOOTWEAR TYPES) and tiny drainage holes in sides and heel.

lineman's boot   High-top or above-the-ankle leather boot, usually black with laces up the center front, made of retanned leather. May have eyelets at the bottom and hooks for SPEED LACING (see CLOSURES: TYPES OF CLOSURES DEFINED) near the top.

lounger   Pull-on boot for cold weather with full grain cowhide UPPER (see under ANATOMY OF SOME FOOTWEAR TYPES) stitched to rubber shoe. Made with cushioned innersole vulcanized to chain-tread crepe outer sole. Sometimes lined and insulated with wool pile and sheepskin innersole.

lumberman's overboot   Man's heavy laced 10″ high boot with oiled-leather top, rubber VAMP, and SOLE (see under ANATOMY OF SOME FOOTWEAR TYPES) worn over felt inner boot. Worn by men in early 20th c., especially when working in lumber industry. *Der.* Boot originally worn in lumbering trade.

Maine hunting boot   Waterproof boot consisting of leather uppers sewn to waterproof, vulcanized rubber bottoms. Developed by Leon Bean, owner of L.L. Bean Company of Maine, and first sold by his firm in 1913.

majorette boot   Calf-high white boot worn by majorette or cheerleader at athletic events since the 1940s. Some have long white tassel attached to front.

Mexican wedding boot   Soft white leather above-the-calf boot made in moccasin style fastened down the outside with four large buttons. Colorful embroidery extends from VAMP (see under ANATOMY OF SOME FOOTWEAR TYPES) up to top of boot.

mod boot   Various types of boots inspired by those worn by boys and girls in mid-1960s in imitation of English mod fashions, e.g., see FOOTWEAR STYLES DEFINED: BOOTS: BEATLE BOOT.

molded boot   A ski boot, sometimes of glass fiber, closed with buckles, made with entire sole and part of shoe molded in one piece. Introduced for skiwear in the late 1960s.

mountain climbing boot   See FOOTWEAR STYLES DEFINED: BOOTS: HIKING BOOT.

mukluk   **1.** Boot reaching to lower calf worn by Alaskan Eskimos made of walrus hide or sealskin in MOCCASIN (see under FOOTWEAR STYLES DEFINED: SHOES) construction, tanned with the hair left on. Copied for winter wear for men, women, and children in same style since 1960s. **2.** Slipper socks made in moccasin construction.

pac boot   Laced boot coming to the lower calf of the leg, sometimes made with traction-tread for SOLE and HEEL (see under ANATOMY OF SOME FOOTWEAR TYPES). Insulated and pile-lined, sometimes made in rubber. Basic type boot originally made in MOCCASIN-type construction (see under FOOTWEAR STYLES DEFINED: SHOES: MOCCASIN-TYPE SHOES) worn by sportsmen, hunters, and workmen.

paddock boot   A less formal type of riding boot that laces to close in order to provide adjustable ankle support.

pants boot Ankle-high shoe-boot designed to wear with pants.

police boot Black leather boot reaching to below the knee made in shiny, stiff leather. Similar to a RIDING BOOT (see under FOOTWEAR STYLES DEFINED: BOOTS). Worn by motorcycle police, some state police, and by mounted police in U.S. and Canada.

rain boot **1.** Lightweight plastic or rubber stretch GALOSHES (see under FOOTWEAR STYLES DEFINED) that may be folded and carried in the purse. See FOOTWEAR STYLES DEFINED: BOOTS: TOTES®. **2.** Clear fold-up plastic coverings extending to ankle with zip front. Made with hole at heel through which high heel of shoe can be worn.

riding boot High boot coming to below the knee made of high-quality leather, usually custom-ordered to fit leg. Worn with breeches for horseback riding. May have boot straps at top for ease in dressing.

riding boot

rubber boot Molded rubber waterproof boot with or without insulated lining but usually fabric-lined, worn over the shoe (especially by children), or in place of the shoe as protection against rain or snow. Currently made in many colors, e.g., red, yellow, or purple.

skating boot See FOOTWEAR STYLES DEFINED: ATHLETIC SHOES AND OTHER SHOES FOR SPORTS: FIGURE SKATE and ROLLER SKATE.

ski boot Waterproof, thick-soled ankle-high boot of molded plastic, closed with laces or buckles. Sometimes has an inner boot or foam lining. Attaches to ski by clamp that grips the sole. Also see FOOTWEAR STYLES DEFINED: BOOTS: MOLDED BOOT. Sometimes has a strap and buckle at ankle, tread soles, and removable felt liners for warmth.

snowmobile boot Waterproof boot with an attached nylon top tightened with drawstring around calf of leg.

squaw boot Below-the-knee boot made of buckskin with fringed turned-down cuff at top, soft sole, and no heel. Originally worn by Native American women, it became a fashion item in late 1960s.

stadium boot Calf-high sheepskin-lined boot popular to wear to football games in the 1950s. At this time this was an innovation, as boots were customarily worn over shoes. Current versions can be made from MANUFACTURED FIBER fabrics. See under TEXTILES IN ACCESSORIES: FIBERS AND YARNS: THE BUILDING BLOCKS OF FABRICS.

stocking boot Fashion boot made of stretch vinyl, leather, or fabric with no zipper fitting the leg closely like a stocking. Sometimes reaches to thigh with attached panties. Also called *body boot.*

storm boot Any type of boot worn in inclement weather.

stretch boot See FOOTWEAR STYLES DEFINED: BOOTS: TOTES®.

Totes® Trademark name for lightweight, fold-up unlined rubber boot, worn over shoes. Also called *stretch boot* or RAIN BOOT (see under FOOTWEAR STYLES DEFINED: BOOTS). The trademark also applies to a wide variety of other apparel products.

waders Pants and boot in one piece reaching to above the waist with suspenders over shoulders. Made of lightweight, flexible vinyl pressed to cotton jersey or rubber, welted to seamless boots with felt liners and cleated nonskid soles. Also called *fishing boot.* Also see FOOTWEAR STYLES DEFINED: BOOTS: HIP BOOTS.

Wellington boot Calf-length or below-the-knee boot with a seam below ankle, making it look like a top has been joined to a man's low shoe with a long tonguelike projection at the VAMP (see under ANATOMY OF SOME FOOTWEAR TYPES). Seams also extend down the sides of the boot to the ankle with boot loops at top. Usually made of water-repellent leather with oak-tanned soles and rubber heels, sometimes leather-lined. *Der.* Named for Duke of Wellington, British military hero who defeated Napoleon in the battle of Waterloo in 1815.

western boot See FOOTWEAR STYLES DEFINED: BOOTS: COWBOY BOOT.

wilderness boot Ankle-high laced boot with reinforced rubber toe, reinforced counter, and strap stitched diagonally from arch over the ankle to aid in arch support. Made with LUG SOLE (see under OTHER COMPONENTS OF FOOTWEAR DEFINED) and upper of olive-drab cotton duck backed with cotton drill for quick drying. Worn for mild weather hiking, wading streams, canoeing, or in African bush country.

SANDALS

alpargata (ahl-par-gah′-ta) Sandal worn in Spain and South America with rope sole and canvas UPPER only around the HEEL. Fastened to foot by cord coming from SOLE in front, crossing at INSTEP, threaded through holes in upper and fastened around ankle. See cross references under ANATOMY OF SOME FOOTWEAR TYPES.

crossover thong sandal See FOOTWEAR STYLES DEFINED: SANDALS: THONG SANDAL #3.

exercise sandal Vinyl sandal held on with two straps. Foot rests on sole made up of tiny rounded projections that massage the foot. Introduced in early 1980s. Also see FOOTWEAR STYLES DEFINED: SANDALS: SCHOLL'S® EXERCISE SANDAL.

flip-flops Sandal made with sponge rubber sole fastened to the foot by two straps that come up between the first and second toes and fasten to the side of the sole. Copied from the original Japanese *zori*, which is a sandal.

Ganymede sandal (gan-e-meed) Open sandal derived from Ancient Greek style, with vertical straps from the sole extending up the legs and crossed at intervals around the leg with additional straps. Introduced in 1960s to wear with minidresses. *Der.* Named for the beautiful boy who was the cupbearer of the gods in Greek mythology.

geta Japanese sandal elevated by means of wooden blocks under the sole and fastened to foot by two straps, meeting between first and second toes, curved to fasten at sides of sole. Adapted for beachwear in 1960s.

gladiator sandal Flat sandal with several wide cross straps holding sole to foot, and one wide strap around ankle. Introduced in late 1960s. *Der.* Copied from sandals worn in Roman arena by "gladiators."

huarache (wah-rah-chee) Mexican sandal consisting of closely woven leather THONGS (see under FOOTWEAR STYLES DEFINED: SANDALS) forming vamp, made with sling back and flat heel. Popular casual shoe in the United States for all ages and both sexes.

kalso Danish open sandal with platform sole, carved from laminated mahogany, finished with rubber walking sole and held on with two wide straps—one over instep and one around heel.

kolhapuri sandal/kolhapure/kolhapur (ko′-lap-poor′) Leather thong-type sandal imported from India, made of hand-tooled water buffalo hide. When sandals are first worn in the shower, the leather becomes permanently shaped to the sole of the foot. Also spelled *kolhapure, kolhapur.*

open-shank sandal High-, medium-, or low-heeled sandal shaped like a D'ORSAY PUMP (see under FOOTWEAR STYLES DEFINED: SHOES) with a strap around the ankle or over the instep, frequently heelless and toeless.

platform sandal Open-type sandal with platform sole, usually made with high heel.

slide Toeless open-back sandal with WEDGE HEEL (see under TYPES OF HEELS DEFINED) of various heights or regular heel made of wood or leather in all heights.

slingback thong sandal See FOOTWEAR STYLES DEFINED: SANDALS: THONG SANDAL #2.

sports sandal Sandal for hiking, running, walking, and other forms of exercise. Invented in 1982 by Mark Thatcher who wanted to devise a shoe that could be used in wading through streams and walking over rough terrain. He used a basic THONG SANDAL (see under TYPES OF FOOTWEAR DEFINED: SANDALS) with a sturdy rubber sole and added sturdy nylon straps to hold it on the foot. This sandal was marketed under the trademark **Teva®**. Other companies have adopted the concept to make a wide variety of sports sandals.

sports sandal

tatamis (tah-tahm′-is) Thong-type sandal with nonflexible rubber sole having a slight wedge. Top of sole is made of woven straw matting. Thong straps are made of wide pieces of durable velvet. *Der.* Japanese, *tatami*, "woven straw mat."

thong sandal 1. Flat, often heelless sandal, held to the foot by narrow strips of leather coming up between first and second toes and attached to sole at either side. Popular for beachwear. 2. In early 1980s, strap was added around heel then called **slingback thong**. 3. Thong sandal with complete strap around big toe is called **crossover thong sandal.**

thong sandal #1

zori See FOOTWEAR STYLES DEFINED: SANDALS: FLIP-FLOPS.

SLIPPERS

acrobatic slipper   Soft flexible slipper made out of sueded splits of leather (see SUEDED and SPLITS under LEATHER: ANATOMY OF LEATHER). VAMP comes up high in center front and a piece of elastic connects it to the QUARTER or back of shoe (see under ANATOMY OF SOME FOOTWEAR TYPES). Worn by dancers and gymnasts and also adopted by avant-garde for streetwear in the 1960s.

Albert slipper   Slipper with a VAMP that extends up to form a TONGUE that rests on the INSTEP (see ANATOMY OF SOME FOOTWEAR TYPES).

après-ski slipper   See FOOTWEAR STYLES DEFINED: SLIPPERS: SLIPPER SOCKS.

ballet slipper (bal'-lay)   **1.** Soft flexible slipper made of kid. UPPER is pulled around to form part of the SOLE, which is very thin and has no HEEL (see under ANATOMY OF SOME FOOTWEAR TYPES). Worn by ballet dancers and children for dancing and in late 1940s for streetwear. Most slippers for professional dancers have been made since 1887 by Capezio, trademark of Capezio Ballet Makers, a division of U.S. Shoe Corp. **2.** Any similarly styled slipper worn indoors or outdoors usually with a heavier type sole. Reintroduced in 1984 with outer sole for streetwear styled in leather or fabric and sometimes worn with ballet laces.

bathing slipper   Woman's flat fabric or rubber shoe that is worn on beach and in water.

bedroom slipper   An older term used for footwear made of fabric, felt, or leather, usually in heelless style and intended for indoor wear.

bootie/bootee   **1.** Bedroom slipper edged with fur or fake fur. **2.** Infant's fabric or knitted footcovering. **3.** Type of sock worn by astronauts in flight.

boudoir slipper (bood-war')   Slipper without back made in fancy fabrics, and sometimes trimmed with marabou.

carpet slipper   19th-c. informal slip-on house slipper made of carpeting, cut in pump style with a standing rounded TONGUE cut in one piece with toe and soft padded leather SOLE with flat HEEL also made in one piece (see cross references under ANATOMY OF SOME FOOTWEAR TYPES). This style is still made in other fabrics and in felt.

Everett   Man's house slipper with low back and high TONGUE curving over INSTEP (see under ANATOMY OF SOME FOOTWEAR TYPES).

Faust slipper   See FOOTWEAR STYLES DEFINED: SLIPPERS: ROMEO SLIPPER.

felts   Slippers with soft SOLE and UPPER frequently made of felt (see under ANATOMY OF SOME FOOTWEAR TYPES).

flokati (flow-kat'-ee)   Handcrafted Greek slipper sock in above-ankle length, made of fuzzy wool, in bright colors, and used as after-ski slipper. Also see FOOTWEAR STYLES DEFINED: SLIPPERS: SLIPPER SOCKS.

folding slipper   See FOOTWEAR STYLES DEFINED: SLIPPERS: PULLMAN SLIPPER.

Harlow slipper   Boudoir slippers, similar to toeless MULES (see under FOOTWEAR STYLES DEFINED: SHOES) with medium to high heel, trimmed with marabou. Copied from slippers worn by Jean Harlow, the Hollywood actress, in the late 1920s and 1930s.

house slipper   Older term for any type of slippers worn indoors.

Juliet slipper   Woman's slipper with a high front and back, and V-shaped elastic gores at the sides. *Der.* Named for heroine of William Shakespeare's play *Romeo and Juliet.*

opera slipper   Man's bedroom slipper similar to D'ORSAY SLIPPER (see under FOOTWEAR STYLES DEFINED: SHOES), but front and back sections overlap at shank.

point shoe   See FOOTWEAR STYLES DEFINED: SLIPPERS: TOE SLIPPER.

Pullman slipper   Man's lightweight, glove leather flat slipper that folds into small envelope for traveling. Also made in patterned stretch fabrics for women. *Der.* Named for railroad sleeping cars designed by George Pullman and Ben Field in 1858–59 and owned since 1864 by Pullman Palace Car Co.

Romeo slipper   Man's pull-on, boot-type slipper with elastic side gores. Also called *Faust slipper.* *Der.* Named for hero of William Shakespeare's play *Romeo and Juliet.*

scuff   Open-back, sometimes open-toe, slipper with flat heel. May be of fur, shaggy fabric, lightweight kid, terrycloth, or other fabrics.

slipper   **1.** Low shoe usually worn indoors. **2.** Sometimes used to refer to some delicate types of shoes, e.g., evening slipper.

slipper socks   Bulky knit socks, frequently handmade with lightweight leather or urethane soles, worn after skiing or around the house.

Also called *after-ski slippers, après-ski slippers, mukluk slippers,* and FLOKATI (see under FOOTWEAR STYLES DEFINED: SLIPPERS).

toe slipper Lightweight kid slipper reinforced with a hard SHANK and toe and usually tied on with satin ribbons crisscrossing across the INSTEP and around the ankle (see under ANATOMY OF SOME FOOTWEAR TYPES). Worn by ballerinas and toe dancers. Made by Capezio, trademark of Capezio Ballet Makers, a division of U.S. Shoe Corp. Also known as a *point shoe.*

ATHLETIC SHOES AND OTHER FOOTWEAR FOR SPORTS

aerobic shoe Laced shoe of nylon mesh with suede outside counter, toe band, and trim. Somewhat higher cut than a SNEAKER (see under FOOTWEAR STYLES DEFINED: ATHLETIC SHOES AND OTHER FOOTWEAR FOR SPORTS), with shock-absorbing midsole and nonskid rubber sole.

basketball shoe High or low OXFORD (see under FOOTWEAR STYLES DEFINED: SHOES) made of canvas or army duck with nonslip molded rubber sole. The shoe laces to the toe and is frequently made with reinforced toe and COUNTER (see under ANATOMY OF SOME FOOTWEAR TYPES). Originally used only for sports, in 1970s accepted for schoolwear. In 1980s and after, sometimes made in real or imitation leather with a padded collar added at top.

basketball shoe

boating shoe Canvas shoe similar to TENNIS shoe, but made with a special nonskid rubber sole for walking on slippery boat decks. Also called *deck shoes.* See FOOTWEAR STYLES DEFINED: ATHLETIC SHOES AND OTHER FOOTWEAR FOR SPORTS: TENNIS SHOE and SHOES: SPERRY TOPSIDERS®.

bowling shoe Soft, supple shoe of OXFORD (see under FOOTWEAR STYLES DEFINED: SHOES) or other type with cushioned insole for comfort. Made with hard rubber sole and heel with an added leather tip on the sole of the right shoe (or left, for left-handed bowlers).

deck shoe See FOOTWEAR STYLES DEFINED: ATHLETIC SHOES AND OTHER FOOTWEAR FOR SPORTS: BOATING SHOE.

figure skate Fancy skating boot with reinforced INSTEP and COUNTER (see under ANATOMY OF SOME FOOTWEAR TYPES), laces to above the ankle with SPEED LACING (see under CLOSURES: TYPES OF CLOSURES DEFINED) to the top. Color is usually white for woman, black for men.

flippers Rubber extensions, shaped like a duck's webbed foot, that fit over the feet and attach with straps around heels. Worn for scuba diving, underwater swimming, and water sports. Also called *fins.*

golf shoe Oxford-style shoe made of oil-treated leather usually given a water-repellent finish, and having a foam-cushioned inner sole. Original shoes had replaceable golf spikes, located on heel and sole, attached to two metal sole plates. In the 1980s, soles of shoes were made with solid rubber sole with rubber spikes.

hockey skate Skate rounded in front attached to boot with reinforced toe. Sometimes has a strap across the instep, worn for ice hockey.

Keds® See FOOTWEAR STYLES DEFINED: ATHLETIC SHOES AND OTHER FOOTWEAR FOR SPORTS: SNEAKERS.

Nike® waffle trainers First true running shoe developed in 1974 by Bill Bowerman (Oregon track coach) who in seeking a way to get more traction without increasing the weight of shoes experimented with making the soles in a waffle iron. Subsequently this textured sole was incorporated into a running shoe manufactured by a then-new company called Nike.

racing shoe See FOOTWEAR STYLES DEFINED: ATHLETIC SHOES AND OTHER FOOTWEAR FOR SPORTS: RUNNING SHOE.

roller blades An updated version of roller skates consisting of shoes with wheels attached.

roller skate Above-the-ankle boot made with polyurethane wheels, rubber toe stop, closed with eyelets and SPEED LACING (see under CLOSURES: TYPES OF CLOSURES DEFINED). Worn for roller skating.

running shoe Sport shoe with crepe or rubber sole and upper made of two or three colors of contrasting leather or fabric. Sometimes laced to the toe and sometimes styled like a regular OXFORD (see under FOOTWEAR STYLES DEFINED: SHOES). Style inspired by the track shoes worn by athletes, which sometimes have contrasting stripes of colored leather on the sides of the shoe. Also called *racing shoe.*

sneakers Formerly used to refer to gym shoes or tennis shoes of white canvas. Now refers to a type of low shoe, similar to TENNIS SHOES (see under FOOTWEAR STYLES DEFINED: ATHLETIC SHOES AND OTHER FOOTWEAR FOR SPORTS) or a high canvas shoe worn by men, women, and boys for school, sportswear, or gym. They originated in 1868 when canvas UPPERS were added to rubber SOLES (see under ANATOMY OF SOME FOOTWEAR TYPES) creating "croquet sandals." These were renamed "sneakers" in 1873. In 1917 U.S. rubber introduced Keds®. (The name derived from the combination of the words "kids"—for whom the first ones were made—and "ped"—Latin for foot.) See also FOOTWEAR: HISTORY AND SIGNIFICANCE OF FOOTWEAR TO FASHION: ATHLETIC SHOES.

sneaker with parts labeled

spiked shoe Shoe with metal appendages on the soles.

tennis shoe Canvas or drill low-cut OXFORD (see under FOOTWEAR STYLES DEFINED: SHOES) with a circular cut VAMP (see under ANATOMY OF SOME FOOTWEAR TYPES). Made with special type of rubber sole for use on tennis courts. Also see FOOTWEAR STYLES DEFINED: ATHLETIC SHOES AND OTHER FOOTWEAR FOR SPORTS: SNEAKERS. Also called *court shoe.*

ADJUNCTS TO FOOTWEAR

gaiter Cloth or leather covering for leg and ankle, buttoned or buckled at side, often held on by straps under foot. Worn by men from end of 18th to early 20th c. and fashionable for women from 1820s to 1840s, and from 1890s to early 20th c. Revived in 1960s in vinyl, leather, or cloth. Fashionable in 1980s and after in water-repellent fabrics for cross-country skiing. Also called *leggings.* Also see FOOTWEAR STYLES DEFINED: ADJUNCTS TO FOOTWEAR: SPATS.

spats Short cloth or leather GAITER (see under FOOTWEAR STYLES DEFINED: ADJUNCTS TO FOOTWEAR) reaching over ankle, buttoned at sides, and held on by strap under instep. First worn by the military, later adopted by civilian men in 1878 to wear with MORNING COAT (see under COATS AND JACKETS) in white, tan, or gray. Also worn by women from 1914 to 1920. Reintroduced at intervals, including the late 1960s for women. Also see FOOTWEAR STYLES DEFINED: ADJUNCTS TO FOOTWEAR: SPATTER-DASHES.

spatterdashes High leggings worn by men from 1670s on, made mainly of leather or canvas, reaching to knees. Fastened down outside of leg with buttons or buckles. Sometimes worn for hunting or traveling through heavy brush.

ACCESSORIES: FOOTWEAR

GLOVES

HISTORY AND SIGNIFICANCE OF GLOVES TO FASHION

The few examples of gloves that survive from prehistory and early civilizations are like bags that cover the hands, or like mittens with a separate section for the thumb. A utilitarian garment, they were generally made of animal pelts with the hair worn on the inside. Gloves with fingers were known to ancient Egyptians, Greeks, and Romans but did not become an important accessory until the Middle Ages. By the beginning of the 17th c., leather, fabric, and knitted gloves were all available. Throughout the Victorian era and early 20th c., gloves were the mark of a lady or gentleman. In the 1960s, gloves declined in use for social occasions and by 1970s were very seldom worn by the general population except for protection from the cold. A wide variety of gloves of synthetic materials and rubber is used to protect the hands from hazardous substances. Mittens are generally used for warmth in cold weather for both adults and children. Mitts, gloves that end at the base of the fingers, are sometimes worn with formal dress and by brides. Specialized gloves have been developed for different athletic activities such as bicycling, golfing, and a variety of other sports.

ANATOMY OF GLOVES

Good quality leather gloves generally consist of eight components. These include: a single piece that is the palm and back of the glove; three narrow pieces that form the sides of the fingers that are called **fourchettes** or **forks**; a thumb; and three **quirks**, small diamond-shaped pieces inserted at

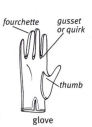

the bottom between the fingers. Leather gloves are cut from a square piece of leather about the size of a glove called a **trank**. **Table-cut gloves** are made from tranks that have been hand-pulled to determine the amount of stretch in the leather, and then cut. Women's fine kid gloves are made in this manner to ensure proper stretch but no bagginess. Leather and cloth gloves may be mass produced by cutting them from multiple layers with a die (a metal pattern with sharp edges that cut through the material).

Variations of the aforementioned structure include **English** or **Bolton thumb,** in which the thumb and quirk are cut in a single piece in order to provide freedom of movement. This is considered to be the strongest and best-fitting thumb. In an **insert thumb,** the thumb is cut in one piece and extends all the way to the cuff edge of the glove. In the **set-in thumb** construction, the thumb is cut in one piece and set into a round opening.

The length of a glove is specified in **buttons.** One button is equal to one French inch (approximately ½″ longer than an American inch), with measurement starting at base of thumb. A one-button glove is wrist length, a six-button glove is halfway to elbow, and a sixteen-button glove is a formal length.

Cloth gloves are made from many different fibers. Although woven fabric can be used, most cloth gloves are knitted. When cloth gloves are die-cut, the glove-sized fabric squares are placed face-to-face so that gloves for the right and left hand are cut at the same time. Triangular pieces called **gores** are placed between the fingers and a separate thumb is cut. In the case of those made of *wool, cotton,* and *manufactured fibers,* knitting machines can shape gloves with or without seams. See cross references under TEXTILES IN ACCESSORIES: FIBERS AND YARNS: THE BUILDING BLOCKS OF FABRICS: GENERIC AND OTHER MANUFACTURED FIBERS DEFINED and NATURAL FIBERS DEFINED.

Gloves can be sewn by hand, but are more likely to be stitched on machines that create stitches that look as if they were done by hand. Different types of stitches can be used to join the pieces of the glove. These are:

full piqué/full P.K. seam Used on expensive kid gloves, all fourchettes are inserted with one piece of leather lapped over the other and stitched on the right side. Also called *kid seam* and *overlapped seam.*

half piqué/half P.K. seam Finger seams on the palm side of the hand are stitched with seams turned to the inside, while those on the outside of the hand are made in piqué manner, with one piece of leather lapped over the other and stitched on the outside. This gives the appearance of a more expensive glove.

inseam Gloves stitched together inside out and then turned so that no stitching shows on the right side. Used on sheer nylon, lace, and cotton gloves.

outseam Glove seams stitched by machine on the right side, leaving edges exposed. Used on sport gloves, e.g., pigskin, and sometimes cotton gloves. **A prix** (pree) **seam/PXM seam** is an outseam stitched on a flat machine that moves horizontally instead of vertically. Used on heavier gloves instead of piqué seam.

overseam Gloves stitched on the right side with an OVERCAST STITCH (see under EMBROIDERIES AND SEWING STITCHES: TYPES OF STITCHES DEFINED) that covers the two raw edges. Used on men's gloves. Also called *round seam.*

saddle-stitched seam Small running stitches visible on the outside of glove that are used to close fingers of the glove.

Laying off is the final step in the construction of leather and cloth gloves in which the glove is placed on a metal hand of the selected size and heated to shape the glove to the correct size.

TYPES OF GLOVES DEFINED

action glove Gloves with cut-outs on the back of hand or over the knuckles to increase flexibility. Originally used for sports such as golf or race car driving, they were adopted for women's daytime wear in mid-1960s and after. Also called *cutout gloves* or *racing gloves.*

bandelet/bandelette (ban-day´-lay or ban-day´-let) Wide hem at wrist of a glove. Also called *bord.*

biarritz glove Slip-on glove with no vent or vertical slit going upward from the hem. Usually of two- or four-button length.

bicycle glove Wrist-length knitted glove with leather palm padded with two layers of foam for comfort. Mesh knit is used for remainder of glove, leaving the tips of the fingers and thumb exposed.

binding Reinforcement or piping of leather or fabric around the wrist and placket or vent.

bord See TYPES OF GLOVES DEFINED: BANDELET.

bracelet length Gloves ending above the wrist.

cocktail glove Dressy suede glove with wide stand-up accordion-pleated taffeta cuffs. Worn in the 1930s and after.

cut-fingered gloves Women's gloves with tips of fingers cut off first worn in early 18th c. Revived as a fad in 1985.

cutout glove See TYPES OF GLOVES DEFINED: ACTION GLOVE.

doeskin glove **1.** Glove made of suede-finished sheepskin. Properly it should be "doeskin-finished sheepskin," but the term doeskin is permissible. **2.** Glove made from the skin of the female deer and frequently sueded. As there are few deerskins available for commercial usage, real doeskins usually come from areas where deer are plentiful (e.g., northern Michigan and where skins are usually processed on Native American reservations).

driving glove Knitted gloves with leather palms made for a good grip on the steering wheel of the car.

Finger-Free® glove Trademark for gloves made with one long strip of material forming all the FOURCHETTES (see under ANATOMY OF GLOVES) between fingers. Designed by Merry Hull in 1938 for greater flexibility.

French thumb Glove thumb construction in which a small diamond-shaped piece (the quirk) is inserted in the arch of the thumb, allowing freedom of movement.

gauntlet (gawnt′-let) Above-the-wrist glove with wide flaring cuff. The cuff may be cut in one with the glove or as a separate piece that is sewn to the glove.

gauntlet

glove length Glove term indicating the length of a glove. Measured in BUTTONS. See under ANATOMY OF GLOVES.

igloo mitt Shaggy fur mitten, frequently with leather palm, worn for sportswear.

insulated glove Glove lined for protection against cold. Lining may be fur, fleece, wool or acrylic knit, or laminated foam.

kid glove Gloves made of genuine kidskin and also of sheepskin. Originally all were kid and as the leather became more scarce, other leathers were used. Fashionable from early 19th c. and still used.

kid seam See ANATOMY OF GLOVES: FULL PIQUÉ SEAM.

lace glove Glove of lace made by hand or machine in white or other colors and used for dress-up summer wear.

mittens **1.** Gloves with a thumb and one other compartment for fingers; worn mainly by children and skiers for warmth. **2.** See TYPES OF GLOVES DEFINED: MITTS.

mitten #1

mitts Fingerless gloves, reaching to or above wrist. Often of kid, net, lace, or sheer fabric and sometimes worn with bridal dresses. Also called *mittens*.

mitt

money mitt Knitted glove with fingers and thumb made with vinyl palm and back. Has zippered slot in center of palm for keys or money.

mousquetaire glove (moos-keh′-tare) Woman's long loose glove made in pull-on style or with buttoned slit at wrist in 14- or 16-button length. Worn crushed down or with hand out of slit, remainder of glove crushed up to elbow with formal evening dress.

opera glove Long-length glove, sometimes made without a thumb.

pointing Ornamental stitching on back of glove, usually in three rows. Same as *silking*.

pull-down cutting The process of cutting gloves by die cutting the pieces.

pull-on Glove that slips easily over the hand and is made without placket or fastening. Also called *slip-on gloves*.

racing glove See TYPES OF GLOVES DEFINED: ACTION GLOVES.

reverse glove Glove thumb construction in which the thumb is set in with a QUIRK (see under ANATOMY OF GLOVES) in such a way that the glove is perfectly flat and can be worn on either hand.

shorty glove Any two-button glove coming to the wrist.

silking See TYPES OF GLOVES DEFINED: POINTING.

slip-ons See TYPES OF GLOVES DEFINED: PULL-ON.

snowmobile glove Similar to SNOWMOBILE MITT (see under TYPES OF GLOVES DEFINED) made with fingers.

snowmobile mitt Water-repellent gloves with polyester fiberfill or down as insulation. Made with suede-leather palms, rubberized nylon back, knitted cuffs, and leather pull-on tabs.

thermal glove Short gloves made of glacé leather with silk lining and inner lining of polyfoam. Worn for warmth, especially for riding or driving.

wrist length Short gloves ending at the wristbone.

wrist length glove

HANDBAGS *and* RELATED ACCESSORIES

HISTORY AND SIGNIFICANCE OF HANDBAGS TO FASHION

A **handbag** is an accessory now carried primarily by women and girls to hold such items as money, credit cards, and cosmetics. The word is often shortened to **bag** and also called a *purse* or *pocketbook*. Related items include briefcases, backpacks, and other containers in which to carry personal items. LUGGAGE is closely related, and is discussed in a separate section. There are also a number of small accessories that serve some of the same purposes, and may even be used in conjunction with handbags. Examples include change purses, wallets, and cosmetic cases. Luggage and handbags serve many of the same purposes and are not easy to separate. In this work, luggage is listed as a separate category and considered to be a container designed to carry the belongings of a traveler. For information about luggage, see ACCESSORIES: LUGGAGE.

Bags in which to carry things have probably been used as a basic tool since prehistoric times and in all civilizations. The oldest mummified body ever found intact (dating from c. 3300 B.C. and found in the Alps) was that of a man who was carrying a leather pouch. From the 13th to 16th c. in Europe, a small leather pouch was worn suspended from a man's belt in order to have money for charity readily available. A **pocketbook** was originally an envelope-like container for written materials and paper money carried by men in the 17th and 18th c. It was made of leather and often tooled or decorated or made of silk or wool worked in col-ored or metal yarns. Eventually this term became a synonym for a women's handbag.

Before pockets were sewn into skirts, a practice that began only in the 19th c., women wore separate pockets tied around their waists under their clothing. They put essential objects in these pockets, which they could reach through slits in their skirts. Around 1800, the popular silhouette narrowed too much for these pockets to be used without creating unsightly bulges, and so women carried small handbags, called **reticules,** instead. Use of these handbags decreased after pockets were added to skirts around mid-century, and small purses were carried inside pockets. By the late 19th c., various types of handbags began to be carried, mainly for traveling, although **chatelaine bags** with a clip that fastened to a belt also gained in popularity. By the 1920s, a handbag had become a necessary accessory for a woman. The need for larger handbags with more space for personal items arose from the newly accepted practices of women's smoking and wearing makeup. Handbags have been constructed in many styles and made of a variety of materials; the specific choices may be dictated by practicality or by fashion or both. Plainer, larger, and more functional handbags tend to be used during the daytime; and smaller, decorative handbags in the evening. A man who needs to carry papers and other items uses a **briefcase** (also called an *attaché case*), a large, usually flat case with a carrying handle, most often made of real or synthetic leather that is large enough, or can expand suffi-

chatelaine bag

ciently, to hold documents and books. A man carries his money and cards in a **wallet** (see under TYPES OF RELATED ACCESSORIES DEFINED). In 1968, the **manbag,** a handbag for men, was introduced.

ANATOMY OF A HANDBAG

Although there is wide variation in handbag structure, many handbags have the following parts. They have a visible exterior that can be made of one or of several different materials, such as leather, patent leather, textile fabric, straw, vinyl, metal, and plastic. That exterior material may be a decorative woven fabric, tooled leather, or may have decoration added to the surface. Decoration can be applied by embroidery, beading, jeweled decorations, printed or painted motifs, or other ornamentation. Many handbags have handles. Some are mounted on a **frame,** which is usually made of brass or steel but may be made of a more valuable metal, such as gold or silver, or made of wood or strong plastic. An **inverted frame** is a frame covered with fabric or leather, so the metal frame does not show at the top of the bag.

Closures (usually either a zipper, snaps, magnets, a buckle, or a drawstring) are often required, though some handbags are made to be open at the top (example: tote bag). The interior generally has a lining, compartments or pockets, and sometimes padding and reinforcements. Bags may come with a coin purse, which is usually removable.

For making mass-produced, less expensive handbags, designers create a basic pattern for the exterior and interior parts. These parts are assembled by sewing and gluing, as needed. If the handbag requires a frame, the outside and the lining are completed and inserted into a frame by a highly skilled worker.

TYPES OF HANDBAGS DEFINED

accordion bag Bag made like an expandable filing envelope that is narrow at the top and pleated at sides and bottom. Usually made with a handle and frequently with a zipper compartment in the center. *Der.* From resemblance to pleats on the musical instrument of this name.

American Indian Bag See TYPES OF HANDBAGS DEFINED: SQUAW BAG.

Apache bag See TYPES OF HANDBAGS DEFINED: SQUAW BAG.

attaché case See TYPES OF HANDBAGS DEFINED: BRIEFCASE.

baguette bag (bah-get´) Popular woman's handbag originated by Italian design house of Fendi. An extended oblong shape, the bag closes with a flap over the front and may have both a shoulder strap and handles. It is made in a wide variety of materials. *Der.* Named after a long, narrow loaf of French bread.

barrel bag Handbag shaped like a stubby cylinder with a zipper closing and handles attached to the sides. *Der.* From the shape similar to a small barrel.

barrel bag

basket bag Applies to many types of handbags. Originally woven only of reed in typical basket shapes. Now made of reed, straw, cane, interwoven plastic strips, or other materials such as leather or plastic in the shape of a basket. One popular style resembles a small picnic hamper. Sometimes decorated with shells, beads, sequins, brass, or leather.

basket bag

beaded bag Any ornate small bag covered with varicolored pearls or glass beads or a fabric bag, often satin, with a design worked in beads.

beaded bag

belt bag **1.** A small bag worn at waist having slots in the back through which a belt is drawn. Usually has a flap closing and is worn with sportswear. **2.** A pouch bag with handle through which a belt is drawn.

book bag Slim oblong bag the size of notebook cinched around center with strap that forms loop handle.

box bag Handbag with rigid frame, similar to small suitcase or lunchbox, made in leather, metal, or vinyl.

bracelet bag Type of handbag with one or two BANGLE BRACELETS (see under JEWELRY: TYPES OF JEWELRY DEFINED: BRACELETS) as handles. It may be a soft pouch made of leather or fabric, or may be made with a frame.

briefcase **1.** Large, usually flat case with a carrying handle, most often made of real or synthetic leather and is large enough or can expand sufficiently to hold documents, books, and the like. Also called *attaché case.* **2.** Handbag of briefcase size for woman executive that features small outside pockets for personal items.

bucket bag   Round handbag made in the shape of a bucket.

canteen bag   Circular-style bag frequently made with a shoulder strap and zipper closing. Made in the shape of a flat canteen used to carry water in dry climates.

caravan bag   See TYPES OF HANDBAGS DEFINED: SAFARI BAG.

carpet bag   Handbag made of patterned carpeting or heavy tapestry, in a large satchel style. Popular in 19th c., late 1960s, and revived in mid-1980s in lighter-weight fabrics. *Der.* From carpet valises popular with Northerners for travel just after the Civil War. Southerners alluded to the travelers by the derisive term "carpetbaggers."

carpet bag

carryall   See TYPES OF HANDBAGS DEFINED: TOTE BAG.

carryall clutch   Woman's wallet designed to hold coins, bills, photographs and credit cards. Usually the size of U.S. paper money, with snap closing on long edge and purselike sections for coins.

Chanel bag   Handbag designed by French couturiere Gabrielle Chanel that has become a classic. Of quilted leather with gold chain handles, it has a gold House of Chanel logo on the front.

Chanel bag

clutch bag/clutch purse   **1.** Regular-sized handbag without a handle. **2.** Type of handbag frequently used for an evening bag. Sometimes has a strap on back through which hand may be inserted, or a fine gold chain attached in such a manner that it is of optional use. Frequently made in envelope style, in which case it is called an **envelope bag. Mini-clutch** bags are tiny versions of this style.

clutch purse

cordé bag   (kor-day′)   Any type of handbag made out of a fabric composed of rows of GIMP (see under LACES AND BRAIDS: TYPES OF BRAID

cordé bag

DEFINED) stitched to a background fabric to make a pattern.

courier bag   See TYPES OF HANDBAGS DEFINED: MESSENGER BAG.

cross-body bag   Handbag with long strap designed to be worn with the strap over one shoulder and the bag on the other side of the body, which causes the strap to cross the chest. A variation of the SHOULDER BAG (see under TYPES OF HANDBAGS DEFINED) that developed when women started placing shoulder straps across the body in order to make the bag more secure.

doctor's bag   Large handbag shaped like the bag traditionally carried by a physician. It has two handles, one on either side of hinged top opening.

drawstring bag   Any handbag that is closed by pulling a cord, usually of pouch type.

duffel bag   **1.** See LUGGAGE: TYPES OF LUGGAGE DEFINED. **2.** Barrel-shaped canvas bag with a zipper or drawstring top copied in various sizes for handbags and beach bags. May have an extra piece of fabric on outside that forms large pockets around outside of bag. **3.** Small taffeta evening bag in pouch style with large ruffled top closed with tasseled drawstring.

duffel bag #2

envelope bag   See TYPES OF HANDBAGS DEFINED: CLUTCH BAG.

fanny pack   An envelope or pouchlike bag mounted on a strap that fastens around the waist. Intended to be worn with the bag in the back, resting on the hips (or in slang, *fanny*), the bag is made in materials ranging from sturdy nylon to leather and in many sizes. Originally a day pack for hiking, by 2000 it had become acceptable daytime street wear and is especially popular with travelers.

feed bag   Cylindrical leather or canvas bag with flat round bottom and top handles copied from canvas bags used for feeding horses. Forerunner of many open tote bags.

fold-over clutch   Small ENVELOPE BAG (see TYPES OF HANDBAGS DEFINED) that may be open at the top or with zippered closing. Bag is folded over double and carried in the hand or under arm.

Grace Kelly bag See TYPES OF HANDBAGS DEFINED: KELLY BAG.

Greek bag Square or rectangular wool open-top bag. Handwoven in Greek-key designs, trimmed around edge with cable yarn that also forms the handle.

hat box bag Handbag made to look like a HATBOX (see LUGGAGE: HISTORY AND SIGNIFICANCE OF LUGGAGE TO FASHION).

hippie bag See TYPES OF HANDBAGS DEFINED: SQUAW BAG.

Indian bag See TYPES OF HANDBAGS DEFINED: SQUAW BAG.

interchangeable bag Complete handbag with extra covers that snap or button over frame to change colors.

Kelly bag Handbag favored by the Princess Grace of Monaco (actress Grace Kelly) in the 1950s. After Grace Kelly was seen frequently carrying an alligator TOTE (see

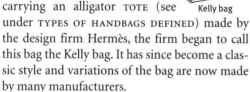

Kelly bag

under TYPES OF HANDBAGS DEFINED) made by the design firm Hermès, the firm began to call this bag the Kelly bag. It has since become a classic style and variations of the bag are now made by many manufacturers.

Kikuyu Open-top straw tote bag with leather handles. Handwoven of natural sisal in horizontal strips of red and blue alternating with natural color. Made by Kikuyu craftsmen of Kenya.

lunchbox bag Identical in shape to the traditional deep lunchbox with a curved lid. Introduced from Italy in 1967, this handbag was first made in papier-mâché and later in metal. Distinctive feature is a collage effect of decorative pictures pasted on the outside and then shellacked.

manbag Handbag, usually a SHOULDER BAG style (see under TYPES OF HAND-BAGS DEFINED) or with a wrist strap, that is carried by a man. A fashion that gained in popularity in early 1970s as an outgrowth of the wide use of camera bags by men.

manbag

mesh bag Tiny links of metal joined to make a flexible bag. The links may be white or colored enamel with matching plastic frames.

messenger bag Large bag with an envelope-like main compartment that usually closes with a zip-per and has a large flap over the front that fastens with a buckle or snap. May have either shoulder straps or handles. Inspired by bags carried by messengers. A smaller version with a more tailored, square appearance is called a **courier bag.**

minaudiere (min-oh′-dee-yehr′) Small, rigid, metal evening bag made in oval, oblong, or square shapes and used to hold cosmetics. Carried in the hand or by short chain. Decorated by engraved designs or set with jewels, this expensive jeweler's product gained popularity when sold by Cartier in New York. *Der.* French, *simper,* "to smirk."

mini bag Small bags that became important in the 1960s with the introduction of miniskirts. Tiny bags were introduced in all styles. Some had double and triple frames, usually with attached shoulder chains or straps.

mini-clutch bag See TYPES OF HANDBAGS DEFINED: CLUTCH BAG.

Moroccan bag 1. Tooled leather handbag made in Morocco of MOROCCAN LEATHER (see under LEATHER: TYPES OF LEATHER DEFINED). Decorated with elaborate designs and color combinations, such as saffron and wine. 2. Handbag made with stitched allover design in saffron on wine-colored leather.

muff bag Basically a muff, an accessory used to keep the hands warm, frequently styled in fur. A zippered compartment to hold small items was added to the muff, and this became a classic item used by little girls.

newsbag TOTE BAG style (see under TYPES OF HANDBAGS DEFINED) with separate section on the outside to slip in a rolled magazine or newspaper.

pannier bag (pan-yeh′) A bag with zipper compartment in the center and two open compartments on either side. A single broad handle extends from one side to the other on the outside of the bag at the middle.

pianta bag (pee-ahn′-tah) Small evening bag introduced from Italy in mid-1960s resembling a tiny umbrella made from a square of fabric with four corners folded to the center and a looped center handle.

pokey Small drawstring pouch made of sueded leather, sometimes with tiny pocket on front. Popular in the late 1960s. *Der.* Copied from a small leather bag used by '49ers to carry gold nuggets and gold dust.

pouch Basic style originally made of soft shirred leather or fabric with a drawstring closing. Now also made with a frame and handles.

pouch

purse See HISTORY AND SIGNIFICANCE OF HANDBAGS TO FASHION.

saddle bags Pair of soft leather bags joined to central strap handle. *Der.* From large bags thrown over horse's saddle to carry provisions.

safari bag Double-handled bag made like a small flight bag with a zippered closing. Characteristic features are the small pockets placed low on the outside of the bag. Also called *caravan bag.*

safari bag

satchel Leather bag with a rigid flat bottom. The sides slope to close on metal frame hinged about halfway down the bag. Often fastened with extra snap locks and with metal reinforcements at corners. Sides are usually recessed. Handle is generally rigid and curved. Similar to a DOCTOR'S BAG (see under TYPES OF HANDBAGS DEFINED).

sea bag See LUGGAGE: TYPES OF LUGGAGE DEFINED: DUFFEL BAG.

shigra Handmade handbag of tote type sold to American tourists or exported to the United States from Ecuador, made from fibers taken from the leaves of the cabuya plant. Artisans use a looping system done with a needle to form distinctive patterns with natural and colored yarns. Originally used for storage of grain and flour. Made in patterns characteristic of different communities in Ecuador.

shoulder bag Handbag in any shape or size with long chain or strap to place over the shoulder. Some types of shoulder straps convert to double chain handles, others may be shortened by unbuckling a section of the strap.

signature bag Handbag of leather or canvas with designer's initials or signature stenciled or printed in an allover repeat pattern. Originating with Louis Vuitton in Paris, later copied by Hermés, Saint Laurent, Mark Cross, Gucci, etc., and considered a fashion status symbol.

Vuitton©
signature bag

sporran bag (spo'-an) Adaptation for women of a bag called a sporran that was worn as part of traditional dress by the Scots Highlander. This shoulder bag is made of leather with long strands of horsehair hanging from it. The frame is metal.

squaw bag Handbag inspired by bags used by Native Americans. May be made of genuine doeskin in natural color or made of tiny geometric contrasting patches of colored leather. Most bags are trimmed with fringe. Popular handbag of the late 1960s. Also called *American Indian bag, Apache bag,* and *hippie bag. Der.* Name by which settlers called Native American woman.

suitcase bag Handbag made of metal and shaped like a miniature suitcase complete with lock and reinforced corners.

swagger pouch Bag with double handles and two open sections on either side of zippered compartment. Classic style since the 1930s.

swinger bag See TYPES OF RELATED ACCESSORIES DEFINED: CONTOUR CLUTCH.

tooled leather bag Typical Western-type handbag made of natural colored cowhide with hand-stamped pattern. Each individual character is stamped with a metal die.

tote bag **1.** Utility bag, large enough to carry small packages, sometimes with inner zippered compartment for money. Copied from shape of common paper shopping bag. Made with open top and two handles, sometimes with outside loop to hold umbrella. **2.** Any large bag with open top and two handles.

tote bag

travel bag See LUGGAGE: TYPES OF LUGGAGE DEFINED: FLIGHT BAG.

triplex/triple-framed bag Triple-framed bag with three separate clasps. Each section is an individual compartment. Introduced in 1967, many were styled as tiny MINI BAGS (see under TYPES OF HANDBAGS DEFINED).

umbrella tote **1.** TOTE BAG (see under TYPES OF HANDBAGS DEFINED), but with a pocket at side for holding an umbrella. **2.** Bag shaped like a briefcase with a zipper around it and the umbrella attached to the side with a plastic loop. **3.** Conventional SATCHEL-type bag with zippered compartment at bottom for umbrella (see under TYPES OF BAGS DEFINED).

TYPES OF RELATED ACCESSORIES DEFINED

backpack Bag with straps fitting over shoulders so that it can be worn on the back. Originally called a *knapsack*. Small, back-packs are often used in place of a handbag. They are usually made

backpack

of nylon or other MANUFACTURED FIBERS (see under TEXTILES IN ACCESSORIES: FIBERS AND YARNS: THE BUILDING BLOCKS OF FABRICS) and sometimes of real or synthetic leather. Variations now include a back pack designed to be carried over one shoulder and called a **one-shoulder backpack.** Also see LUGGAGE: TYPES OF LUGGAGE DEFINED: BACKPACK.

billfold See TYPES OF RELATED ACCESSORIES DEFINED: WALLET.

briefcase See TYPES OF HANDBAGS DEFINED: BRIEFCASE.

calculator case Small, pocket-sized case for holding a calculator.

card case Holder for business cards that may be hard or soft.

change purse Small purse that closes by a snap clasp on the rigid frame or by a zipper. Usually carried inside handbag to hold coins and made in leather, clear plastic, or matched to the larger handbag. Also called a *coin purse.*

cigarette case Case for holding a pack or loose cigarettes. May be made of soft material such as leather or can be made of hard materials, and in some cases can be highly ornamental.

coin purse See TYPES OF RELATED ACCESSORIES DEFINED: CHANGE PURSE.

contour clutch WALLET similar to a CLUTCH purse, but curved on top edge, sometimes with attached leather carrying loop at one end. See TYPES OF RELATED ACCESSORIES DEFINED: WALLET and TYPES OF HANDBAGS DEFINED: CLUTCH BAG. Also called *swinger* or *swinger clutch.*

cosmetic bag Small bag with a zipper or snap closing that is usually plastic-lined for holding cosmetics. Also see LUGGAGE: TYPES OF LUGGAGE DEFINED: COSMETIC CASE.

credit-card case Small case with plastic inserts for holding credit and other cards of the same size.

document case A rectangular bag for carrying papers, it has no handles and closes with a zipper that runs from the bottom of one side, across the top, and down the other side.

eyeglasses case Hard or soft case for holding one or more pairs of eyeglasses. It may be hinged so that it snaps to close, may have a fold-over flap, or may be open at one end.

French purse Fold-over wallet for bills. One half incorporates a change purse with metal clasp closing at the top that is actually one end of the wallet.

jewelry roll Soft bag that has compartments to hold different items of jewelry that rolls or folds up and usually closes with a tie.

keycase Hard or soft case with metal rings to which keys may be attached that generally snaps or zips to close.

one-shoulder backpack See TYPES OF RELATED ACCESSORIES: BACKPACK.

passport case Case with compartments of an appropriate size to hold passports, airline tickets, and other travel documents.

portfolio A flat case that, although it has no obvious handles, may have handles that telescope into the bag. It closes with a zipper or a locking envelope flap. Portfolios can be quite large and are often used for carrying artwork.

travel kit Bag that may have a waterproof lining to hold toiletries when traveling. It usually can hang up when open, and rolls up into a fairly small size when ready to pack.

vanity bag See LUGGAGE: TYPES OF LUGGAGE DEFINED: COSMETIC CASE.

wallet **1.** Accessory used to carry money, credit cards, and photographs. Sometimes with change purse attached and/or space for checkbook and note pad. Originally used only by men, now also used by women and children. Also called a *billfold* when designed to hold paper money, credit or other cards, and photos, and made to fold in center. **2.** In 1980s, smaller sizes, closed with VELCRO® (see under CLOSURES: TYPES OF CLOSURES DEFINED), were introduced to wear on wrist, ankle, or belt, primarily when engaging in sports, e.g., jogging.

HEADWEAR, VEILS, *and* HAIR ACCESSORIES

HISTORY AND SIGNIFICANCE OF HEADWEAR, VEILS, AND HAIR ACCESSORIES TO FASHION

Headwear is a covering for the head, often called a *headcovering* or *headdress*. It may be decorative or utilitarian, or both. It may also serve as a symbol of status, for example the crown worn by a king or queen or the special headdress worn by the Pope and other clerics. Earliest recorded headwear probably had two utilitarian purposes, to keep the head warm and to protect it from injury. Headwear most likely also had ceremonial functions. Cave paintings from prehistoric periods depict individuals wearing headgear that are thought to have signified the status of the wearer.

Artistic works from early civilizations such as those of Egypt and Assyria show a variety of headdress worn by royalty, priests, and soldiers. In ancient Greece travelers wore broad-brimmed hats to protect themselves against the sun. During the early Middle Ages in Europe, headwear was relatively simple, often consisting of practical hoods or scarves for warmth. But by the late Middle Ages when fashion had permeated all forms of dress, headwear included tall steeplelike constructions, elaborately draped turbans, and jewel-encrusted, padded rolls that covered the hair. The variety of hat styles multiplied century after century. Hat-making developed into a highly skilled craft. Those who made women's hats were known as **milliners,** and those who made men's were called **hatters.** Hats were considered an essential part of the wardrobe of both men and women

until the latter part of the 20th c. Men's formal hats became less important after President John Kennedy went hatless to his inauguration in 1961. Women's hats also became less important as casual wear became more and more acceptable for most occasions. Even so, many women continue to wear hats as a decorative element of their wardrobes, and both men and women wear headwear for warmth or to protect from sun exposure.

A **veil** is an accessory usually made of lace, net, tulle, or other sheer fabric that is placed over the head and either draped down the back or over the face and shoulders. A veil may also be a piece of sheer fabric attached to a hat. Veils are an important part of the tradition of some cultures in which religious or social mores require that women cover their faces or even their entire bodies when in public. It is likely that women were veiled when outdoors in ancient Greece. This practice is still followed in some non-Western countries. In Europe in Medieval times, veils were worn over the hair. From the late 18th to end of the 19th c., a piece of net, lace, or gauze attached to a woman's outdoor bonnet or hat might be arranged to cover part or all of the face, or might be draped to the back as trimming. In the 20th and 21st c., veils have been worn intermittently, following the dictates of fashion. At present they are mostly used as trimmings. They may also be worn for special occasions such as weddings and funerals.

Hair accessories are ornaments worn in the hair as decorations or to hold the hair in place. Their use varies according to the current fashion in hairstyles. Certain hair accessories were developed to complement or to manage specific hairstyles. They are generally small and do not cover the hair.

ANATOMY OF HEADWEAR

Many items of headwear have a **brim.** This is the rim of the headwear and may be narrow to wide; may be horizontal, or may be angled, or turned up or down. A thick rolled-back brim is called a **bumper brim** and is used in various widths on different styles of hats. A **dressmaker's brim** is usually part of a fabric hat and has closely spaced rows of machine stitching or stitched tucks around the brim. An **umbrella brim** is the brim of a woman's hat set in *umbrella pleats* that open out to resemble an umbrella.

parts of a hat

Headwear also generally has a **crown,** which is the portion that covers the top of the head. Some headwear, especially caps, have a visor instead of a brim. A **visor** (also called a **bill**) is a stiffened semicircle attached to a headband or to the front of a cap to protect the wearer's eyes from the sun.

Other elements frequently found on hats include: a **sweatband,** a band usually made of sheepskin leather placed around the inside of a hat where the crown joins the brim. It protects the hat from sweat. A **hatband** may be placed at the bottom edge of the crown. These are often made of ribbon or sometimes of a decorative fabric.

Headwear is often divided into various groupings. It is often difficult to assign specific characteristics to one group, as features may overlap. The following are the most frequently used subdivisions:

hat   Sometimes used as a generic term for headwear. It is more specifically applied to headwear that consists of a crown and a brim and usually does not tie under the chin. Hats can be made of felt, straw, fur, fabric, leather, or synthetic materials.

bonnet   Applied to headwear for women, children, and infants that fits over the back and top of the head and ties with strings under the chin. However, in contemporary usage the word "bonnet" is frequently used interchangeably with "hat." For this reason, definitions of hats and bonnets are listed together in the following section.

cap   Headcovering fitting more snugly to the head than a hat, frequently made with a visor-type front. Caps can be constructed from materials such as felt, leather, or fabric. They are worn for sports or informal occasions.

helmet   Protective covering for the head worn primarily to prevent injury; particularly by the armed forces, those working in law enforcement, laborers working in dangerous settings, and participants in various sports and recreational activities. In the 1960s, helmet-shaped hats were introduced as a fashion accessory.

Other examples of headwear do not fit easily into the above categories. These are defined below under TYPES OF HEADWEAR DEFINED: OTHER HEADWEAR.

Hats and bonnets may have fairly complex structures. They may employ a foundation material, most often a BUCKRAM (see under TEXTILES IN ACCESSORIES: DIFFERENT TYPES OF FABRIC STRUCTURES: WOVEN FABRICS DEFINED) or material. Wire is commonly used to reinforce crown and brim edges. A wide variety of trimmings may also be attached to hats and bonnets. These can include various textiles, beads, feathers, veiling, artificial flowers, lace, and the like. Headwear can be made from straw, felt, leather, fur, fabric, or synthetic materials. For information about these materials, see the headings under COMPONENTS OF ACCESSORIES.

If made of straw or felt, headwear must be blocked. **Blocking** is the shaping of a hat. It can be done by hand or by machine, although when a new style with a unique shape is developed, a sample or model hat must be made. The model hat is first blocked by hand. The moistened straw or felt crown is formed over a balsa wood block in the shape of a human head. While the crown dries, the brim is pulled over the head form and shaped. The brim is stiffened, and when both crown and brim are dry, they are sewn together by hand. For mass-produced hats, a metal form, called a **pan,** is made from the model hat. The pan will be used on a machine to impress the form of the hat onto felt or straw.

After blocking, the hat is sewn, if necessary, and trimmed. When appropriate to the material from which they are made, hats are finished by steaming or ironing. Finally they are generally checked for quality. Most women's hats are made in one size: 22.5 inches or 57.15 centimeters.

TYPES OF HEADWEAR DEFINED

HATS AND BONNETS

Alpine hat Various types of hats adapted from Bavarian and Austrian Tyrolean hats. One contemporary version for men is of fur felt, with a slight surface texture, a slightly peaked CROWN with a crease in the center, and an upturned BRIM in the back (see under ANATOMY OF HEADWEAR). Popular since 1940s as a man's sport hat, it was first introduced in the late 1890s. Also called a *Tyrolean hat. Der.* Named for alpine Tyrol region in Austria and Bavaria where this type of hat is worn.

alpine hat

baby bonnet Infant's cap, often made of batiste and lavishly trimmed with lace and ribbons, that is fitted to shape of head and tied under chin.

balaclava (bal-ah-kla′-vah) Hood covering the head and shoulders exposing the face, made of knitted wool. Worn by soldiers in 1890s and in World War I and II in cold weather. Now worn by mountain climbers and skiers. *Der.* Named for Crimean War, Battle of Balaklava, fought October 25, 1854.

balaclava

bambin/bambino hat (bam-been) Woman's hat with a halo-shaped brim rolling away from the face.

basque beret See TYPES OF HEADWEAR DEFINED: HATS AND BONNETS: BERET #1.

beach hat Hat used as a sunshade on the beach or at a resort. Made of real or synthetic straw in natural or bright colors in any of a variety of shapes. Frequently has a wide brim and is sometimes decorated with felt, sequins, or shells.

beanie See CAPS: SKULLCAP.

beefeater's hat Distinctive hat worn by Yeomen of the Guard in England, consisting of a narrow brim and soft high crown pleated into headband with crown flaring slightly at the top.

beret (beh-ray′) General name given to a round, flat hat, usually synonymous with TAM (see under TYPES OF HEADWEAR DEFINED: HATS AND BONNETS). Some specific types include: **1. basque beret** (bask beh-ray′) Round, flat, soft woolen cap worn by Basque peasants who inhabit the western Pyrenees region of France and Spain. **2. pancake beret** Flat molded felt tam. Worn tilted to one side of the head and associated with the dress of an artist. Also called a *French beret.* **3. bubble beret** Large bouffant beret, usually without a brim, worn tilted to side of head in the early 1960s.

French or pancake beret

bergère hat (ber-zher′) Woman's straw hat with low crown and a wide floppy-type brim, sometimes tied under chin. Worn from 1730 to 1800, revived in 1860s and currently used to describe similar hats. Worn by Marie Antoinette (1755–1793), wife of Louis XVI of France, when she played at farming on the grounds of the palace at Versailles. Also called *milkmaid hat* or *shepherdess hat. Der.* French, "shepherdess."

bergère hat

bicorne/bicorn (by′-korn) Man's hat of the Napoleonic era in shape of a crescent, with front and back brims pressed against each other making points on either side. Now applied to any hat of the same shape. *Der.* Latin, *bicornis,* "two-horned."

bicorne

bicycle-clip hat Tiny half-hat fastened over CROWN (see under ANATOMY OF HEADWEAR) and side of head by piece of springy metal. Often used for a child's hat of fur. *Der.* From metal clip worn around leg when riding a bicycle to keep trousers from catching in chain or wheel spokes.

bluebonnet Small-sized Scotch TAM (see under TYPES OF HEADWEAR DEFINED: HATS AND BONNETS), of blue wool with narrow tartan plaid band fitting around head, black streamers in back, and colored pompon on top. Originally made in leather for protection when fighting. Also called *bonaid. Der.* Scottish, "bonnet."

boater Man's flat-topped, flat-brimmed straw hat with an oval CROWN (see under ANATOMY OF HEADWEAR) worn in the 19th c. and later also adopted by women. This style is often copied in plastic for wear at political conventions.

boater

bobby's hat Hat with high domed CROWN and narrow turned-down BRIM worn by English policemen. See under ANATOMY OF HEADWEAR. *Der.* From slang British term "bobbies," meaning policemen.

bowler See TYPES OF HEADWEAR DEFINED: HATS AND BONNETS: DERBY.

breton (breh′-ton) Woman's off-the-face hat made with medium-sized rolled-back brim worn on back of head. Copied from hats worn by peasants of Brittany, France.

breton

bubble beret See TYPES OF HEADWEAR DEFINED: HATS AND BONNETS: BERET #3.

bubble hat Puffed-out felt or straw hat, usually stiff rather than soft, made with or without a tiny brim. Worn perched on top of head over bouffant hairstyles. Also called a *dome hat.*

bucket hat Casual hat made of fabric that has a moderate-sized, sloping brim that may be stitched in concentric circles and is attached to flat-topped, slightly cone-shaped crown.

busby Tall cylindrical black fur or feathered military hat with cockade at top of center front. A bag-shaped drapery hangs from crown and is draped to the back. Worn by Hussars and certain guardsmen in the British army.

bush hat Large-brimmed Australian-type hat worn turned up on one side. Worn in Australia and in Africa for safaris, also worn as part of uniform by Australian soldiers in World War II. Also called *caddie* or *caddy.*

bush hat

caddie/caddy See TYPES OF HEADWEAR DEFINED: HATS AND BONNETS: BUSH HAT.

canotier See TYPES OF HEADWEAR DEFINED: HATS AND BONNETS: BOATER.

cape hat Woman's half-hat made by attaching felt or fabric capelet to a springy metal clip that crosses the head from ear to ear, letting capelet fall over back of head.

Capulet (cap-yew-let′) Small hat conforming to shape of head and placed back from brow, sometimes with cuffed brim in front. *Der.* For cap worn by Juliet Capulet, heroine of Shakespeare's play *Romeo and Juliet.*

cartwheel hat Woman's hat with extra wide stiff BRIM and low CROWN (see under ANATOMY OF HEADWEAR) frequently made of straw.

cartwheel hat

casque (cask) Hat shaped like a helmet. *Der.* French, "helmet."

cavalier hat 1. A wide-brimmed velvet hat trimmed with ostrich plumes. 2. Brimmed hat with one side turned up like that worn by Theodore Roosevelt and his Rough Riders in Spanish-American War.

chain hat Decorative close-fitting cap made with lengths of chain—some linked together, others dangling. Decorative item of body jewelry introduced in the late 1960s.

chapeau (cha-po′) French word meaning hat or cap.

chechia Adaptation for women in the late 1930s and early 1940s of a felt hat with a tassel—similar to a FEZ (see under TYPES OF HEADWEAR DEFINED: HATS AND BONNETS) but more peaked in shape—that was worn by Algerian and Moroccan children.

chef's hat Tall, white full-crowned fabric hat starched to stand up stiffly. Set into the headband with 100 pleats, which originally indicated that the chef could cook eggs 100 ways. Also called *hundred pleater.* The more important the chef—the taller the hat.

chignon strap Band of ribbon fastened to woman's hat that passes around back of head and under the chignon to hold hat firmly.

chou (shoo) choux (*pl.*) Soft, crushed-crown hat similar to MOB CAP (see under TYPES OF HEADWEAR DEFINED: CAPS). *Der.* French, "cabbage."

chukka hat (chuh′-ka) Domed hat with small brim copied from hats worn by polo players. Similar to, but not as high as, English policeman's hat. *Der.* Named for divisions of polo game called chukkars.

clip hat See TYPES OF HEADWEAR DEFINED: HATS AND BONNETS: BICYCLE-CLIP HAT.

cloche (klohsh) Deep-crowned hat with very narrow brim or brimless, fitting head closely, almost concealing all of the hair. Worn pulled down almost to eyebrows, fashionable in 1920s and revived periodically. *Der.* French, "bell."

cloche

coolie hat Chinese hat made of straw that may take many forms—mushroom-shaped with knob at top, bowl-shaped, flared-cone shape, and a flared shape with a peak in the center. All are made of bamboo, palm leaves, or straw, and stand away from the head, forming almost a parasol against the sun. Copies of this style are made in felt and straw for fashionable hats. *Der.* Chinese, "kuli," an unskilled worker.

cossack hat   Tall brimless hat of fur worn by Russian horsemen and cavalrymen. Copied for men's winter hat in United States and England periodically.

Courrèges hat (Koor′-rej)   Fashion HELMET (see under ANATOMY OF HEADWEAR) shaped similar to World War I aviator's helmet. Introduced in 1964 by French couturier André Courrèges as a result of universal interest in astronauts. The style reappears occasionally.

cowboy hat   Large, wide-brimmed felt hat with crown worn creased or standing up in cone shape and the brim rolled up on both sides and dipping in front. Sometimes with hatband of leather and silver. Worn in United States by Western cowboys to shade face and neck. Also called **ten-gallon hat** when extra tall and uncreased.

cowboy hat:
ten gallon type

Also see TYPES OF HEADWEAR DEFINED: HATS AND BONNETS: SOMBRERO and STETSON.

crusher hat   Comfortable man's snap-brim felt hat that can be made into a compact roll to fit in pocket or pack for travel. Introduced about 1900 and popular in the 1920s and again in the 1980s and after.

dandy hat   Woman's high-crowned, roll-brimmed hat decorated with jet embroidery, feathers, and a veil. Introduced by New York milliner Sally Victor in mid-1950s.

deerstalker   Checked or tweed CAP with VISOR on both front and back and ear flaps that can be buttoned or tied to top of CROWN, worn from 1860s on (see cross references under ANATOMY OF HEADWEAR). Associated with pictures of Sherlock Holmes, the fictional detective created by Sir Arthur Conan Doyle. *Der.* Originally worn in England for hunting, including "stalking deer." Also called *fore-and-after.*

deerstalker

derby   American name for a hat, called a **bowler** in England, which was first worn about 1860, made of hard felt with a domed CROWN and

derby
or bowler

narrow stiff BRIM rolled up on the sides (see under ANATOMY OF HEADWEAR). Usually black, but brown and fawn colors have been worn. *Der.* The British version was named for the hatter, William Bowler, about 1850 to 1860, although shape dates from 1820s. The American version was named for Earl of Derby and an English horse race called the Derby; pronounced *"darby"* in England.

doll hat   Miniature hat worn in different ways at different time periods. In the late 1930s, pushed forward on the head and held on with an elastic band around back of head. Popular after being worn by Jacqueline Kennedy when she was First Lady in early 1960s, when it was attached to the back of head with combs or pins and sometimes had a veil. Reintroduced in 1984 to perch on the front of the head in various shapes—square, round, etc.

dome hat   See TYPES OF HEADWEAR DEFINED: HATS AND BONNETS: BUBBLE HAT.

drum major's hat   Very tall hat with chin band, frequently made of fur in black or white, worn by the leader of a band or drum major for parade functions. Similar to BEARSKIN CAP (see under TYPES OF HEADWEAR DEFINED: CAPS).

Easter bonnet   Another name for an Easter hat. May be any type of hat, not necessarily tied under the chin.

envoy hat   Man's winter hat similar to COSSACK HAT (see under TYPES OF HEADWEAR DEFINED: HATS AND BONNETS) with leather or fur crown and fur or fabric edge. Popular in late 1960s.

Eugénie hat (yoo-je′-nee)   Small hat with brim rolled back on either side, worn by Greta Garbo in a film about the Empress Eugenie, and popular in the 1930s and revived periodically. Worn tilted sideways and to the front, and often trimmed with one long ostrich plume in the side roll. *Der.* Named for Eugénie, Empress of France.

Eugenie hat

fedora   Felt hat with medium-sized BRIM and high CROWN (see under ANATOMY OF HEADWEAR) with lengthwise crease from front to back. Originally worn by men but now also styled for women with turned-up back brim. *Der.* Became popular for

fedora

men after Victorian Sardou's play *Fedora* was produced in 1882.

fez   Red felt hat shaped like truncated cone with long, black silk tassel hanging from center of crown worn by Turkish men until 1925; also worn in Syria, Palestine, and Albania. Also worn by the "Shriners," an auxiliary order of the Masons. This basic shape, without tassel, has been copied for women's hats in the West. *Der.* Named for town of Fez in Morocco.

fold-up hat   Straw sun hat with pleated BRIM and CROWN (see under ANATOMY OF HEADWEAR) that folds to a 6-inch roll for carrying in pocket or purse.

fore-and-after   See TYPES OF HEADWEAR DEFINED: HATS AND BONNETS: DEERSTALKER.

French beret   See TYPES OF HEADWEAR DEFINED: HATS AND BONNETS: BERET #2.

French sailor hat   Large navy blue or white cotton TAM (see under TYPES OF HEADWEAR DEFINED: HATS AND BONNETS), stitched to stiff navy blue headband and trimmed with red pompon at center of crown. Originally worn by French seamen pulled down on forehead with top exactly horizontal.

funnel hat   Brimless tall conical hat of felt or fabric worn by women.

Gainsborough hat   Large, graceful, brimmed hat worn from late 1860s to 1890s. Made of velvet, straw, or beaver, frequently turned up on one side and trimmed with ostrich plumes. The style is revived periodically. *Der.* Named after the 18th-c. British painter Thomas Gainsborough, who painted many portraits of ladies in this type of hat, including portrait of *Duchess of Devonshire.*

Garbo hat   Slouch hat worn so frequently by Greta Garbo in the 1930s that it is sometimes called by her name. See TYPES OF HEADWEAR DEFINED: HATS AND BONNETS: SLOUCH HAT.

garden hat   Large-brimmed floppy hat of horsehair or straw worn in 1920s and 1930s for afternoon teas and garden parties. Currently worn when gardening to protect face from the sun.

gaucho hat (gow-cho)   Wide-brimmed black felt hat made with medium-high flat crown. Fastened under chin with leather thong. Originally worn by South American cowboys, it was adapted for women in late 1960s and worn with gaucho pants, a style of women's pants inspired by the dress of Argentinian cowboys. Also called *sombrero córdobes* (som-brer'-oh kor-dob'-ehs). *Der.* Spanish "cowboy" of Argentina, Chile, and Uruguay.

gob hat   See TYPES OF HEADWEAR DEFINED: HATS AND BONNETS: SAILOR HAT.

gondolier's hat (gon-doh-leer')   Straw hat with a medium-sized brim and a shallow, slightly tapered crown with a flat top. Wide ribbon trims the crown and long streamers extend down the back; the color of the ribbon denoted length of service. Worn formerly by gondoliers of Venice, Italy. Often purchased as a tourist souvenir by visitors to Venice.

halo hat   See TYPES OF HEADWEAR DEFINED: HATS AND BONNETS: PAMELA.

hard hat   Protective covering for the head. Made of metal or hard plastic in classic PITH HELMET shape (see under TYPES OF HEADWEAR DEFINED: HELMETS) or similar to a baseball BATTER'S CAP (see under TYPES OF HEADWEAR DEFINED: CAPS). Held away from the head by foam lining to absorb impact. Worn by construction workers and others subject to work hazards. In late 1960s, the term "hard hat" took on right-wing political connotations when U.S. construction workers expressed their sentiments against peace advocates.

harlequin   Hat with brim, wide at sides and cut straight across front and back. *Der.* From *Harlequin,* a part played by an actor, in 16th- to 18th-c. Italian comedies called *commedia dell'arte.*

high hat   See TYPES OF HEADWEAR DEFINED: HATS AND BONNETS: TOP HAT.

homburg   Man's hat of rather stiff felt with narrow rolled BRIM and lengthwise crease in the CROWN (see under ANATOMY OF HEADWEAR) worn from 1870s on for formal occasions. Made fashionable by Prince of Wales, later Edward VII, who visited Bad Homburg in Germany many times. Revived after President Dwight Eisenhower wore one to his inauguration in 1952. *Der.* Homburg, Prussia.

homburg

hundred pleater   See TYPES OF HEADWEAR DEFINED: HATS AND BONNETS: CHEF'S HAT.

hunt derby/hunting derby   Stiff protective DERBY (see under TYPES OF HEADWEAR DEFINED: HATS AND BONNETS) made with reinforced strong plastic shell covered with black felt and worn with riding habit.

leghorn hat/leghorn bonnet Woman's hat or bonnet in leghorn straw, a fine, smooth straw braid plaited with thirteen strands. The straw is made from the upper part of wheat stalks grown near Livorno, a town in Tuscany, Italy. Fashionable at intervals since latter half of 19th c. *Der.* Named for place of export for the straw, Livorno, Italy. The British anglicized the name of the city to "Leghorn."

matador hat (mat-ah-door) Hat shaped like the top of a bull's head—rounded over forehead with two projections like bull's horns covered with black tufts of fabric, with the center of the crown made of embroidered velvet. Worn by bullfighters in Spain and Mexico.

Merry Widow hat Very wide brimmed hat, sometimes a yard across, frequently of velvet and ornately trimmed with ostrich plumes. *Der.* Named for 1905 light opera *The Merry Widow*, with music by Franz Lehár.

milkmaid hat See TYPES OF HEADWEAR DEFINED: HATS AND BONNETS: BERGÈRE.

Montgomery beret Military cap, a bit larger than the conventional BASQUE BERET (see TYPES OF HEADWEAR DEFINED: HATS AND BONNETS: BERET) but set on a band like a Scottish *tam-o-shanter* and decorated with regimental insignia. Became popular after it was worn by field marshal Bernard Law Montgomery, 1st Viscount Montgomery, commander of British ground forces in World War II.

mortarboard Academic headgear consisting of large, square black brim attached horizontally to a cap. A large tassel in center of the flat top hangs to right side before graduation, to the left after. Worn all over U.S. today and since 14th c. at universities such as Oxford and Cambridge in England.

Mountie's hat Wide-brimmed hat with high crown creased into four sections with a small peak at the top. Similar to World War I army hat worn with dress uniform. Worn by state policemen, forest rangers, and by the Royal Canadian Mounted Police.

mushroom hat Woman's straw hat with small round CROWN and downward-curved BRIM, shaped like the cap of a mushroom (see under ANATOMY OF HEADWEAR).

open-crown hat Woman's hat made without a crown—may be of the HALO or TOQUE hat type (see under TYPES OF HEADWEAR DEFINED: HATS AND BONNETS).

Paco Rabanne hat (pak'-oh rah'-bahn) Unusual cap fitted to conform to the head and covered with tiny diamond-shaped mirrors linked together. Introduced in late 1960s and named for French couturier *Paco Rabanne.*

pamela **1.** Straw bonnet worn from 1845 to late 1860s, made of a "saucer-shaped" piece of straw or fabric placed on top of the head. Fastened with bonnet strings that bent it into a U-shape around the face. Trimmed on top with foliage, flowers, or feathers. **2.** Continued to be a basic hat style with a rounded crown and wide brim and now often called a **halo hat.**

pamela or halo hat #2

Panama hat Hat made of fine, expensive straw obtained from the leaves of the *jipijapa* plant handwoven in Ecuador. Worn in different styles from 1855 on. By extension, any man's summer hat regardless of type of straw.

panama hat

pancake beret See TYPES OF HEADWEAR DEFINED: HATS AND BONNETS: BERET #2.

Peter Pan hat Small hat with brim extended in front and turned up in back. Made with a conical crown trimmed with long feathers. *Der.* Named after the hat worn by actress Maude Adams in 1905 when starring in J. M. Barrie's play *Peter Pan.*

picture hat Hat with large brim framing the face frequently made of straw. Also see TYPES OF HEADWEAR DEFINED: HATS AND BONNETS: LEGHORN HAT.

pillbox hat Classic round brimless hat that can be worn forward or on the back of the head. Introduced in late 1920s and worn since with slight variations. *Der.* From small round pillboxes formerly used by chemists or druggists.

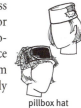
pillbox hat

planter's hat Wide-brimmed white or natural handwoven straw hat with high dented crown, banded with dark ribbon. Worn by Southern gentlemen in the United States and popular for women in late 1960s.

polo hat   See TYPES OF HEADWEAR DEFINED: HATS AND BONNETS: CHUKKA HAT.

pork-pie hat   Classic snap-brim man's hat, flat on top with crease around edge of crown, made of fabric, straw, or felt. Worn in 1930s and copied for women in the 1940s. Still a basic hat for men.

pork pie hat

profile hat   Woman's hat with brim turned down sharply on one side, silhouetting the profile.

Puritan hat   Black, stiff, tall-crowned man's hat with medium-wide straight brim trimmed with wide black band and silver buckle in center front. Worn by Puritan men in America in early 17th c. and copied for women in 1970s.

rain bonnet   Accordion-pleated plastic covering for head that ties under chin. Folds up to fit in purse when not in use.

rain hat   Any waterproof hat worn in the rain. Some hats are made of vinyl and styled with a high crown and a floppy brim. Also see TYPES OF HEADWEAR DEFINED: HATS AND BONNETS: SOU'WESTER.

ranger's hat   See TYPES OF HEADWEAR DEFINED: HATS AND BONNETS: MOUNTIE'S HAT.

Rex Harrison hat   Man's snap-brim hat of wool tweed with narrow brim and matching tweed band. Popular after being worn by actor Rex Harrison in his role as Professor Henry Higgins in the musical *My Fair Lady,* in 1956.

Robin Hood hat   Hat with high peaked CROWN, BRIM (see under ANATOMY OF HEADWEAR) turned up in back, down in front, and trimmed with one long feather. *Der.* From hat in illustrations of books about Robin Hood, legendary British outlaw of the 12th c.

roller   Hat with close-fitting CROWN and narrow curved BRIM (see under ANATOMY OF HEADWEAR) worn rolled up or with the front turned down. Popular for women and girls in 1930s and 1940s, revived in early 1970s.

safari hat   Lightweight straw or fabric hat shaped somewhat like a shallow soup dish with medium-sized brim. Hat is somewhat similar to a TOPEE (see under TYPES OF HEADWEAR DEFINED: HELMETS) with a shallower crown. Worn to deflect heat in warm weather. *Der.* Shape of hat is similar to those worn on African hunting trips called "safaris."

sailor hat   **1.** Hat worn by naval enlisted personnel made of white duck fabric with gored crown and stitched upturned brim worn either on the back of the head or tilted over the forehead. Also called *gob hat* and *tennis hat.* **2.** Women's straight brimmed hat with shallow flat crown worn since 1860s. Very popular in 1890s for sportswear and bicycling and worn intermittently since.

sailor hat #1

Saint Laurent hat   Cap designed by French couturier Yves Saint Laurent in 1966, made of leather studded with nailheads and styled similar to World War I aviator's helmet.

Salvation Army bonnet   High-crowned black straw bonnet with short front brim raised off forehead to show a pale-blue lining. Has dark blue ribbon around crown and ties under chin; worn by women of the Salvation Army, a religious and charitable organization.

scarf hat   **1.** Woman's soft fabric hat made by tying a scarf over a lining or base, sometimes shaped like a PILLBOX (see under TYPES OF HEADWEAR DEFINED: HATS AND BONNETS) and sewed in place. **2.** A triangular piece of colorful print or plain fabric quilted on long side. Worn with quilted part in center front and tied on the head like a KERCHIEF (see under TYPES OF HEADWEAR DEFINED: OTHER HEADWEAR).

scottie   A brimless hat styled somewhat like the GLENGARRY (see under TYPES OF HEADWEAR DEFINED: CAPS) with narrow recessed crown. Veiling, ribbon, or feathers are sometimes placed on top toward the back.

shako   (shay'-ko)   Cylindrical stiff tall cap with attached visor. Top is sometimes tapered, sometimes flared, with feather cockade in front. Worn by marching bands, it was adapted from an earlier style of military cap. Also see TYPES OF HEADWEAR DEFINED: HATS AND BONNETS: DRUM MAJOR'S HAT.

shepherdess hat   See TYPES OF HEADWEAR DEFINED: HATS AND BONNETS: BERGÈRE.

shoe hat   Hat designed by Elsa Schiaparelli in the 1930s that looked like a woman's shoe. This design was reflective of the designer's interest in Surrealism.

shoe hat 1930s

silk hat   See TYPES OF HEADWEAR DEFINED: HATS AND BONNETS: TOP HAT.

skimmer   SAILOR HAT or BOATER (see under TYPES OF HEADWEAR DEFINED: HATS AND BONNETS), with exaggerated shallow crown and wide brim.

sleep bonnet   Any net, snood, or cap worn to bed to protect hairstyle.

slouch hat   Woman's hat similar to a man's FEDORA (see under TYPES OF HEADWEAR DEFINED: HATS AND BONNETS) made with a flexible brim that may be turned down in front. Also called a GARBO HAT (see under TYPES OF HEADWEAR DEFINED: HATS AND BONNETS).

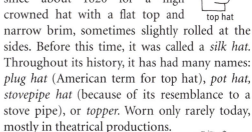
slouch hat

snap-brim hat   Man's or woman's hat with the brim worn at several different angles according to the preference of the wearer. Also see TYPES OF HEADWEAR DEFINED: HATS AND BONNETS: REX HARRISON HAT.

sombrero (som-brer'-oh)   Mexican hat with a tall, slightly tapered crown and large upturned brim. Worn in Mexico by peons in straw and by wealthier citizens in felt lavishly trimmed around the edge, sometimes with silver lace. Also worn in Spain and the southwestern United States, where it is made of felt and somewhat similar to a *ten-gallon hat*. *Der.* Spanish, *sombre*, "to shade."

sombrero córdobes   See TYPES OF HEADWEAR DEFINED: HATS AND BONNETS: GAUCHO HAT.

sou'wester/southwester   Rain hat made with a dome-shaped sectioned crown and broad stitched brim—larger in back. Originally made of yellow oiled silk—now made of any waterproof fabric for children's rainwear and fishermen. *Der.* First worn by fishermen in New England where a wind from the southwest meant rain.

Stetson®   Trade name for a man's hat manufacturer of all types of hats, but often used to mean a wide-brimmed Western-style hat, especially the COWBOY style (see under TYPES OF HEADWEAR DEFINED: HATS AND BONNETS).

stroller   Casual mannish felt hats worn by women for town and spectator sports in 1930s and 1940s.

sun bonnet   Wide-brimmed fabric bonnet tied under chin especially worn by infants and children for protection against the sun. Often made with pockets into which pieces of cardboard or other firm material could be slipped in order to provide stiffness to the brim. Worn originally by early pioneers on western treks across the United States for protection against the sun.

Revived for Centennial celebrations throughout the United States.

swagger hat   Informal sports hat, often felt, with medium-sized brim turned down in front.

tam/tam-o-shanter   **1.** "Tam" is a shortened form of the Scottish "tam-o-shanter" used in United States. It is a flat cap made in several ways: *a)* out of two circles of fabric—one complete and one with hole cut in center—sewed together at the outer edge; *b)* crocheted with pompon on top for trim; *c)* made out of piece of circular molded felt and also called a BERET (see under TYPES OF HEADWEAR DEFINED: HATS AND BONNETS). **2.** Genuine Scottish tams are frequently made out of long, shaggy, striped-wool fabric and cut in segments so that stripes form a pattern on the top. Usually larger than other tams with a pompon at center of crown. *Der.* From the name of the main character of Scottish poem written by Robert Burns about 1791 called "Tam O'Shanter."

tam

ten-gallon hat   See TYPES OF HEADWEAR DEFINED: HATS AND BONNETS: COWBOY HAT and SOMBRERO.

top hat   Man's tall hat with narrow brim made of shiny silk or beaver cloth. This term has been used since about 1820 for a high crowned hat with a flat top and narrow brim, sometimes slightly rolled at the sides. Before this time, it was called a *silk hat*. Throughout its history, it has had many names: *plug hat* (American term for top hat), *pot hat, stovepipe hat* (because of its resemblance to a stove pipe), or *topper*. Worn only rarely today, mostly in theatrical productions.

top hat

toque (tok)   A basic hat type that has a high CROWN and is generally brimless or may have a very small BRIM (see under ANATOMY OF HEADWEAR). Can be made in various shapes, often turbanlike.

toque

toreador hat (tor-ayah'-dor)
1. See TYPES OF HEADWEAR DEFINED: HATS AND BONNETS: MATADOR HAT.

tricorne (try'-korn)   19th-c. term for a three-cornered hat made by turning up the

tricorne

brim of a round hat to form three equidistant peaks with one peak in center front. Also spelled *tricorn*. The name is applied to contemporary hats of this shape.

turban Contemporary draped hat worn by women that is similar to the headdress of some Middle Eastern men, which consists of a long scarf wound around the head.

turban

Tyrolean hat See TYPES OF HEADWEAR DEFINED: HATS AND BONNETS: ALPINE HAT.

western hat High-crowned hat with a flat top and wide brim frequently trimmed with a leather thong pulled through holes punched at regular intervals around the crown. Has a leather adjustable strap worn under the chin to secure the hat, or permit it to hang down the back. Similar to GAUCHO HAT (see under TYPES OF HEADWEAR DEFINED: HATS AND BONNETS).

wig hat Soft hat, often crocheted, that fits tightly around the face but blouses in the back. Some hats are entirely covered with feathers, some with flowers. No hair shows from beneath the hat. Popular in mid-1960s.

William Penn hat Medium-sized BRIM with high-rounded CROWN worn forward on the head. Introduced in late 1960s (see under ANATOMY OF HEADWEAR). *Der.* Similar to hat worn by William Penn (1644–1718) when he colonized Pennsylvania.

wind bonnet Lightweight foldup covering for head made of net, point d'esprit, or chiffon to protect hair.

CAPS

applejack cap See TYPES OF HEADWEAR DEFINED: CAPS: NEWSBOY CAP.

army cap Caps worn by U.S. Army. See TYPES OF HEADWEAR DEFINED: CAPS: FATIGUE, OVERSEAS, and SERVICE CAPS.

astronaut's cap Cap similar to a BASEBALL CAP (see under TYPES OF HEADWEAR DEFINED: CAPS) with elaborately embroidered gold braid on visor, band of gold braid around edge of crown, gold button on top of crown, and adjustable back strap. Copied from caps worn by astronauts and World War II naval commanders, the gold braid is sometimes facetiously called

"scrambled eggs." Also called *commander's cap* and *flight deck cap*.

baseball cap Cap with dome-shaped crown, sometimes made with alternate panels of nylon net for coolness, and an adjustable band or elastic at the back. May have any type of "patch," slogan, or picture on front, e.g., major league football, baseball and Little League team names, makes of cars or trucks, sports insignia, soft-drink brands, cartoon characters, and the like. When first introduced, cap fit more closely to the head like a skullcap. In the 1990s, wearing these caps backward became a fad among the young. Also see TYPES OF HEADWEAR DEFINED: CAPS: BATTER'S CAP.

baseball cap

bathing cap Tight-fitting cap made of rubber or stretchable fabric, with or without strap under chin. May be decorated. Worn to protect hair while swimming.

batter's cap/batter's helmet Duck-bill visored cap with hard crown for protection, worn by baseball players when taking turn at bat.

bearskin cap Tall cylindrical cap of black bearskin with a chain or strap under lower lip or the chin. Worn by some personnel of the British army, also by military guards of Buckingham Palace in London and Parliament buildings in Ottawa, Canada. Also see TYPES OF HEADWEAR DEFINED: HATS AND BONNETS: DRUM MAJOR'S HAT.

bebop cap See TYPES OF HEADWEAR DEFINED: CAPS: NEWSBOY CAP.

bellboy/bellhop cap Small fabric pillbox, often trimmed with gold braid, sometimes with chin strap, worn by hotel or restaurant bellboys.

calotte (ca-lot′) **1.** A SKULLCAP (see under TYPES OF HEADWEAR DEFINED: CAPS) frequently made of leather or suede with a small matching projection like a stem on center top. **2.** Woman's small skullcap worn in 1940s and 1950s, sometimes with large jeweled pin. **3.** A cap worn by schoolboy, called a BEANIE (see TYPES OF HEADWEAR DEFINED: CAPS: SKULLCAP).

Carnaby cap See TYPES OF HEADWEAR DEFINED: CAPS: NEWSBOY CAP.

chapel cap Small round cap that fits on the back of the head, sometimes lace-trimmed, matched to choir robes, and worn by women of choir for church services.

chignon cap   Small cap made in a variety of colors and fabrics worn over the chignon in the 1930s and 1940s. Popular again in the 1960s and 1970s—usually made of crocheted wool—and called a *bun-warmer* or *bun snood.*

chapel cap/chapel veil   Small circle of lace or tulle, frequently edged with a ruffle, worn by women over top of head while inside a church.

commander's cap   See TYPES OF HEADWEAR DEFINED: CAPS: ASTRONAUT'S CAP.

conductor's cap   Cap with crown shaped like a pillbox with visor-shaped brim, frequently trimmed with braid around the crown and an insignia in front. Worn placed straight on forehead by train conductors.

cossack forage cap   Visored cap with soft crown set on band worn toward back of head rather than pulled down on forehead. Made in napped suede fabric in natural, black, or loden green. Adapted from caps worn by Russian Cossacks and accepted for general wear by men and women in the late 1960s. Also see TYPES OF HEADWEAR DEFINED: CAPS: FORAGE CAP.

crocheted cap   (kro-shade′)   Any type cap that is hand crocheted. Styles vary—some are helmet-shaped—others made like TAMS (see under TYPES OF HEADWEAR DEFINED: HATS AND BONNETS). Some styles are trimmed with metal or plastic PAILLETTES (see under OTHER DECORATIVE MATERIALS USED TO ORNAMENT ACCESSORIES: SPANGLES) attached at intervals.

Davy Crockett cap   Coonskin (raccoon fur) cap with tail of animal hanging down back. Worn in Colonial America by woodsmen and pioneers and named after David Crockett, frontiersman and politician, who fought and died at the Alamo in Texas in 1836. Popular for young boys in 1950s and 1960s after wide exposure on television programs, at which time the term was copyrighted. Copyright now applies to a wide variety of apparel.

dink/dinky   See TYPES OF HEADWEAR DEFINED: CAPS: SKULLCAP.

desert fatigue cap   VISOR cap of cotton poplin made with soft CROWN set on wide band, worn with top crushed down at sides (see under ANATOMY OF HEADWEAR). Copied from German forage cap worn in World War II and accepted for general wear in late 1960s and after.

dunce cap   Tall conical cap, sometimes marked with a **D**, formerly worn in school by students who failed in their lessons. Although this cap is no longer worn, the term is still used.

Dutch-boy cap   Cap with VISOR and soft wide CROWN usually made of navy blue wool. See under ANATOMY OF HEADWEAR.

Dutch cap   Cap worn by women and girls in Volendam, Holland, made of lace or embroidered muslin fitted to the head with a slight peak at the crown and flaring wings at sides of face. Made fashionable by *Irene Castle,* famous ballroom dancer in 1920s. Sometimes used as bridal cap. Also called *Dutch bonnet.*

eight-point cap   Policeman's cap, or utility cap, with soft CROWN and a stiff VISOR in front (see under ANATOMY OF HEADWEAR). Crown is made by sewing together eight straight-edged wedges of fabric making an octagon-shaped crown.

engineer's cap   Round cap with visor worn by railroad workers, usually of blue-and-white striped cotton. The crown is box-pleated onto the band. Adopted in 1960s by young people for sportswear.

Eton cap   Close-fitting cap with a short visor, modeled after those worn at Eton College in England. Often worn by small boys.

fatigue cap   U.S. armed forces cap usually made of twill fabric in style similar to ENGINEER'S CAP (see under TYPES OF HEADWEAR DEFINED: CAPS).

flight deck cap   See CAPS: ASTRONAUT'S CAP.

forage cap   Small cap similar to a KEPI (see under CAPS), formerly worn by soldiers in U.S. Army. Also see TYPES OF HEADWEAR DEFINED: CAPS: DESERT FATIGUE CAP.

frigate cap   Utility cap with visor and a flat top slanting toward back. Made of water-repellent black fabric with cord and buttons on front for trim. Copied from caps worn by merchant seamen in the 19th c.

garrison cap   See TYPES OF HEADWEAR DEFINED: CAPS: OVERSEAS CAP.

glengarry cap   Military cloth cap creased to fold flat like an OVERSEAS CAP (see under TYPES OF HEADWEAR DEFINED: CAPS), usually with tartan band at edge, regimental badge at side front, and two black ribbon streamers in back. Part of the uniform of Scottish Highland regiments, and adapted for sportswear by women and small boys in mid-19th c. and after. *Der.* After Glengarry, a valley in Invernessshire, Scotland.

Greek fisherman's cap Soft cap of denim or wool with CROWN higher in front than in back. Elaborately trimmed with braid on VISOR and at seam where visor meets crown. Styled in black wool, blue denim, or white and worn for sportswear or boating in 1980s by both men and women. See cross references under ANATOMY OF HEADWEAR.

havelock Originally a cloth covering for military cap extending to shoulders in back in order to protect the neck from sun. Now also worn for outdoor activities. *Der.* Named for Sir Henry Havelock, British general in India.

hunt cap Cap cut in six segments with small visor, elastic chin strap, and button on center top, sometimes of cloverleaf shape. Worn with riding habit, it is sometimes made with a plastic shell covered with velvet or velveteen and a padded lining.

hunting cap Stiff protective DERBY (see under TYPES OF HEADWEAR DEFINED: HATS AND BONNETS) made with reinforced strong plastic shell covered with black felt worn with riding habit.

jockey cap Visored cap with crown usually of bicolored sateen cut in gores, similar to BASEBALL CAP (see under TYPES OF HEADWEAR DEFINED: CAPS) but with deeper crown, worn by racetrack jockeys. Similar caps worn by women in mid-1960s.

Juliet cap SKULLCAP (see under TYPES OF HEADWEAR DEFINED: CAPS) of rich fabric worn for evening or with wedding veils. May also be made entirely of pearls, jewels, or chain. *Der.* Medieval costume of Juliet in Shakespeare's play *Romeo and Juliet.*

Legionnaire's cap See TYPES OF HEADWEAR DEFINED: CAPS: KEPI.

kepi High-crowned, flat-topped visored cap frequently worn with HAVELOCK (see under TYPES OF HEADWEAR DEFINED: CAPS) in back as protection from sun. Worn by French Foreign Legion and French General and statesman Charles de Gaulle. Also called *Legionnaire's cap.*

miner's cap Stiff cap with short duck-billed visor and battery-powered light attached to front of crown.

mob cap Woman's indoor cap of 18th and 19th c. made of white cambric or muslin with gathered crown and ruffled edge forming a bonnet. Had side lappets, called *kissing strings* or *bridles* that tied under the chin. Has served as a basis for contemporary women's hat styles.

mod cap Cap similar to NEWSBOY CAP (see under TYPES OF HEADWEAR DEFINED: CAPS), popular in United States in mid-1960s.

newsboy cap Soft fabric cap with flat, bloused crown and visor that sometimes snaps to the crown. Formerly worn by newsboys and made famous by child actor Jackie Coogan in silent films of the 1920s. Revived in exaggerated form in 1960s and 1970s and continues to be fashionable. May be referred to by various names, e.g., *Carnaby, bebop, soul, applejack cap.*

newsboy cap

nightcap Any headcovering worn to bed at night.

nurse's cap White stiffly starched fabric cap received by nurses at graduation. At one time, but no longer, worn pinned to the crown of the head when dressed in uniform and on duty in hospitals. Each school of nursing has an individual style of cap.

overseas cap Flat folding cloth cap of khaki or olive drab fabric, worn by men and women in the armed services. Has a lengthwise pleat from front to back in center of CROWN (see under ANATOMY OF HEADWEAR) to enable it to fold flat. Worn overseas in World Wars I and II. Also called *garrison cap.*

painter's cap Lightweight duck-billed fabric cap made with a round, flat-topped CROWN (see under ANATOMY OF HEADWEAR). Sometimes imprinted with school name, team name, or resort on front of crown. *Der.* From cap worn by house painters.

scarf cap Long, tubular knitted or crocheted scarf with opening for head in one end, similar to STOCKING CAP (see under TYPES OF HEADWEAR DEFINED: CAPS).

service cap Army cap worn with dress uniform, made with a stiff, round, flat top and stiff visor of leather or plastic.

shower cap Plastic or waterproof cap, usually shirred into an elastic band, worn to keep the hair dry when taking a shower.

skullcap   Gored cap, usually made in eight sections, which fits tightly to crown of the head, often part of ecclesiastical garb or national costume. A **beanie** is a skullcap cut in gores to fit the head. Worn by children and by freshmen students as a part of hazing by upperclassmen, it is also called a *dink* or *dinky*. A **yarmulke/yarmulka** (yahr-muhl′-kuh) is a skullcap made of plain, embroidered, beaded, or crocheted fabric that is worn by Orthodox Jewish males for day wear and in the synagogue. Worn by less traditional Jewish men for special occasions and religious services. Also see TYPES OF HEADWEAR DEFINED: CAPS: CALOTTE.

beanie

soul cap   See TYPES OF HEADWEAR DEFINED: CAPS: NEWSBOY CAP.

stocking cap   A knitted or crocheted cap with a long pendant tail worn hanging down the back or side frequently with a tassel on the end. Also called *toboggan cap*.

stocking cap

tea-cozy cap   Cap introduced in late 1960s that fits head closely to cover hair completely. *Der.* Quilted padded cover for teapots used to keep the tea hot at the table.

toboggan cap   See TYPES OF HEADWEAR DEFINED: CAP: STOCKING CAP.

touring cap   Leather or fabric cap with snap-down visor, frequently treated for water repellency. Popular in the 1980s, it is copied from earlier cap worn when "touring" in early 20th-c. automobiles.

trooper cap   Man's or boy's cap of leather or leatherlike plastic with fur or pile lining and a flap around sides and back. Flaps can be folded down to keep ears warm or up to reveal lining. *Der.* Originally worn by state police or "troopers," now used by mail carriers, police officers, etc.

watch cap   Knitted cap, fitting closely over head with turned-up cuff, made of navy-blue wool yarn. Worn by sailors on watch or other work duties, or as a replacement for white duck hat. Adapted in other colors for sportswear by men, women, and children.

watch cap

welding cap   Cap similar to a BASEBALL CAP (see under TYPES OF HEADWEAR DEFINED) but with a relatively short visor.

yachting cap   Cap, usually white, with flat CROWN and black or navy blue VISOR, decorated with yacht-club emblem (see under ANATOMY OF HEADWEAR). Styled similar to a naval officer's cap, and also worn by yacht-club members on boats.

yarmulke/yarmulka   See under TYPES OF HEADWEAR DEFINED: CAPS: SKULLCAP.

HELMETS

aviator's helmet   **1.** helmet made of high-impact plastic, sometimes fitted with an oxygen mask, worn by a pilot and crew of planes flying at high altitudes. **2.** World War I helmet fitting the head snugly and fastened under the chin. Made of leather with wool or shearling lining for warmth. Goggles were worn on top. Also called *Red Baron helmet* after a famous World War I ace.

bicycle helmet   Helmet not covering the ears, with dark adjustable visor and air inlets for ventilating and cooling, held on by a strap under the chin. Shell is high-impact PVC plastic lined with polystyrene, and foam-lined for comfort.

fashion helmet   Any helmet designed as a fashion item rather than for protection. May be made of leather, fabric, fur, plastic, or other materials.

football helmet   Molded plastic helmet that conforms closely to the head, covering the ears. Made with nose guard, consisting of curved plastic strips attached to sides, and decorated with symbols indicating team. Worn by all contact football players.

German helmet   Metal helmet made with small visor and a spike on the top decorated with large gold eagle on front. Worn by Germans in World War I and adopted by teenage boys in the late 1960s. Also called a *pickelhaube.*

motorcycle helmet   Molded plastic helmet with foam lining worn when riding a motorcycle. Usually has a large dark-colored plastic shield that snaps on to protect eyes and face.

pickelhaube   See TYPES OF HEADWEAR DEFINED: HELMETS: GERMAN HELMET.

pith helmet   See TYPES OF HEADWEAR DEFINED: HELMETS: TOPEE.

Red Baron helmet   See HELMETS: AVIATOR'S HELMET.

space helmet   Helmet made of molded plastic covering the head and neck completely and fastening to collar around the top of the space suit. Front section is made of see-through plastic with mirror-like reflective finish.

topee/topi   Tropical helmet shaped more like a hat with a wide brim, originally made of cork ½″ thick. Worn particularly in the jungles as a protection from the sun. Does not fit close to the head, because constructed with an air space between head and helmet. Also called *pith helmet. Der.* Name refers to European cork.

OTHER HEADWEAR

American Indian headband   Narrow band of leather, fabric, or beadwork placed low on the forehead and tied at side or back, sometimes with feather in back, worn by American Indians and adopted by hippies in the 1960s and worn periodically since.

bandeau (band-oh′)   Narrow piece of ribbon or fabric, sometimes decorated, worn around head as substitute for a hat.

brow band   Ribbon, fabric, beaded band, or braid of hair around head worn low on forehead. See also TYPES OF HEADWEAR DEFINED: OTHER HEADWEAR: HEADBAND.

coronet (kor′-o-net)   **1.** Crown that denotes rank below that of sovereign. Nobility of Great Britain have seven different styles of crowns for prince of the blood, younger son, nephew, duke, marquis, earl, viscount, and baron. **2.** Band or wreath worn by women like a TIARA (see under TYPES OF HEADWEAR DEFINED: OTHER HEADWEAR) on the head.

crown   **1.** Circlet of precious metal and gems worn by kings and queens. **2.** Bridal headpiece worn with veil. **3.** A garland or wreath worn on the head as an ornament or sign of honor.

crusader hood   Snug-fitting hood cut in one piece with a small shoulder cape. Originally made of chain mail—later copied in knits for winter sportswear.

diadem (dy′-ah-dem)   **1.** A crown. **2.** Decorative headdress resembling a crown.

doo rag   Headcovering with the appearance of a head scarf tied in the back with long, hanging tail. Usually made from brightly colored fabrics or leather.

diamanté headband (dya-mahn-tay′)   Band of fabric set with artificial sparking jewels (for example, rhinestones) and worn around head, low on forehead.

earmuffs   **1.** Two disks of wool, fur, felt, or other fabric worn to keep the ears warm in winter. Disks may be fastened to a strap that goes overhead and ties under the chin, or fastened to a springy metal band that fits over top of the head. **2.** A pair of flaps on sides of a cap that may be turned up and buttoned at top of cap, or left down to cover the ears.

fillet   See TYPES OF HEADWEAR DEFINED: OTHER HEADWEAR: HEADBAND #1 and #2.

hair net   Fine, cap-shaped net worn over the hair to keep it in place. Sometimes made of knotted human hair and nearly invisible. Also made of chenille, gold, or silver threads and worn as decoration. Also see TYPES OF HEADWEAR DEFINED: HEADWEAR: SNOOD.

headband   **1.** Strip of leather, cord, or fabric bound around the head horizontally across the forehead. Also called a *brow band.* **2.** Band worn over top of the head from ear to ear as an ornament or to keep hair in place since ancient times.

headband

head wrap   In 1980s, a scarf, bandanna, ribbon, or piece of fabric worn wrapped around the head to frame the face or as a BROW BAND (see under TYPES OF HEADWEAR DEFINED: OTHER HEADWEAR).

hood   **1.** Preliminary, shaped piece of felt or straw from which the milliner works. Has a high rounded nondescript crown and an extra-large floppy brim. **2.** Accessory worn on the head and sometimes the shoulders that is frequently attached to a jacket or coat. Differs from a hat in that it has no specific shape and usually covers the entire head, sometimes tying under the chin. Popular item for winter wear, it is made in all types of fabrics and fur. Although there are a great variety of styles, there are no specific names for these items.

kerchief   A large triangle of cloth, or a square folded in triangular fashion, worn as a headcovering or around the neck.

snood   Hairnet made from CHENILLE, MESH, or other material worn at the back of the head and nape of neck to confine the hair—sometimes attached to a hat. See under TEXTILES IN ACCESSORIES: HOW YARNS MAY BE IMPORTANT: TYPES OF YARNS DEFINED and DIFFERENT TYPES OF FABRIC STRUCTURES: WOVEN FABRICS DEFINED.

snood

Statue of Liberty visor   Headband with seven spikes and visor in front worn during "Liberty Weekend" in 1986 in celebration of the renovation of the Statue of Liberty in New York harbor.

sweatband   A stretch terrycloth band worn in 1980s around the head during exercise to absorb sweat.

tiara (tee-ar´-ah)   Curved band, often of metal set with jewels or flowers, worn on top of woman's head from ear to ear, giving effect of a crown. Sometimes used to hold a wedding veil. Also called *demi-coronal*.

TYPES OF HAIR ACCESSORIES DEFINED

barrette (ba-ret´)   Clip worn in the hair. May be small and worn one on either side of head, or larger and worn in back of head or at nape of the neck. Made of plastic, metal, wood or other materials in various shapes (e.g., bar or bow knot). *Der.* French, diminutive of *barre*, "bar." Also spelled *barret, barette*.

bobby pin   Small flexible piece of metal bent in half with prongs held together by the spring of the metal; worn to keep hair in place or to set hair in pin curls.

bobby pin

hairpin   A two-pronged device, usually of tortoise shell, plastic, or metal. Used to hold the hair in place, especially hair styled in a bun, knot, updo, or French twist. The classic hairpin is a wire bent double with crimps halfway down each side to give flexibility. Pins of very fine wire tinted to match hair are called **invisible hairpins**. Decorated hairpins are worn as jewelry and made of exotic materials or jeweled.

hairpin

hair sticks   Long stiletto-like pieces of wood, plastic, or metal worn for decorative effect. Usually thrust through hair knotted at the back of the head.

rat   Sausage-shaped padded roll of nylon mesh (formerly of hair or felt) worn by women under natural hair to create high pompadour effect in early 20th c. and since.

hair sticks

scrunchy   Elastic band covered with fabric for confining ponytails.

Spanish comb   Comb with ornamental top, sometimes five inches high, worn at crown of head to support a MANTILLA (see under TYPES OF VEILS DEFINED) or separately for decorative effect.

scrunchy

TYPES OF VEILS DEFINED

bird cage   Dome of stiff wide-mesh veiling pinned to crown of head covering face and ears. Worn in place of hat.

bridal veil   Traditionally a length of white net, lace, tulle, or silk illusion reaching to waist, hips, ankles, or floor in back. Chest length in front and worn over face during wedding—turned back after ceremony.

communion veil   A sheer net elbow-length veil worn by girls for first communion in the Catholic Church.

mantilla (man-til´-ah)   Large oblong, fine lace veil, usually in rose pattern of black or white, worn wrapped over head and crossed under chin with one end thrown over shoulder. Frequently worn to church instead of a hat in Spain and South America. Popular after it was worn in early 1960s by U.S. first lady Jacqueline Kennedy.

mourning veil   Semi-sheer black veil to the shoulders, usually circular, sometimes edged with wide band of black fabric worn under or over hat at funerals or during periods of mourning.

prayer veil   Small triangular lace veil worn instead of hat for church services.

ACCESSORIES: HEADWEAR, VEILS, AND HAIR ACCESSORIES

HOSIERY

HISTORY AND SIGNIFICANCE OF HOSIERY TO FASHION

Hosiery is a knitted item of wearing apparel covering the foot and/or leg. Many other names are also given to hosiery. The term **stockings** is generally applied to knitted coverings for the foot and most of the leg. **Socks** usually applies to knitted coverings for the foot and may extend some distance up the leg. The distinction between socks and stockings is not entirely clear-cut, although socks are generally thought of as shorter and stockings as longer. The term "sock" derives from the Latin *soccus,* which was a soft Roman shoe that covered the foot and ankle, whereas "stocking" derives from a type of leg covering called *stocks* that was worn in the 15th and 16th c. and covered the foot and leg, extending to the waist. The upper section was called the upper stocks, and the lower section, the lower stocks. When the garment was eventually divided into two separate parts in the 16th c., the lower part, which extended to the knee or above, became known as a stocking. **Hose** is another synonym for hosiery. Current usage suggests that hose tends to be used when referring to the more transparent and decorative varieties of hosiery, while "stockings" is used for heavier varieties of a more utilitarian nature.

Although hand-knitted articles were in use before the 16th c., knitted foot coverings only came to predominate in hosiery after the invention of a knitting machine in the 16th c. Prior to this, garments that covered the legs were usually made of woven fabric. These garments were baggy and fit poorly. William Lee, inventor of the first knitting

stocking

machine, presented Queen Elizabeth I with a pair of knitted silk stockings in the late 1500s. He was refused a patent because she found them too coarse and, again later, because of the fear that his machine would put hand-knitters out of business. By the early 1600s, however, this machine, which still serves as the basis of certain modern knitting machines, found acceptance and was the only knitting machine used for centuries. Hosiery was made from cotton, linen, wool, and silk yarns.

With the advent of shorter skirts in the 20th c., hosiery took on more importance because it was now a much more visible part of dress. Among 20th c. innovations in hosiery were "flesh-colored" or beige silk hosiery in the 1920s, the introduction of NYLON (see TEXTILES IN ACCESSORIES: FIBERS AND YARNS: THE BUILDING BLOCKS OF FABRICS: GENERIC AND OTHER MANUFACTURED FIBERS DEFINED) hose in 1940, textured hose in the 1960s, and PANTYHOSE (see under WOMEN'S NYLON HOSIERY) in the 1960s.

ANATOMY OF HOSIERY

When stockings and socks are shaped like the foot, they may have reinforced sections for the toes and the heel. The **heel** is that portion of the hose that fits over the heel of the foot. If hosiery has no double reinforcement at the heel,

cuff
toe
heel pocket
sock

it is called **heelless hose.** In a stocking that runs the length of the leg, the **boot** is that part of pantyhose or stocking that extends from the panty or the welt to the toe. The **welt** is the part at the top of a stocking that is reinforced so that it is strong enough to fasten a support device. It may be a separate piece of fabric machine-sewn to the top of the stocking or may be knitted in heavier yarn and folded double.

Specialized knitting machines are used to create various types of hosiery. Prior to the development of circular knitting machines in the mid-19th c., hosiery had to be knitted flat and sewn shut. Today hosiery is generally seamless. Both sheer hosiery and heavier socks are made in a PLAIN KNIT, a knit stitch that is elastic and stretches to conform to the shape of the foot and leg. Many socks have a cuff that is worn either turned down or against the leg. This part of the sock is usually made in a RIB KNIT variation of the plain knit because rib knits are more elastic (see under TEXTILES IN ACCESSORIES: DIFFERENT TYPES OF FABRIC STRUCTURES: KNITTED FABRICS and KNITTED FABRICS DEFINED).

Even if a circular knitting machine is used, the stocking must have some shaping. **Reciprocated construction** used in the making of some hosiery begins at the top and moves toward the toe. A semicircular or "reciprocating" motion of the machine shapes a pocket for the heel. A toe may also be formed. A **nonreciprocated** stocking has no shaped heel or toe (see ANATOMY OF HOSIERY: STOCKINGS: TUBE SOCK). The toe of a stocking made in a nonreciprocating construction is called a **fishmouth toe**. In this stocking, the seam runs parallel to the bottom of the foot rather than across the top of the toe.

WOMEN'S NYLON HOSIERY

The term **nylons** is now virtually synonymous with women's hose because of the almost universal use of NYLON (see under TEXTILES IN ACCESSORIES: FIBERS AND YARNS: THE BUILDING BLOCKS OF FABRICS: GENERIC AND OTHER MANUFACTURED FIBERS DEFINED) in dress hose for women. Trademarked nylon yarn was introduced in 1939, making possible a much sheerer type of hose that was also more durable than the silk hosiery worn previously. Although it was possible to make seamless hose, when this hosiery was made of silk or rayon, it tended to bag and wrinkle. Shaping a flat stocking and seaming it up the back achieved a smoother fit. In the 1950s, techniques developed for making seamless hose fit better by using heat-setting treat-

ments or stretch yarns. Seamless hose now dominate the market.

Yarn size of filament yarns such as nylon is measured in **denier**: the higher the denier number, the thicker the yarn. **Gauge** is a measure of the number of needles per inch on the knitting machine. A higher gauge number means that stitches are closer together. The yarn size and the gauge together determine the weight or sheerness of hosiery. A low denier yarn and a low gauge produce sheer hosiery, which is less durable than hosiery with higher denier and higher gauge. **Sheer hose** are nylon hose made with a fine or low denier yarn, thus making them more translucent. **Ultra sheer** hose are made with exceptionally fine yarns; **day sheer** or **business sheer** hose are less translucent and more durable. **Opaque** (oh-pake′) **hose** are textured or plain hose or pantyhose that are not sheer and come in all colors.

Sheer or opaque women's hosiery is available in the following length variations:

ankle-length hosiery Sock-length hosiery made out of conventional nylon yarn. Women wear them with full-length slacks or pants.

knee-high hose Also called *trouser socks* or abbreviated to *knee-hi;* these are hose of conventional nylon yarn or of NYLON and SPANDEX (see under TEXTILES IN ACCESSORIES: GENERIC AND OTHER MANUFACTURED FIBERS DEFINED). They end just below the knees and are finished at the top with elastic. Though first made in beige and worn when dresses were long, they are now worn with various types of pants and are made in various colors.

thigh highs NYLON or nylon and SPANDEX stockings that end at the top of the thigh and have elasticized tops. See under TEXTILES IN ACCESSORIES: FIBERS AND YARNS: THE BUILDING BLOCKS OF FABRICS: GENERIC AND OTHER MANUFACTURED FIBERS DEFINED.

full-length stockings Stockings that extend to the top of the leg and must be held in place with a garter or elastic.

pantyhose Hosiery, made with textured and sheer nylon yarns and follows the design of tights, having stockings and panties cut in one piece. Pantyhose were introduced in the United States about 1963. First made in sizes for tall, medium,

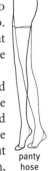

panty hose

and petite heights, and later made in larger sizes. They were introduced for men in fall 1970. In the mid-1980s, interest in unusual pantyhose was revived and currently they are made in many patterns, colors, and textures. Those pantyhose with a knitted-in panty of heavier weight nylon or cotton are known as **all-in-one pantyhose.** **Control pantyhose** are those in which the panty portion is knit of nylon and stretch yarns (see TEXTILES IN ACCESSORIES: GENERIC AND OTHER MANUFACTURED FIBERS DEFINED: ELASTOMERS) to provide the control of a lightweight girdle. **Bodyshaper pantyhose** are control pantyhose with the control section extending to cover the thighs in addition to the abdomen and the hips. In all-nude pantyhose, a finger band, which is a reinforcement just under the waistband, protects the hose against fingernail punctures.

Women's stockings also may have such features as resistance to running. **Proportioned hose** are designed to fit different types of legs, e.g., extra long, full, above-the-knee, long, short, and average. For wear with various types of shoes, women may use **sandalfoot hose,** hosiery with no reinforcement at the toe. These are popular for wearing with open-toed shoes or sandals. There are also **nude heel stockings** or pantyhose that have no reinforcement at the heel so they can be worn with backless or sling-back shoes.

In nylon stockings or pantyhose, size is generally indicated on a chart on the package and may vary from one brand to another. These sizes are generally based on the weight of the customer.

STOCKINGS

Socks may be divided into categories according to their use. The categories that have been identified by the *The Hosiery Association* are:

everyday comfort socks Casual socks for daily wear.

performance socks Those socks with special construction or finishes that make them particularly suitable for athletic activity.

coordinate socks Fashionable socks for use with more dressy clothing.

dress or novelty socks Ornamented or decorated socks intended for special occasion use. Often worn by children, especially if they have cartoon characters depicted on them.

Dress stockings for men are frequently made from nylon or other manufactured fibers, or blends with natural fibers. Usually conservative in design and color, these stockings are frequently chosen to blend with the shoe and trouser colors. The stockings intended for use in sports and casual wear are more likely to be made from cotton or cotton blends that absorb moisture and are therefore more comfortable when feet are hot and perspiring. Manufactured fibers such as acrylic or polypropylene that carry moisture away from the foot are also used. Often sports stockings are white, as fabrics that have been dyed to bright colors are less absorbent.

Stockings are available in a variety of different lengths. These are:

socklet Very low-cut socks, usually light-weight and not visible above pumps or other shoes, styled to keep feet comfortable while maintaining bare-leg look in summer. PEDS® (see under TYPES OF HOSIERY DEFINED) is a trademark for the first widely available socklet made in a number of fibers and styles. These are also called *"no-shoe" socks.*

footsock/footie Sock that ends below the ankle bone. When these socks have a pompom sewn on at the back, they may be called **poms.**

ankle sock Short sock reaching only to the ankle that may be worn turned down or have elastic top on the cuff. Also called *anklet.*

crew sock Heavy sock extending to lower calf with foot knitted in plain stitch, the upper part with rib stitch. Originally white and worn for rowing and other sports. Now made in colors, especially for men and boys. Also known as *work socks* and *boot socks.*

half-hose Standard-length stocking for men that ends halfway between the ankle and the knee.

knee-hi sock Sock that reaches to below the knee.

over-the-knee sock Sock or stocking with an elastic top that reaches above the knee. This elastic top holds up the stocking without a garter.

tube sock Calf or knee-length sock made of stretch yarn that does not have a knitted-in heel or toe.

Socks and stockings carry size numbers that are quite different from those of shoes. Generally hosiery has enough stretch that sizes are given as a range. Women's size 9–11, for example, would be a "medium" size, equivalent to a shoe size of 4.5 to 10.5. Large is 11–12.5 (shoe size 10–13). Men's medium is 10–13 (shoe size 6–12) and large would be 12–16 (shoe size 11–18).

TYPES OF HOSIERY DEFINED

all-in-one pantyhose See ANATOMY OF HOSIERY: WOMEN'S NYLON HOSIERY: PANTYHOSE.

all-sheer pantyhose Sheer nylon pantyhose made with no reinforcements. Also called *sheer pantyhose*.

anklet See ANATOMY OF HOSIERY: STOCKINGS: ANKLE SOCK.

anti-embolism stocking A stocking specially constructed with graduated compression that aids blood flow and prevents blood clots from forming. Also called *surgical stockings*.

argyle socks Sock knitted in a diamond pattern of several colors by hand or on a JACQUARD LOOM (see under TEXTILES IN ACCESSORIES: DIFFERENT TYPES OF FABRIC STRUCTURES: WOVEN FABRICS). Heel, toe, and top areas are of solid color while the other part is of a multicolored, diamond-patterned plaid. *Der.* Tartan of Duke of Argyle and Clan Campbell of Argyll, a county in West Scotland. Also spelled *argyll, argyl*.

Art Deco hose Hose printed with geometric designs derived from Art Deco styles, which underwent a revival in the late 1960s. *Der.* French, *art decoratif*, "decorative art."

Art Nouveau hose Stylized single or multiple printed designs placed on the calf or climbing the leg, usually on opaque or colored hose, based on Art Nouveau designs. An innovation of the late 1960s. *Der.* French, "new art."

astrolegs hose Hose imprinted with signs of the zodiac, introduced in the late 1960s.

athletic sock See TYPES OF HOSIERY DEFINED: SWEATSOCK.

bed sock Knit sock worn when sleeping to keep foot warm. Often hand-knit in a variety of fancy stitches. Also called *foot warmer*.

bikini pantyhose Pantyhose with low-slung top for wear with bare-midriff dresses, hip-hugger skirts, or low-slung pants.

blazer sock Boys' and girls' socks decorated with bands of color. Similar in effect to competitive stripes on knit shirts.

bobby sock Ankle sock, usually with turned-down cuff, worn by children and so universally popular with female teenagers during 1940s and 1950s that young girls were called "bobby soxers."

bodyshaper pantyhose See ANATOMY OF HOSIERY: WOMEN'S NYLON HOSIERY: PANTYHOSE.

checkerboard hose Hose knitted in a checked design with some squares sheer and some opaque, or knitted in two colors.

clocked hose Hose or stockings with designs running partway up the sides of the legs. Designs may be knitted in or embroidered on after hose are knitted.

clocked hose

control pantyhose See ANATOMY OF HOSIERY: WOMEN'S NYLON HOSIERY: PANTYHOSE.

Courrèges flower sock See TYPES OF HOSIERY DEFINED: KNEE-HI SOCK.

cushion-sole sock Sock worn for active sports knit with a special sole that keeps the foot from blistering—often a layer of cotton and stretch-nylon terry cloth. Frequently given a special finish to help protect the foot from fungus, bacteria, and odor.

detachable pantyhose Three-piece pantyhose made with patented bands on panties to attach replacement stockings.

dress sock Man's sock in lightweight, silky type, nonbulky yarns in conservative colors.

electric sock Heavyweight knee-high sock, usually made of a combination of fibers, with a specially designed heating element operated by a battery held on by strap around the leg. Worn by spectators at winter sports events. Trademarked by Timely Products Corp. and called *Lectra-Sox.®*

English rib sock Man's sock knit with a wide rib or wale and a narrow depression between the wales (raised areas).

fancies Men's socks in multicolor designs.

fishnet hose Openwork hose in a diamond-shaped pattern.

flat-knit hose See TYPES OF HOSIERY DEFINED: FULL-FASHIONED HOSE.

foot warmers See TYPES OF HOSIERY DEFINED: BED SOCK.

full-fashioned hose Hose knit in flat pieces and seamed up the back, leaving fashion marks where knitting is increased or decreased. Also called *flat-knit hose*.

garter belt hose Hose attached to two elastic strips that connect at waistline to an elastic band around waist.

glitter hose Hose made of shiny yarn—some are made with metallic yarn that reflects silver, gold, and copper tones. Also called *glimmer, silver, gold,* or *metallic hose.*

gold hose See TYPES OF HOSIERY DEFINED: GLITTER HOSE.

gym sock See TYPES OF HOSIERY DEFINED: SWEATSOCK.

jacquard hose (ja-kard′) Hosiery knitted on a jacquard knitting machine, which permits much variation in colors and patterns. Argyle and herringbone designs would be examples of jacquard patterns.

jeweled pantyhose Sheer pantyhose with embroidery at ankle trimmed with rhinestones.

knee hi sock Sock ending just below the knee. Became very fashionable when featured by the French couturier Courrèges in his collection in 1965. In 1967, he introduced a variation called the **Courrèges flower sock** (coor-rej′), which was a dainty feminine sock coming to several inches below the knee usually styled in white with lacy top, embroidered with flowers. Now available in many colors, styles, and fabrics. Also called *knee sock, trouser sock.*

knee sock See TYPES OF HOSIERY DEFINED: KNEE-HI SOCKS.

lace hose Knitted hose in lacelike patterns.

lace pantyhose Pantyhose made of patterned stretch lace in openwork styles.

legwarmer Knitted covering for legs extending from the ankle to the knee or above. Originally worn by ballet and toe dancers when exercising and subsequently became a fashion item.

leg warmers

lisle hosiery (lyle) Socks and hose made of cotton LISLE YARN (see under TEXTILES IN ACCESSORIES: HOW YARNS MAY BE IMPORTANT: TYPES OF YARN DEFINED), smooth, lustrous cotton yarn. Nearly as fine as silk, usually white, brown, or black, lisle hosiery was worn by men, women, and children throughout 19th and early 20th c. until replaced by silk in 1920s and nylon in 1940s. Revived in the 1960s when longer opaque socks were popular. See ANATOMY OF HOSIERY:

WOMEN'S NYLON HOSIERY: OPAQUE HOSE. *Der.* Early spelling of Lille, France.

mesh hose Nylon hose knit with a milanese stitch, forming tiny diamond designs that make hose run-resistant.

metallic hose See TYPES OF HOSIERY DEFINED: GLITTER HOSE.

mini-pane hose See TYPES OF HOSIERY DEFINED: WINDOWPANE HOSE.

mock seam Hosiery industry term for seam sewed into circular-knit hose to give appearance of FULL-FASHIONED HOSE (see under TYPES OF HOSIERY DEFINED).

neats Solid color socks ornamented with small, evenly spaced designs such as dots.

neon sock Ankle- or knee-length sock styled with ribbed tops in extremely bright colors of 100% nylon.

novelties Women's hosiery that has unusual patterns, designs, or coloring.

patterned hose Hosiery woven in a design, usually on a Jacquard knitting machine, e.g., POINT D'ESPRIT, CHECKERBOARD, and ARGYLE hose. See under TYPES OF HOSIERY DEFINED.

Peds® Registered trademark of American Corporation for a broad range of hosiery products of varying types and uses. Also see ANATOMY OF HOSIERY: STOCKINGS: SOCKLET.

point d'esprit hose (pwan des-pree′) Netlike machine-manufactured hose of cotton or NYLON (see under TEXTILES IN ACCESSORIES: FIBERS AND YARNS: THE BUILDING BLOCKS OF FABRIC: GENERIC AND OTHER MANUFACTURED FIBERS DEFINED) with some of the holes made solid to form a decorative pattern.

poms See ANATOMY OF HOSIERY: STOCKINGS: FOOTSOCK.

quarter socks Sock, shorter than ankle length, made of ACRYLIC and NYLON with colored terry knit top in colors. See under TEXTILES IN ACCESSORIES: FIBERS AND YARNS: THE BUILDING BLOCKS OF FABRIC: GENERIC AND OTHER MANUFACTURED FIBERS DEFINED.

replaceable legs Waist-length garment in which one or both legs can be replaced. Made either as a separate panty to which legs attach at the bottom or as two separate legs, each with a half panty and a full waistband.

ribbed hose   Textured hose knit with vertical wales.

run resistant   Hosiery and knit term for stitches with locked or displaced loops that inhibit runs, but do not prevent them.

sandalfoot hose   Hosiery with no reinforcement at the toe. Popular for wearing with open-toed shoes or sandals.

sanitary sock   An athletic sock, usually white, worn under a stirrup pants or hose as part of an athletic uniform.

seamed hose   Full-fashioned hose with a seam up the back, originally made by the flat-knit process and sewed together. Worn until the 1960s when textured yarns were invented with more "stretch," making it possible to make well-fitting hose without the seam. By 1968, very few seamed hose were sold. In 1970s, circular knits with black lines up the back were made in imitation.

seamed pantyhose   Conventional pantyhose with black seam up the back.

seamless hose   Circular-knit hose without seam in back.

sheer hose   See WOMEN'S NYLON HOSIERY.

sheer pantyhose   See TYPES OF HOSIERY DEFINED: ALL-SHEER PANTYHOSE.

silver hose   See TYPES OF HOSIERY DEFINED: GLITTER HOSE.

slipper sock   Crocheted or knit sock attached to soft, moccasin-type sole.

slouch sock   Anklet with shirred tricolor top, made of acrylic and stretch nylon, designed to be pushed down and gathered around the ankle.

sneaker sock   Type of SOCKLET (see under ANATOMY OF HOSIERY: STOCKINGS) that is shaped higher in front to conform to laced instep of the sneakers. Worn instead of socks for the bare-legged look.

stay-up hose   Regular hose knitted with a special top that holds the hose up without garters. Also called *stretch top*.

stirrup hose   Hosiery in which the foot portion is fashioned without a heel or toe but has a strap that fits under the instep of the foot. Often this construction is part of an athletic uniform.

stretch hose   Hosiery made with textured nylon stretch yarns. When such hose are not on the leg, they look very small.

stretch socks   Socks knitted with textured yarns. Made so flexible that one size usually fits any size foot. Also made for men, women, and children.

support legwear   Hosiery for men or women knitted of stretch NYLON combined with SPANDEX yarns to provide support to the muscles and veins of the legs (see under TEXTILES IN ACCESSORIES: FIBERS AND YARNS: THE BUILDING BLOCKS OF FABRIC: GENERIC AND OTHER MANUFACTURED FIBERS DEFINED). These fabrics keep pressure on the blood vessels so they will not dilate. This improves the circulation and prevents leg fatigue. They are made as hose and pantyhose for women and socks or stockings for men.

surgical stocking   See TYPES OF HOSIERY DEFINED: ANTI-EMBOLISM STOCKING.

sweatsock   Sock made of combination of fibers (e.g., wool, acrylic, cotton, sometimes with cushioned sole). When this type of sock was first worn, it was always white and made of coarse cotton yarns that stretched out of shape easily. The cotton versions were known as **gym socks**, which were worn instead of wool socks for active sports and gym classes because of their washability. Blends now make these socks more washable and shape retentive. Usually they have a ribbed top and plain foot. Also called *athletic sock*.

tattoo pantyhose   Very sheer pantyhose with legs painted in twining floral designs that appear at a distance to be tattooed on the leg.

textured hose   Any style of hose patterned with thick and thin sections, e.g., lace, striped, or windowpane hose.

thermal sock   Heavy boot-length sock worn for winter activities; made of fibers with good insulating qualities.

tights   Knitted pants and stockings in one piece usually made of opaque textured yarns. Worn originally by athletes and dancers, later worn by children and now an alternative to pantyhose.

tights

toelet   Hosiery designed to cover only the toe portion of the foot. Worn with heelless shoes such as mules or clogs.

trouser sock   See ANATOMY OF HOSIERY: STOCKINGS: KNEE-HI SOCK.

ultra-sheer pantyhose   See under ANATOMY OF HOSIERY: WOMEN'S NYLON HOSIERY.

U seams Pantyhose in which one leg is sewn to the other with a continuous U-shaped seam, As a result, they have no crotch.

windowpane hose Textured hose made in geometric squares in thin and thick sections. Heavier part looks like the frame of the window, sheerer section looks like the glass. **Mini-pane** hose have smaller squares. Made in white, black, and all colors, e.g., shocking pink, chartreuse, and orange.

JEWELRY

HISTORY AND SIGNIFICANCE OF JEWELRY TO FASHION

Jewelry is a purely decorative accessory made of material considered to be precious or aesthetically pleasing. Archeological remains indicate that such materials as shells, worked bone or ivory, and amber or shiny rocks were made into jewelry in prehistoric times. As technological skills developed and new materials were discovered, metals and gems were also used (see COMPONENTS OF ACCESSORIES: OTHER MATERIALS USED IN ACCESSORIES and GEMS, GEMCUTS, AND SETTINGS).

The use of expensive materials, such as gold and silver, and gems, such as diamonds and rubies, increase the value of jewelry. Artists often design jewelry, and skilled craftsmen create the pieces. In the 19th c., only the wealthy could afford fine jewelry. After the Industrial Revolution, when mechanized equipment for making less-costly jewelry from inexpensive materials was available, men and women of more modest means were also able to purchase and wear jewelry. In the 20th c., jewelry made of less precious materials became known as **costume jewelry.** Its popularity is credited to French couturière Gabrielle Chanel, who in the 1920s introduced imitation pearls, emeralds, and rubies—copies of her own real jewels—for daytime wear. In the second half of the century, new terms were introduced to describe costume jewelry. **Fashion jewelry** is a term coined in the 1980s for high-quality, expensive costume jewelry. **Faux** (foh) **jewels** are fashion jewelry that is obviously fake. Some of the materials used in costume, fashion, and faux jewelry include **paste,** which is made of highly reflective transparent types of flint glass faceted or molded to make imitation gems. One variety called **strass,** named for Josef Strasser, a German jeweler, is used in making replicas of expensive jewelry.

By contrast, **fine jewelry** is made only from precious metals and precious and semiprecious stones. **Bridge jewelry** is an umbrella term applied to several types of jewelry including those made from silver, gold (14K, 12K, 10K), and from less-expensive stones. It is jewelry designed by artists using a variety of materials.

Jewelry styles are subject to changes in fashion. Many people purchase antique or collectable jewelry not only because they hope that its value will appreciate, but also because of its beauty. Experts can establish the date of an item of jewelry by examining the materials used, the cut of the stones, the settings used, and the overall design.

The individual items of jewelry that are most likely to be worn are:

brooch or **pin**   Ornamental jewelry made with a pin fastener on the back that may have a safety catch. Made in all types of materials—e.g., gold, silver, plated metals—brooches are frequently set with gems or imitation stones.

ring   Decorative jewelry worn on the finger, sometimes on the thumb, and infrequently on one of the toes. Before the mid-1960s, rings were worn on the third finger and the little finger. After this time, it was fashionable to wear rings on any of the fingers. This was a revival of styles of the 16th c., when many rings were worn and two rings were sometimes worn on the same finger.

necklace   Decorative accessory worn around the neck. Frequently made of beads or a chain, and sometimes of real or imitation gems set in gold, silver, or other metals, necklaces can be made from an enormous variety of materials. An expensive necklace is frequently a status symbol.

bracelet Decorative band or circlet worn on the arm, wrist, or ankle as an ornament. Bracelets can be made of metal, chains, plastic, wood, leather, textiles, or Lucite, either in one piece or in links.

earring Decorative jewelry accessory worn on the ear. The ear may be pierced and small wires or posts inserted. For unpierced ears, earrings are held in place with SCREW or CLIP-BACKS (see under TYPES OF JEWELRY DEFINED: EARRINGS). From the 17th c. to the 1980s, men rarely wore earrings, but over the last two decades the fashion of earrings for men returned. In the early 1980s, double and triple ear piercing became a fashion with two and three sets of earrings being worn at the same time on either one or both ears.

parure (pah-roor´) Matched set of jewelry that may consist of a necklace, earrings, pin, or bracelet.

Some jewelry is attached to garments, some wraps around arms, legs, fingers, or necks. And some jewelry is attached by **body piercing**. This requires making a hole at some place in the body through which an item of jewelry can be fastened. Earlobes have long been pierced for the insertion of earrings. In the late 1990s, a fashion for piercing almost any part of the body spread, especially among young people. The jewelry for insertion in these openings is called **body jewelry**.

ANATOMY OF JEWELRY

For more detailed descriptions of the components of jewelry, see the discussion under GEMS, GEM CUTS, AND SETTINGS. As items of jewelry even within the same grouping can differ widely, see the definitions of TYPES OF JEWELRY given below for more detailed description of the structure of specific styles.

Precious metals are often used in making jewelry. Among the treatments given to these materials in order to enhance their attractiveness are:

chasing Fine lines engraved on metals.

damascening (dam´-ah-sehn-ing) Engraving steel, bronze, or iron and filling up the incision with gold or silver wire. An inferior style of damascening can be made by etching the pattern on steel then depositing gold or silver in the engraved lines electronically. *Der.* Named for Damascus, where the technique was formerly used.

filigree (fill´-ee-gree) Ornamental metal work for jewelry or accessories made of fine silver, gold, or copper wire intricately arranged—or similar pierced metal openwork.

gold-filled Gold of 10 to 22 karats fused to a base metal, e.g., nickel, silver, or brass. The layer of gold should weigh at least one-twentieth of the weight of the entire metal used. What one-tenth 18K means is that the gold used is 18 karat and that it represents one-tenth of the weight of the metal.

gold-plated Describing jewelry with a thin surface of gold electrolytically plated to a base metal.

gold-washed Describing jewelry with a thin coating of gold applied to a base metal by dipping or washing it in a solution of gold.

plated As applied to jewelry a thin film of precious metal applied to an inexpensive base metal—usually by electrolysis.

washed gold Thin coating of gold applied to a base metal by dipping or washing it in a solution of gold salts.

TYPES OF JEWELRY DEFINED

BROOCHES OR PINS

bar pin Long narrow pin secured by back fastener the same length as the pin. Fashionable since early 20th c.

bar drop pin Long narrow pin made with attached pendants.

chatelaine (shat-len´) Pin worn on the lapel or chest with hook on back to secure a watch, or two decorative pins joined by a chain. Also called *fob pin*. *Der.* Keys worn at the waist on a chain by medieval mistress of the castle or "chatelaine."

chatelaine

collar pin Pin that is placed through holes embroidered into the points of shirt collars.

duet pins   Two pins worn together as a set.

fob pin   See TYPES OF JEWELRY DEFINED: BROOCHES OR PINS: CHATELAINE.

fraternity pin   Pin selected and specially made for a high school or college fraternity group. Usually contains the Greek letters of the fraternity in gold on an onyx background. Tiny pearls may be mounted around the edge. Sometimes a small guard chain is attached with individual symbol.

friendship pin   Tiny colored beads threaded on small safety pin and worn fastened to shoelaces. Exchanged as tokens of friendship or love, colors of the beads have various meanings (e.g., red, best friend; pink, sweetheart; green, enemy; purple, good friend; yellow, pal; blue, going steady). A school fad of the 1980s.

kilt pin   Pin that is shaped like a safety pin and worn on the front of a kilt skirt.

lapel pin   Woman's pin originally worn on the lapel of a suit. Almost all medium-sized pins are now called lapel pins.

necktie pin   See TYPES OF JEWELRY DEFINED: BROOCHES OR PINS: STICKPIN.

pendant pin   Pin with a clasp at back and a hook at center top so it can be worn on a chain, cord, etc., as a necklace or a pin.

safety pin   An item of jewelry shaped like a utilitarian safety pin that may have beads hanging suspended from the long bar or decorating the head.

scarf pin   See TYPES OF JEWELRY DEFINED: BROOCHES OR PINS: STICKPIN.

sorority pin   Similar to FRATERNITY PIN (see under TYPES OF JEWELRY DEFINED: BROOCHES OR PINS), but worn by high-school and college girls as an emblem of their club or sorority.

stickpin   **1.** Straight stiletto-type pin with an ornamental top worn by a man to secure a four-in-hand necktie or ascot. Popular from late 19th c. to 1930s. Now *tie tacks* are more usually worn. Also called *scarf pin* and *tie pin*. **2.** Same type of pin styled as a LAPEL PIN for women (see under TYPES OF JEWELRY DEFINED: BROOCHES OR PINS).

stickpin #1

tie pin   See TYPES OF JEWELRY DEFINED: BROOCHES OR PINS: STICKPIN.

RINGS

adjustable ring   Ring made with band with overlapping ends so that it can be fitted to any finger size. Usually an inexpensive ring.

ankh ring   (angk)   Gold or gold-finished ring made in the shape of the ankh, the ancient Egyptian symbol of life—a cross with a loop at the top.

birthstone ring   Ring set with a stone representing the birth month of the wearer, e.g., an amethyst for February. Also see GEMS, GEM CUTS, AND SETTINGS: TYPES OF GEMS DEFINED: BIRTHSTONE.

bracelet ring   See TYPES OF JEWELRY DEFINED: BRACELETS: SLAVE BRACELET.

bridal set   Matching engagement ring and wedding band.

class ring   High school or college ring of individual design for each school with class year included. Sometimes uses large stones, crests, or individual initials. Also called a *school ring.*

cluster ring   Type of ring set with many large and small stones grouped together. Sometimes made of precious stones, frequently diamonds.

cocktail ring   Large showy ring, either a piece of costume jewelry or fine jewelry, set with precious or semiprecious stones. Sometimes called *dinner ring.*

damascene ring   (dam′-ah-sehn)   Blackened metal inlaid with fine gold-tone wire to form a delicate design.

Decatur ring   Gold band, similar to a wedding ring, with two inset bands of black enamel. Copied from ring given to Stephen Decatur, American naval officer, by Lieutenant Richard Somers in 1804 as a friendship ring. Original ring is in the Smithsonian Institution, Washington, D.C.

dinner ring   See TYPES OF JEWELRY DEFINED: RINGS: COCKTAIL RING.

dome ring   Ring with a high rounded top, similar to a dome, usually set with many stones or made of metal.

engagement ring   Ring given to a woman by a man signifying that they plan to be married—for many years a diamond SOLITAIRE (see under TYPES OF JEWELRY DEFINED: RINGS)—now most any type of ring.

eternity ring   Full or half circlet of diamonds, rubies, or sapphires set in a narrow band of gold or platinum, sometimes given by husband to wife as a pledge of love on a special occasion (e.g., birth of a child or wedding anniversary). This tradition started in England in 1930s.

family ring Rings for all members of the family (i.e., father, mother, daughter, grandmother, etc.). Rings are of various sizes and shapes, but all incorporate several birthstones representing birthdays of various members of the family.

filigree ring (fill′-ee-gree) Gold or silver wire twisted in a lacy intricate pattern to make a ring, usually protruding upward to make a dome.

fraternal ring Emblematic ring only used by members of fraternal organizations (e.g., Masons, Elks, and Knights of Columbus). Frequently made of gold or silver with an onyx setting on which symbols of the organization are placed in gold, silver, and gems.

free-form ring Contemporary ring that may be almost any shape other than the conventional round ring. Frequently made of a long piece of metal shaped to the finger but having the two ends lapped over each other, often made with gemstones at the ends. *Der.* From free-form sculpture.

friendship ring An older term for a simple metal ring exchanged by good friends and worn for sentimental value. Formerly called a TALISMAN RING (see under TYPES OF JEWELRY DEFINED: RINGS.

gemel ring A ring fashionable in the Middle Ages, it was really two identical rings joined together and worn together. Popular style had clasped hands on the front. The rings were traditionally separated at betrothal—the man and woman each wearing one. After marriage the rings were joined together and worn by the woman. Later, triple and quadruple rings of this style were worn. Revived in the mid-1980s. *Der.* From the Italian word *gemelli,* or Latin, *gemini,* "twins."

initial ring See TYPES OF JEWELRY DEFINED: RINGS: SIGNET RING.

nugget ring Ring with stone made from a piece of metal in its natural shape (e.g., a gold nugget).

peace ring Simple ring designed of metal with "peace symbol" consisting of a circle intersected with straight bar down the center and inverted Y-shaped bars to the outer edge.

perfume ring Large ring that is hinged under the stone so that solid perfume may be placed inside.

poison ring Novelty item sometimes used to contain perfume, similar to a ring worn from Roman period through the 17th c. that was designed to hold a dose of poison. Cesare Borgia's ring, dated 1503 and still in existence, has a small sliding panel which opened into a small cavity in which poison was placed.

posy/poesy ring Plain gold band, sometimes with small decorative design in center, given as a love token. Inside was inscribed "let love endure" or "faithful and true." Popular in the 16th c., revived in the 1980s.

rolling ring Bands of three circlets of gold in different colors—rose, yellow, and white—interlocked to make a ring. First designed and made by Cartier since the 1920s. Also made with six interlocking circles.

school ring See TYPES OF JEWELRY DEFINED: RINGS: CLASS RING.

serpent ring Ring shaped like snake curled around the finger.

signet ring Ring with large, flat stone cut with an engraved design (see GEMS, GEM CUTS, AND SETTINGS: ANATOMY OF GEM CUTS: INTAGLIO). Formerly used to make an impression in sealing wax to seal letters.

solitaire Ring set with a single stone, frequently a diamond, sometimes a pearl or another gem.

solitaire

spoon ring The handle of a small sterling silver spoon molded to wrap around the finger to form a ring.

talisman ring (tahl′-iss-mahn) "Charm" ring worn in Ancient Greece and the Middle Ages to ensure the wearer of good health, the strength of ten, love, wealth, and happiness. Worn in recent times as a pledge of friendship. Also see TYPES OF JEWELRY DEFINED: RINGS: FRIENDSHIP RING.

toe ring Any ring worn on one of the toes, usually the big toe. In 1967, plastic, papier-mâché, or felt rings were popular.

wedding band/wedding ring Used in wedding ceremony and traditionally a band of gold in any of various widths worn by both men and women on the third finger of the left hand.

wedding trio Woman's engagement ring and wedding band—plus men's wedding band, similarly styled and sold together. Also see TYPES OF JEWELRY DEFINED: RINGS: BRIDAL SET.

Zuni snake eye ring Sterling silver ring set with 25 turquoise stones, mounted 5 to a row in 5 rows, alternating with rounded silver beads. Copied from ring in the Smithsonian Institution. *Der.* Originally made by Zuni, Native Americans of the southwestern United States.

NECKLACES

Afro choker Necklace made of strand of springy metal wound around the neck many times, *Der.* Copied from necklaces worn by Ubangi tribe in Africa. Also called *Ubangi necklace.*

American Indian necklace **1.** Long, flat necklace made with tiny glass beads of various colors, usually woven on small loom. **2.** Necklace of tiny colored beads worked in rope effect with Native American motif as center pendant, made by Native Americans.

bayadere Seed pearl necklace made up of multiple strands twisted together.

beaded necklace See TYPES OF JEWELRY DEFINED: NECKLACES: AMERICAN INDIAN NECKLACE.

beggar beads Hand-carved ornamental gemstones in elongated shape strung on necklace between gold beads. Stones include MOSS AGATES, green JASPERS, BLOODSTONES, brown or orange CARNELIANS, and other nonprecious stones (see specific stones under GEMS, GEM CUTS, AND SETTINGS: TYPES OF GEMS DEFINED). Originally worn in India for good luck.

bib necklace Necklace fitting close to base of neck and extending in the shape of a child's bib. Sometimes made of linked metal, looking like a short triangular scarf, sometimes made of several irregular strands of beads or chains arranged like a fringe.

bib necklace

birthstone necklace **1.** Medium-length fine-linked chain with individualized birthstones in the form of a bead placed about every three to four inches. Also see TYPES OF JEWELRY DEFINED: NECKLACES: DIAMONDS BY THE YARD. **2.** A short fine-linked chain with an attached pendant containing a colored gem representing an individual birthstone. Also see GEMS, GEM CUTS, AND SETTINGS: TYPES OF GEMS DEFINED: BIRTHSTONE.

byzance (bi-zance′) Beads alternating with chain in long necklace with dangling ends similar to a rosary. Created by Christian de Gasperi (nephew of former prime minister of Italy) and given this name by Pierre Cardin in 1968 when it became popular at the Riviera resort of St. Tropez, France.

chain necklace Necklace consisting of links of metal sometimes interspersed with gems or imitation stones. May be short or long and looped around neck several times. Worn at intervals since 16th c. and very popular during the late 1960s and 1980s.

charm necklace **1.** Gold- or silver-toned chain worn around the neck with a cluster of metal objects attached in center front (e.g., hearts, initials, animals, sports motifs, some engraved with slogans or names). **2.** Young girls' plastic chain necklace with dangling miniature plastic replicas of keys, telephones, tennis rackets, roller skates, pencils, and other ornaments.

choker Necklace fitting snugly around base of neck, may be one or more strands of beads, a suede or ribbon band, or a dog collar.

choker

chute A single strand of pearls.

cloisonné necklace **1.** A medallion made of brass enameled with luminous colors and fired. Usually attached to a braided cord of silk, nylon, or polyester with an additional cord pendant hanging from base of medallion. **2.** Necklace of beads with some of the beads being made in the cloisonné manner.

coin necklace Antique coin (e.g., a five-dollar gold piece, a silver dollar, an Indian head penny, or a buffalo nickel) worn on a chain around the neck, sometimes enhanced by a circlet of gold, silver, or other metal around edge.

collar necklace **1.** Necklace shaped and fitted to neck like a collar. Frequently of metal. **2.** Tiny beads interlaced to form a separate collar.

diamond necklace **1.** Any necklace made of genuine diamonds. May be single or large diamonds set in PAVÉ fashion (see under GEMS, GEMCUTS, AND SETTINGS: ANATOMY OF GEM SETTINGS) in a band of precious metal, or diamonds set in precious metals and mounted in medallions linked together with chains of the same metal. **2.** Single large diamond suspended from a chain.

diamonds by the yard   Chain of 18K gold interspersed with a diamond at intervals, sold by the yard. Worn wrapped around the neck, wrist, or waist. Introduced in 1974 by Elsa Peretti of Tiffany's, New York City. Also made from rubies, emeralds, or sapphires.

dog collar   **1.** Wide CHOKER (see under TYPES OF JEWELRY DEFINED: NECKLACES), similar to a dog's collar, often consisting of pearls or of a band of metal set with diamonds or rhinestones. Introduced in early 20th c., popular in 1930s, and again in 1960s, at which time it was also called *throat belt.* **2.** Band of colored suede or leather worn tightly around neck.

floater necklace   Necklace of beads or pearls strung on a cord that is almost invisible, such as nylon fishing line, so that the beads seem to "float" on the skin of the wearer. Also called *invisible necklace.*

hippie beads   Beads adopted by hippies, a group of young people in the United States in the mid-1960s. For necklaces, usually small beads worn chest-length by both sexes. Influenced conventional men to adopt the fashion of wearing chains or medallion necklaces. Also called *love beads.*

hippie beads

lampshade beads   Short lengths of tiny strung beads, hung in a fringe from a ribbon tied close to neck, worn in early 1970s. *Der.* Beaded fringe on lampshades popular in late Victorian era and 1920s.

lariat necklace   **1.** Long strand of beads or metal, sometimes ending in tassels, that is not fastened by a clasp. Worn looped into a knot or uses a slide so that the two ends hang free. **2.** Man's short necklace (or tie) usually made of leather that has a silver slide and two ends tipped with silver hanging free.

lavaliere (lav-al-yer´)   Pendant, sometimes set with precious stones, worn as a necklace on a fine chain. *Der.* Named after Louise de la Baume Le Blanc La Vallière, mistress of Louis XIV of France.

locket   Chain necklace with a gold or silver disk that opens to reveal picture of loved one or lock of hair. Very popular from mid-19th to early 20th c. and still worn, especially by children.

love beads   See TYPES OF JEWELRY DEFINED: NECKLACES: HIPPIE BEADS.

matinee-length necklace   Bead necklace, usually of pearls or simulated pearls, 30″ to 35″ long.

medallion necklace   Heavy chain necklace with large disk as a pendant, worn by women during various eras and introduced for men in late 1960s.

mizpah medallion necklace (miz´-pah)   Large medallion with a quotation from Genesis cut in half in zigzag fashion to form "his" and "hers" medals worn on a chain.

neck ring   Single narrow band of springy metal worn as choker, sometimes with dangling ornament.

opera-length necklace   Necklace of beads, usually of pearls or simulated pearls, 48″ to 120″ long, usually worn wrapped twice around the neck. Also see NECKLACES: ROPE NECKLACE.

pearl beads   PEARLS (see GEMS, GEM CUTS, AND SETTINGS: ANATOMY OF GEMS: PEARLS) all of one size or graduated in size. Usually strung on thread, often with a knot after each bead, made in a variety of lengths and worn in single strand or several strands. A classic fashion for many centuries.

pendant necklace   Ornament such as a locket, medallion, or single jewel suspended around neck from a chain, thong, or cord.

rope necklace   Extra-long beaded necklace, usually of pearls, that may be wrapped around neck several times or worn long and knotted. Very popular in 1920s and worn continuously since then.

sautoir (so-twar´)   Pendant-type necklace with a dangling piece in front that may appear to be fringed at base. *Der.* French, woman's watch chain or a medal of honor worn around the neck.

seed bead necklace   Necklace in various styles that is made from very small beads.

squash blossom necklace   Traditional necklace made of tiny pieces of turquoise set in sterling silver. Stones are mounted in a manner to imitate flowers with many petals. *Der.* Handcrafted by Zuni Native Americans of the southwestern United States. Some necklaces are in

squash blossom necklace

the collections of the Museum of Natural History and the Smithsonian Institution.

tassel necklace Long linked chain necklace with cluster of as many as twelve short chains forming a tassel at the end.

throat belt See TYPES OF JEWELRY DEFINED: NECKLACES: DOG COLLAR.

torsade Several strands of pearls, chains, or beads twisted together to form a single necklace.

Ubangi necklace See TYPES OF JEWELRY DEFINED: NECKLACES: AFRO CHOKER.

utchat Ancient Egyptian necklace with a depiction of the sacred eye as a pendant. Sometimes imitated in contemporary jewelry based on ancient forms.

zodiac necklace Any necklace, usually of the pendant type, with medallion engraved with a personal sign of the zodiac.

BRACELETS

ankle bracelet Ornament worn around the ankle; may be a chain or I.D. bracelet. Worn in Eastern countries and Egypt since earliest times. Also called *anklet*.

ankle bracelet

anklet See TYPES OF JEWELRY DEFINED: BRACELETS: ANKLE BRACELET.

armband Bracelet for the upper arm frequently made of a band of metal. Fashionable in matching sets with anklets in ancient Egypt and reintroduced in 1969.

baby bracelet Tiny beads with letters on them. Originally used in hospitals to spell out the name of the newborn child on a bracelet. Now used for personalized bracelets, barrettes, and necklaces.

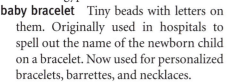
armband and bangles

bangle bracelet Narrow, round, rigid bracelet of metal, plastic, wood, or other material, worn singly or several at a time. Popular since 1900s and originally worn in sets that jingled when the arm moved. Also called *hoop bracelet*. Shown at TYPES OF JEWELRY DEFINED: BRACELETS: ARMBAND.

boot bracelet Linked bracelet, sometimes with dangling charms, worn either around the ankle or calf of the boot.

bubble bracelet Oversized spherical beads, often hollow, used for bracelets.

bugle bracelet Long tubular-shaped glass beads, often black, white, or silver, that are made into bracelets.

chain bracelet One or more chains of varying width worn on the wrist.

charm bracelet A metal (often gold or silver) chain bracelet on which one or more matching metal charms, e.g., disks, zodiac signs, or hearts—are hung often to commemorate personal events.

charm bracelet

coiled bracelet Bracelet made from a long gold- or silver-tone finished strip of metal curled like a spring to fit the arm.

cuff bracelet Oval-shaped rigid bracelet styled with opening in back. May be wide or narrow and usually made of metal.

diamond bracelet Bracelet made of expensive metals, e.g., gold or platinum, set with many small faceted diamonds and other precious gems. Also worn as watch bracelet with diamond watch.

elastic bracelet Bracelet made of beads or sectional motifs of various types strung on elastic that slips over the hand.

eternity bracelet See TYPES OF JEWELRY DEFINED: BRACELETS: SLAVE BRACELET.

expandable bracelet Spring-link metal bracelet that stretches and needs no clasp. Since 1940s frequently used as watch bracelet.

friendship bracelet See TYPES OF JEWELRY DEFINED: BRACELETS: WOVEN FRIENDSHIP BRACELET.

hinged bracelet Any bracelet with a hinge allowing it to open wide for removal.

hoop bracelet See TYPES OF JEWELRY DEFINED: BRACELETS: BANGLE BRACELET.

Hopi bracelet Narrow sterling silver cuff bracelet with symbols of Hopi Native American tribe in black. *Der.* From Hopi Indians of the southwestern United States.

I.D./identification bracelet Bracelet of large links attached to oblong metal plaque engraved with name or initials. First used by soldiers in wartime, later adapted for adults and children.

Mali bracelet Handmade bracelet made of leather approximately 1 inch wide and decorated with very small European glass beads (called *American Indian beads* in the United States) in a variety of colors and designs.

Introduced from the Republic of Mali in Africa in 1980s.

medic alert bracelet Bracelet worn to indicate blood type and allergies to certain drugs.

mesh bracelet Metal bracelet made of minute links or a continuous piece of woven metal. Used in gold for expensive watches and bracelets.

ring bracelet See TYPES OF JEWELRY DEFINED: BRACELETS: SLAVE BRACELET.

scarab bracelet Bracelet made of several oval semiprecious stones (e.g., LAPIS LAZULI or CHALCEDONY, see under GEMS, GEM CUTS, AND SETTINGS: TYPES OF GEMS DEFINED) engraved to look like beetles, outlined in gold, and connected by gold links. *Der.* Ancient Egyptian sacred beetle.

slave bracelet **1.** Ring connected by a chain to a bracelet worn around the wrist. Also called a *bracelet ring*, a *ring bracelet*, and more recently an *eternity bracelet*. Originally copied from bracelets worn in Eastern countries for centuries. Popular in the 1880s and the 1990s. **2.** A TOE-ANKLE CHAIN (see under TYPES OF JEWELRY DEFINED: BRACELETS) is also called by this name.

slave bracelet

sleeve bracelet Ornate bracelet worn around upper arm over full sleeve to make a double puffed sleeve.

slide bracelet Bracelet with small piece of pierced metal through which fine flat chains are threaded. Needs no clasp as it is adjusted by pulling the chains. Popular in late 19th c., and revived by using antique watch chains in 1960s.

snake bracelet Metal bracelet in form of a serpent worn coiled around the arm. Worn by ancient Greeks and fashionable in 1880s and in late 1960s.

spring bracelet Beads strung on flexible wire in a spiral that expands to permit entry of hand.

toe-ankle chain Unusual ankle bracelet with chain attached to toe ring. Also called SLAVE BRACELET (see under TYPES OF JEWELRY DEFINED: BRACELETS).

watch bracelet Band, strap, or other device attached to wristwatch made of all types of metals, leather, plastic, or fabric that holds the watch on the wrist.

woven friendship bracelet Bracelet made from different colored strands of yarn woven, knotted, or plaited together.

wrist strap Wide band of leather buckled around wrist, usually trimmed with metal studs. Introduced in late 1960s.

EARRINGS

Art Deco earring Earring made in geometrical forms. Derived from patterns of the 1920s shown in the 1925 Paris Exhibition and revived in the late 1960s and after.

ball earring Earring in the shape of a round bead usually suspended from a tiny linked chain, made of gemstones, plastic, glass, or other material.

button earring Round flat earring shaped like a button. Made in various sizes of materials such as imitation pearls, metal, wood, or plastic.

button earring

chandelier earring

chandelier earring Long dangling oversized earring made of metal or beads hanging like crystals on a chandelier.

changeable earring Earring usually made with a selection of colored plastic disks that may be snapped into a metal circlet. Parts of the PEEKABOO EARRING (see under TYPES OF JEWELRY DEFINED: EARRINGS) can also be interchanged.

clip-back earring Earring that fastens to the ear by means of a spring clip that snaps against back of the ear to secure it.

cluster earring Groups of pearls, gems, or beads fastened together to make a large earring.

diamond earring Earring made with single diamond attached to a post for pierced ears or long strings of diamonds with larger stones set at the top. The former has been a popular wedding gift for the groom to give to the bride. Marie Antoinette, Queen of France in the late 18th c., had a famous pair of the latter type. Elaborate types of diamond earrings were popular from the 1920s on for evening wear.

door knocker earring Elongated hoops hanging free from ear clips—may be interchangeable.

drop earring Any earring in which the lower part swings free. One of the earliest styles, and one that was popular for single genuine gemstones or pearls, was called a **pendant earring.**

ear band Earring that clips on middle edge of ear with dangling portion.

ear clip Synonym for earring.

gypsy earring Large hoop earring usually of brass or gold-colored metal, worn in pierced ear, inspired by plain brass circles worn by gypsies. For unpierced ears, hoop is suspended from a small button top that clips to the back of the ear.

hoop earring **1.** Circlet (or oval) of metal, plastic, or wood that swings free from a small button. Also see TYPES OF JEWELRY DEFINED: EARRINGS: GYPSY EARRING. **2.** Incomplete circlet that fastens around the earlobe. May be hinged and clip into place.

hoop earring #1

jacket earring Earring consisting of post plus various shaped separate pieces with holes in top that may be interchanged by placing post through hole. "Jackets" may be in shape of shells, roses, hearts, butterflies, etc. Introduced in early 1980s.

mobile earring (mo-beel) Delicate wire drop earring like small mobile sculpture carefully balanced so it is constantly in motion.

peek-a-boo earring Earring for pierced ears with small object or stone showing where ear is pierced and three or four stones showing at lower edge of ear. The latter group is attached to back of earring.

pendant earring See TYPES OF JEWELRY DEFINED: EARRINGS: DROP EARRING.

pierced earring Earring designed to be worn in pierced ears. A wire or post is inserted through the ear lobe and should be made of gold or surgical steel rather than plated metals to prevent infection. Until the introduction of screw-back earrings, all types of earrings were made for pierced ears.

pierced-look earring Earring designed for unpierced ears. Has a delicate band of metal coming under the ear to the front giving the appearance that it goes through the ear.

posts See TYPES OF JEWELRY DEFINED: EARRINGS: STUDS.

screw-back earring Earring for unpierced ears, with screw behind the ear that can be tightened to hold it in place. An innovation of the early 20th c. that enabled people without pierced ears to wear earrings.

Statue of Liberty earring Dangling earring with head of Statue of Liberty enclosed in circle. *Der.* Inspired by the July 4, 1986, celebration in New York harbor of the restoration of the Statue of Liberty.

studs Earrings similar to posts designed for pierced ears. One part of earring goes through the ear and in back screws into a **post.** Basic type of earring for pierced ears. Some studs are secured by pushing back piece onto straight post, with notch in post securing back.

wedding band earring Wide gold hoop earring similar in style to a wide gold wedding ring.

wires Earrings for pierced ears that have a thin curved wire, usually gold, that passes through the ear. Usually dangling objects are attached to the wire or the wires may be worn separately.

OTHER TYPES OF JEWELRY

ankh Egyptian symbol for eternal life, somewhat like a cross with a vertical bar forming a loop at the top. Popular as jewelry motif, especially as necklaces and rings, in late 1960s and 1970s. Also called *ansate cross.* See TYPES OF JEWELRY DEFINED: RINGS: ANKH RING.

breastplate Solid metal bra or metal breast ornaments worn by women as body jewelry in late 1960s.

chain Series of connected loops or links made of metal, plastic, or tortoise shell used for closings or worn as ornamental accessory in form of necklace, bracelet, or belt. Chains are called by various names according to shape of links—**cobra chain** is composed of two rows of triangular-shaped links that alternate in a flat effect. **Herringbone chain** is made of small slanting links giving a flat effect. **Rope chain** is composed of two (or more) pieces of chain twisted and wound together like rope.

chain   rope chain

charm Small amulet, usually of metal, consisting of all sorts of mementos, e.g., heart, disk, or zodiac signs, worn on bracelet or necklace.

clip Ornament similar to a pin but with spring clasp on back that snaps closed over the edge of fabric. Set with diamonds or rhinestones. Introduced in 1930s and 1940s.

cross A depiction, stylized or realistic, of an instrument used by Romans for executing individuals. An actual cross would have been made from an upright post of wood with a cross piece near the top, a form that is known as a **Latin cross.** Crosses have been worn by Christians as a symbol of their religious belief from the early days of Christianity and as a badge on the clothing worn by Crusaders during the Middle Ages. Different representations of crosses in badges, jewelry, or as motifs of various kinds have developed and have been given such names as: (1) **ansate cross** See TYPES OF JEWELRY DEFINED: OTHER TYPES OF JEWELRY: ANKH; (2) **Eastern Orthodox cross** With two cross pieces more than halfway up the central post and a diagonal crosspiece a short distance from the bottom; (3) **Greek cross** With the cross piece the same length as the vertical piece and located at its center; (4) **Maltese cross** With four arms of equal length that are shaped like arrowheads decreasing in size as they approach the center; (5) **St. Andrew's cross** With diagonal arms, like an X; (6) **tau cross** With the crosspiece at the top of the post, like the Greek letter *tau.*

Eastern Orthodox cross

Greek cross

Maltese cross

St. Andrew's cross

cuff link Decorative jewelry consisting of two buttons or disks, joined by a link or short chain, worn to close the french cuff of a shirt. May be metal, engraved, set with stones, or made in wide variety of materials. Worn originally by men and adopted by women.

ferronnière (fehr-ohn'-yair) **1.** Delicate chain worn as a band across the brow with single jewel hanging in center of forehead. Fashion originated by La Belle Ferronnière, a favorite of Francis I (1515–1547), as shown in a portrait attributed to Giovanni Boltraffio or Leonardo da Vinci. **2.** Narrow brow band, with jewel in center, worn on the forehead with evening dress.

ferronnière

fronts Around 2001 fans of rap music began to wear clip-on covers for their teeth made of gold and set with diamonds or other gems.

hat pin Straight pin from 3″ to 12″ long with bead or jewel at top. Used by women to secure their hats.

religious medal A pendant necklace worn by Christians of various sects.

stud Small ornamental closure, used since the mid-18th c., that consists of a broader section, a short post, and a smaller buttonlike end that is inserted through an eyelet to fasten a shirt front, neckband, or cuffs. Also called *collar button.*

tie clasp/clip Jewelry consisting of a decorative metal bar bent double that slides over a man's tie and behind his shirt front placket clipping the tie in place. May also have spring-clip back.

tie tack Small ornament with a sharp-pointed back worn pierced through both parts of a man's necktie to hold them together. Back portion is usually screwed into a round metal stud.

Wedgwood® cameo Usually blue in color, with the head of a woman in raised design on the surface. Made by casting Wedgwood pottery material. Can be distinguished from cut cameos by the tiny air bubbles on the surface. *Der.* Made by the Wedgwood China Company in England.

worry beads Short string of beads, often made of semiprecious stones. Originally carried in hand to fidget with by men in Middle Eastern countries, Greece, and Turkey. Popular in America in late 1960s. *Der.* From string of 33 beads used to count the 99 names of Allah during prayers in Moslem countries.

Zuni jewelry Beautiful, exotic, and unusual bracelets, pins, necklaces, and rings of sterling silver set with genuine turquoise gems. *Der.* Made by the Zuni, a Native American tribe inhabiting the largest of the Indian pueblos in western New Mexico.

LUGGAGE

HISTORY AND SIGNIFICANCE OF LUGGAGE TO FASHION

Luggage are containers designed to carry the belongings of a traveler. The distinction between luggage and handbags is somewhat imprecise; however, use of the term "luggage" generally implies containers that are larger and that will hold clothing as well as personal objects.

Humans have been on the move since prehistoric times and must have had specialized containers for carrying personal objects, but remains of specific examples are few. A mummy found in the Alps that dated from c. 3300 B.C. was carrying a skin bag containing arrows. The word luggage apparently derived in the Middle Ages from the idea of something that has to be "lugged" around. As early as the 16th c., there are literary references to the use of a *portmanteau,* a leather bag for carrying clothing. By the 19th c., more types of luggage are identified by name. **Carpet bags** were made from carpet fabric. **Gladstone bags,** named after a British Prime Minister, opened into two equal-sized compartments. And women carried **hat boxes,** made in sizes and shapes to accommodate large hats. Some of these terms and styles are still in use. Innovations of the 20th c. included rigid aluminum and plastic bags that were merchandised with an emphasis on their strength. In the post–World War II period, a variety of synthetic textiles were incorporated into luggage, and by the turn of the century, high-strength materials were in use. Fashion trends influenced color, fabric, shape, and special features.

ANATOMY OF LUGGAGE

Such a wide variety of bags can be classified as luggage that generalization as to structure is difficult. One might divide luggage into rigid, semirigid, and soft types. Rigid luggage can be made from such materials as aluminum and rigid plastics. Some leather luggage can also be quite rigid. Semirigid luggage generally has an internal frame in order to maintain its shape, but is usually made from some type of fabric or flexible plastic so that it can expand to some extent to accommodate the contents, while also keeping its shape. Soft luggage is made of fabric or flexible plastic and is essentially a soft bag with handles to permit carrying. Usually such bags have some method of closure, such as a zipper.

The development of high tech-fabrics and special finishes has increased the variety of materials used for semirigid and soft luggage. Such diverse fabrics as cotton canvas, brocade, or tapestry; nylon ballistic cloth; rip-stop nylon or polyester; textured nylon and polyester fabrics, and carbon fiber materials are in widespread usage. These fabrics can be made water- and tear-resistant by coating with such materials as rubber, PVC (polyvinyl chloride), polyurethane, or ceramic or amino acid compounds.

Other construction features often found in luggage include closures, locks, and pockets. Such brass hardware as buckles and latches enhance appearance. Plastic buckles are mounted on nylon straps that slide into a matching clasp to secure the bag and its contents. Strong, durable, large zippers function even if a few teeth are lost, and built-in locks close with a key or a combination to fasten the bag. Interiors have pockets such as **sleeve pockets** to hold long garments in place, **wet packs** made of plastic to hold wet items, or mesh pockets to hold blouses and shirts firmly into place so they will wrinkle less. Exterior pockets of various sizes and shapes include **coal chute pockets,** which are large patch pockets on the exterior.

TYPES OF LUGGAGE DEFINED

The types of bags identified by luggage makers are:

back pack   Bag with straps fitting over shoulders so that it can be worn on the back. The term *backpack* has largely replaced the earlier term for such a bag, *knapsack.* Made in a wide variety of materials, of various sizes, with various compartments on the exterior and interior, and suitable for many purposes, backpacks are used not only for outdoor sports, but also by students as book bags. They also serve as substitutes for handbags.

carry-on bag   Any bag designed to be small enough to carry on to an airplane. It must be small enough to fit under the seat or in the overhead compartment of the plane. A carry-on case that has wheels is called a **rollaboard.**

computer case   A case of the size to hold a portable computer. Cases may have pockets and sections for papers and other supplies. Some cases are made of rigid material in order to protect the computer while others are made of durable fabrics. Those often have a rigid backing for pockets so as to provide greater protection to the computer.

cosmetic case   Also called a *vanity case.* Either rigid or soft, a cosmetic case is equipped with a mirror and a number of small partitioned sections to hold cosmetics. It usually has an interior that is not harmed by spilled materials.

duffel bag   A large, soft, oblong or barrel-shaped canvas bag with a drawstring or zipper-top closure. Used historically by sailors and soldiers to transport their clothing and other items, duffel bags are now made as luggage in various sizes and shapes. They are also made in smaller versions for handbags and beach bags. Contemporary duffel bags often have pockets on the exterior and generally close with a zipper.

duffel bag

flight bag   **1.** Soft canvas satchel with zippered-top closing and two handles copied from standard carryall issued by airlines to passengers when air travel was less common. **2.** Any bag used for traveling that is larger than a handbag and smaller than a suitcase. Also called a *travel bag.*

garment bag   A soft, long bag that folds in half or in thirds vertically and has a handle at the top for carrying. It is long enough to accommodate a suit or dress and has an interior bar and hangers for clothing. It may also have exterior compartments. Garment bags are also available with rollers. Also called a *suitfolder,* especially if it has no exterior pockets. Sometimes included internally on a PULLMAN BAG (see under TYPES OF LUGGAGE DEFINED).

garment bag

gym bag   A soft bag with zipper top and a handle on either side of the zipper that is designed for carrying clothes used for physical education or workouts. Usually these bags have a separate waterproof compartment for damp towels or clothing.

Other bags that have come into use for travel include:

overnight bag   A bag of a size that will accommodate enough apparel for a stay of one night. It may be soft, semirigid, or rigid.

pullman or upright case   Large suitcase now generally made with wheels at one end and a handle that telescopes into the body of the case. When the case has hangers or an internal compartment for suits and dresses, it may be called a **suiter.**

stuff sack   Small, often mesh, bag to use inside another bag to subdivide various types of contents. Initially developed for backpacking to improve the efficiency of packing, now used in all kinds of bags.

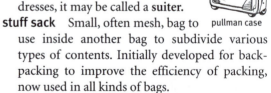
pullman case

A number of cases are sold to businesspersons for carrying documents, computers, and the like. However these may be more closely related to handbags than to luggage, and are discussed under the category of HANDBAGS AND RELATED ACCESSORIES, e.g., BRIEFCASE, ATTACHÉ CASE, PORTFOLIO, etc.

SHAWLS, SCARVES, *and* HANDKERCHIEFS

HISTORY AND SIGNIFICANCE OF SHAWLS, SCARVES, AND HANDKERCHIEFS TO FASHION

Shawls, scarves, and handkerchiefs are among the simplest of garments. They have been used throughout history, and probably originated in prehistoric times. A **shawl** is a decorative or utilitarian wrap that is worn draped over the shoulders and sometimes over the head. Shawls may be oblong, square, triangular, or can be made by folding a square diagonally. Wrapped garments of this type have been used throughout history, often as outerwear. In contemporary practice, they are more often used as a decorative accessory. Shawls became especially fashionable in Europe around the second half of 18th c. when hand-woven shawls from India were imported to Europe. Shawls from the Kashmir region of the Indian subcontinent were highly prized, and soon textile mills in Europe, especially those in the town of Paisley, Scotland, produced imitations of these **cashmere shawls.** The characteristic design is a cone or leaf, pattern called a **boteh,** which eventually became known as a **paisley design.** Shawls were very popular throughout the 19th c. and have been worn intermittently since.

A shawl is larger than a **scarf** (pl. *scarfs* or *scarves*), which is also either decorative or utilitarian and is worn draped around the shoulders, the neck, or over the head for warmth or adornment. Scarves may be square,

scarf

oblong, or triangular and made of knitted, crocheted, or woven fabric. Scarves can be so small that they only fit around the neck or large enough to cover the shoulders and much of the upper body. They may be a solid color, printed, or woven in various patterns, or have applied ornamentation such as beads, spangles, or embroidery.

A **handkerchief** is a square of cotton, linen, or silk, sometimes edged with lace or embroidered, that is carried and used for wiping the face or nose. Apparently used in China more than 3000 years ago, in ancient Egypt, and in classical antiquity, the modern version apparently came into general use in Europe around 1500.

Men's handkerchiefs are usually larger than women's. Modern handkerchiefs are made in a wide variety of colors and sizes, although white predominates. Paper handkerchiefs have replaced cloth for many practical uses, but cloth handkerchiefs serve a number of decorative functions. They may appear folded in a pocket and are carried by brides. For more formal occasions, an ornamental cloth handkerchief is often used.

ANATOMY OF SHAWLS, SCARVES, AND HANDKERCHIEFS

The structures of these accessories are largely dependent on the textiles from which they are made. Knitted and crocheted fabrics for shawls or scarves are generally made to the correct size and do not require any finishing of edges. Those made from woven fabrics that are woven to size, such as large shawls, are also generally finished at the edges by the weaver. Scarves and handkerchiefs are more often cut from larger lengths of fabric. If so, the edges of the fabric must be hemmed or finished in some way to prevent raveling. Sewn hems are made either by hand or by machine. Edges may be finished with a fringe.

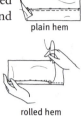

plain hem

rolled hem

These accessories often have a decorative or ornamental aspect that can be achieved by appliqué, embroidery, trimming with lace, braid, or other materials. Designs may be woven or printed. A wide range of colors can be achieved by dyeing. See TEXTILES IN ACCESSORIES and EMBROIDERIES AND SEWING STITCHES for explanations of these processes.

TYPES OF SHAWLS DEFINED

all-purpose poncho See TYPES OF SHAWLS DEFINED: PONCHO.

beach poncho Oblong terrycloth poncho that can be laid flat for use as a towel at the beach.

capelet Any small cape, e.g., a cape collar, attached or detachable, on a coat, dress, or suit.

cashmere shawl Any shawl made from CASHMERE fiber (see TEXTILES IN ACCESSORIES: FIBERS AND YARNS: THE BUILDING BLOCKS OF FABRICS: NATURAL FIBERS DEFINED), which is exceptionally fine, soft, and expensive.

crocheted shawl Fringed shawl made by hand crocheting usually in a lacy pattern. Made in oblong, semicircular, or triangular shapes.

domino A large shawl, usually black, worn with a small mask for traditional carnival and masquerade costume.

fishnet poncho Square medium-sized poncho made of fishnet or see-through fabric with a high large turtleneck collar. The edge of the collar and the hem is trimmed with ball fringe.

fur stole Term used in 20th c. for waist-length fur cape with elongated ends in front, sometimes trimmed with tails of animals. May also be made in an oblong shape.

lapponica Poncho imported from Finland of plaid wool with fringed edges. Colorful plaids are of all varieties, some being in large squares of color; and some in smaller checks similar to glen plaid (see TYPES OF SHAWLS DEFINED: PONCHO).

mantilla (man-til´-ah) Shawl or veil worn by Spanish women, usually of black lace—white lace worn for festive occasions. Worn draped over the head, sometimes over a high comb placed in hair, wrapped around neck, and falling over shoulders. This shawl has influenced 20th-c. fashions. *Der.* Diminutive of Spanish *manta,* "shawl."

paisley (pay´-slee) **shawl** Shawl with a paisley design. This design is a cone or leaf pattern called a **boteh**, which originates in India. Many of the earliest shawls imported to Europe from India in the 18th c. were woven in this design and became so popular that they were imitated by textile mills in the town of

paisley shawl

Paisley in Scotland. They soon became known as **paisley shawls** and the characteristic boteh design became known as a *paisley design.*

piano shawl See TYPES OF SHAWLS DEFINED: SPANISH SHAWL.

poncho Shawl-like fashion item shaped like a square or a small oblong blanket with hole in center for the head. Frequently fringed around the edges. Variations include a utilitarian garment consisting of waterproofed fabric with a slash in the center for the head. When worn, it was used as a rain cape; when not worn, could be used as a tarpaulin or a blanket. Another water-resistant version consisted of a square of nylon fabric, 54″ × 80″, laminated

poncho

with polyvinyl chloride that slips over the head and snaps closed at the sides to make a partial sleeve. One size fits everyone. Usually styled with an attached hood. Originally made of a rubberized fabric and worn by policemen on a rainy day. Also called a *rain poncho* or *all-purpose poncho.*

rain poncho See TYPES OF SHALLS DEFINED: PONCHO.

rebozo (re-bow'-zho) An oblong shawl made of native fabric worn originally by South American Indians and introduced as a fashion item in late 1960s.

serape (say-rah'-pay) Brightly colored oblong rectangle worn over the shoulder by Mexicans. Handmade in horizontally striped patterns, it resembles a small blanket. Usually made with fringed ends.

skoncho A do-it-yourself style poncho made from a brushed wool plaid or striped blanket with a fringe on two ends, similar to a blanket used at a football game. A 16″ slash is cut diagonally in the center. May also be worn as a skirt.

Spanish shawl Large embroidered silk shawl, usually made in China then shipped to Spain, where the long silk fringe was added. When used as a wrap, the shawl was folded diagonally with the point in center at the back and the ends thrown loosely over the shoulders. A fashionable accessory of the early 20th c., it was revived in the late 1960s and early 1970s and has become fashionable periodically. Also called *piano shawl,* because this type of shawl was draped on the top of grand pianos in the early 20th c.

Spanish shawl 1926

TYPES OF SCARVES DEFINED

apache scarf (ah-patch'-ee or ah'-pash) Man's small square or triangular scarf introduced in late 1960s for wear instead of a necktie. Worn knotted or pulled through a slide. *Der.* French slang for gangster or thug, especially as depicted by French nightclub dancers. The French word taken from the southwest American Indian tribe, thought to be very fierce.

ascot scarf Oblong scarf, frequently white, lapped over and worn loosely around the neck by men and women. Reintroduced in late 1960s by St. Laurent, the Paris couturier, who emblazoned it with his initials, making it a status symbol. *Der.* Named for a scarf worn at Ascot racetrack in England.

babushka (bah-boosh'-ka) Triangular-shaped scarf or square folded diagonally, worn draped over head and tied under chin in manner of Russian peasant woman. *Der.* Russian, "grandmother." So called because it was worn by older Russian immigrants to the United States. Also called a KERCHIEF (see under TYPES OF SCARVES DEFINED).

bandanna (ban-dan'-nah) Large square cotton handkerchief, either red or blue, with a distinctive black and white design. Worn in late 19th and early 20th c., tied around the head or neck by workmen, and later adopted in all colors for wear with sport clothes.

boa (bow'-ah) Round, narrow, long scarf made of feathers, pleated silk, fur, or SWANS-DOWN (see FEATHERS: TYPES OF FEATHERS DEFINED). Also called French boa.

boa

calligraphic scarf Letters of the alphabet arranged to form a pattern in much the same manner a picture is "drawn" on a typewriter by using Xs and other characters. Introduced in late 1960s.

comforter Woolen scarf worn around the neck in cold weather.

designer scarf Scarf made in an elaborate design using beautiful or unusual colors. In the late 1960s, it became popular to print the name of a famous company or designer on the pure silk scarves, which were then called **signature scarves**. The fashion started in Paris with Balenciaga, Dior, and Saint Laurent—spread to Italy and United States as a status symbol for most prestigious designers.

dog collar scarf Triangular or oblong scarf folded to go around neck twice, bringing ends back to the front where they are knotted or looped over.

fascinator Large long woolen scarf made in a lacy knit worn over the head or around the shoulders by women. First fashionable in the early 1890s and worn at intervals since.

fichu (feesh'-u) Historic term that is occasionally still used in describing neckwear consisting of a large square of muslin or other soft fabric folded diagonally to

fichu

form a triangle and worn with the point of the triangle at the back and the two points fastening in the center front.

foulard scarf (foo-lahr′) Scarf of silk twill, called foulard, often made with small designs printed on plain ground. Originally imported from India.

fur scarf Neckpiece made of several skins of a small animal or from one large animal skin complete with head, tail, and paws.

hacking scarf Long, oblong scarf doubled and placed at back of neck. Both ends are then pulled through loop and hang down in front. *Der.* Long scarf, originally 72″ worn by four-in-hand coach drivers in Old England.

kerchief Scarf worn as head or neck covering, usually a square folded into triangle with crossed ends fastened on chest. Also called *neckerchief.*

muffler Long scarf approximately 12″ wide; usually knitted or woven of plaid or plain-colored wool, silk, or rayon.

neckerchief Triangular scarf, either cut in shape of a triangle or a square folded diagonally, worn by men and women. Worn from 19th c. on by cowboys instead of a necktie. Also worn by Boy Scouts with uniforms.

neckerchief

neckpiece Boa or scarf, usually of fur.

Paisley scarf **1.** Square or oblong scarf made with paisley designs that are shaped like a tear drop, rounded at one end and with a curving point, and having delicate tracery, done in rich reds, rusts, beiges, and browns. Usually made in an allover design. **2.** Unusual scarf featuring a shell design with elongated blocks around edge, Paisley print inside, and plain cream-colored center sprinkled with a few designs. Comes in 18″ × 62″ size and is copied from a shawl in National Museum of American History's Costume Division of the Smithsonian Institution. Also see TYPES OF SHAWLS DEFINED: PAISLEY SHAWL.

ring scarf Oblong scarf with ends stitched together to form a circle. Worn with jewelry to form a collar on a dress.

sailor scarf Square NECKERCHIEF (see under TYPES OF SCARVES DEFINED) folded diagonally, worn under sailor collar and slipped through loop front of blouse or tied in a knot. Also called *sailor tie.*

signature scarf See TYPES OF SCARVES DEFINED: DESIGNER SCARF.

souvenir scarf Large square scarf imprinted with scene, picture, symbol, or words depicting a special place, e.g., Miami, Paris. Usually bought by tourists to remind them of a special holiday spent at that place.

stock Oblong scarf worn loosely lapped over rather than tied. During 1968 introduced to be worn instead of NECKTIES by men (see under TIES AND NECKWEAR).

stole **1.** Long wide scarf, often fringed at ends, made of fabric, knit, or fur worn since 19th c. as woman's wrap **2.** Long wide scarf matched in fabric to woman's dress worn with bare-top dress in 1950s, especially in the evening.

stole #2

TYPES OF HANDKERCHIEFS DEFINED

embroidered handkerchief A handkerchief with embroidered decoration applied by hand or by machine. Various embroidery techniques can be used and embroidering may be done in colors or white on colored background or in colors or white thread on a white background. The initials of the person carrying the handkerchief may be embroidered on it. Also see EMBROIDERIES AND SEWING STITCHES: TYPES OF EMBROIDERY DEFINED.

embroidered handkerchief

lace handkerchief A handkerchief with a woven fabric center that is framed in lace. Lace used in embroidered handkerchiefs can be hand- or machine-made. Also see LACES AND BRAIDS: ANATOMY OF LACE and TYPES OF LACE DEFINED.

lace handkerchief

printed handkerchief A handkerchief with decorations applied by printing. Handkerchiefs may be printed by machines, by HAND-BLOCK PRINTING, or by SCREEN PRINTING (see under TEXTILES IN ACCESSORIES: ADDING COLOR AND DESIGN TO FABRIC: DESIGNS AND SURFACE EFFECTS DEFINED).

TIES *and* NECKWEAR

HISTORY AND SIGNIFICANCE OF TIES AND NECKWEAR TO FASHION

The contemporary word "tie," a shortened form of "necktie," appeared first about 1820. The word derived from the form of this accessory garment, i.e., something that tied around the neck. For some time after this, "tie" and "cravat," an earlier term, were used interchangeably to describe men's neckwear that was worn over a shirt, and cravat persists in use today as a rather more high-toned way of referring to a necktie.

The precursor of the necktie was a silk scarf worn by Croatian soldiers victorious in a 1660 military campaign. When the French king Louis XIV saw these colorful garments, he adopted the style as a royal insignia and established a regiment that he called the Royal Cravattes, a French word derived from "Croat." Fashionable men throughout Europe soon were wearing a wide variety of "cravats" tied in many different ways. The forms utilized today had crystallized by the early 20th c.

Although women can and do wear neckties, these accessories are more commonly part of a man's wardrobe. Those most often seen are neckties, bowties, ascots, and neckscarves. (Neckscarves are discussed under SHAWLS, SCARVES, AND HANDKERCHIEFS.) The width of neckties, their cut, and the fabrics from which they are made vary according to contemporary fashion trends.

2¾ inches to 3½ inches. Lengths vary from 52 to 58 inches. Even longer ties can be obtained by placing special orders with retailers. The two ends of a tie are usually equal in size, although the under layer may be slightly smaller. Silk has been traditionally the fiber from which tie fabric is made; however, at present many other fibers are also used.

bar tack stitch
loop label
shell
facing (tipping)
slip stitching
interlining
necktie

Better quality ties are cut on the bias, the diagonal direction of the fabric (see TEXTILES IN ACCESSORIES: DIFFERENT TYPES OF FABRIC STRUCTURES: WOVEN FABRICS: BIAS). An inner lining gives the tie body and helps to hold its shape. In high-quality ties, the weight of the lining is indicated by gold bars that can be seen if one opens up the back of the tie. The more gold bars, the more substantial the lining. A stitch called a **bar tack** placed on the back of the tie, where the two sides come together in an inverted V, will help to preserve the shape of the tie. In handmade ties a **slip stitch**, a loose black thread, runs the length of the tie. The tie can move along this thread as it is wrapped, the thread prevents the tie from ripping, and when the tie is removed, the thread brings it back into its proper shape.

Bow ties are either made to tie or may be sold pre-tied and placed on clips that fasten to the shirt collar.

ANATOMY OF A NECKTIE

Neckties can range in width, sometimes growing to as much as 5 inches, but are more likely to be about

TYPES OF NECKTIES DEFINED

apron The wide ends at the front and back of a contemporary necktie.

ascot **1.** Wide necktie worn looped over and held in place by scarf pin. The ends are cut diagonally. **2.** Scarf looped under the chin. *Der.* Fashionable horse-racing spot, Ascot Health, England. Also see SHAWLS, SCARVES, AND HAND-KERCHIEFS: TYPES OF SCARVES DEFINED: ASCOT SCARF.

ascot #1

band bow Pre-tied bow tie on an adjustable-sized band that fastens around the neck.

bar-shaped tie FOUR-IN-HAND TIE (see under TYPES OF NECKTIES DEFINED) with ends of the same width that are parallel.

black tie Man's black BOW TIE (see under TYPES OF NECKTIES DEFINED) worn with dinner jacket or tuxedo, for semiformal occasions.

boater tie Man's FOUR-IN-HAND TIE (see under TYPES OF NECKTIES DEFINED), shorter than average, made with extra-large knot, and usually with square-cut ends. Introduced in late 1960s from England.

bolo tie/bola tie Western-type tie of heavy rounded braid with metal-tipped ends fastening with an ornamental slide. Also called *shoelace tie.*

bolo tie

bootlace tie See TYPES OF NECK-TIES DEFINED: STRING TIE.

bow tie **1.** Man's tie, square-cut or with shaped ends, tied in a bow under the chin. Originally introduced in late 19th c. and worn with formal dress for men since then. See TYPES OF NECKTIES DEFINED: BLACK TIE and WHITE TIE. **2.** Man's tie, already tied in a bow, which clips to the collar.

bow tie #1

butterfly bow tie Bow tie with top and bottom edges that narrow at the middle of the tie to make the center about half the width of the ends. Ends may be either square or pointed. Contrast with TYPES OF NECKTIES DEFINED: CLUB BOW TIE.

clip-on tie Tie, either pre-tied in a knot like a FOUR-IN-HAND or a BOW TIE, that is fastened to the collarband by a metal clip (see under TYPES OF NECKTIES DEFINED).

club bow tie Bow tie in which the top and bottom edges are straight. Ends are either square or pointed. Contrast with TYPES OF NECKTIES DEFINED: BUTTERFLY BOW TIE.

cravat Sometimes used as a synonym for a man's wide necktie worn with morning coat and pinstriped trousers.

cravat

four-in-hand tie Long necktie that goes around the neck with one end looping over the other end twice, then being pulled through the loop making a slip knot. Usually made of bias-cut fabric or knit, narrow in the center back and wider at the ends. Worn continuously since the 1890s in varying widths. Also worn by women with tailored suits.

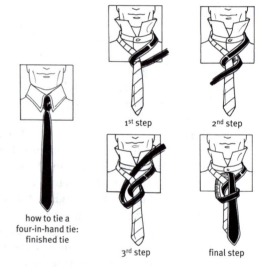
how to tie a four-in-hand tie: finished tie
1st step
2nd step
3rd step
final step

hunting stock Type of wide tie or stock. Worn folded over once to fill in neckline of jacket. Used by equestrians when riding in hunt field or show ring.

kipper Necktie 4 or 5″ wide with ends like a BOW TIE usually of striped or patterned fabric. Introduced from England in late 1960s (see under TYPES OF NECKTIE DEFINED).

Macclesfield tie (mak´-liz-feld) Necktie made from silk fabric of a type produced in Macclesfield, England. Fabric has small DOBBY WEAVE patterns. (See under TEXTILES IN ACCESSORIES: DEFFERENT TYPES OF FABRIC STRUCTURES: WOVEN FABRICS DEFINED).

maharatta tie See TYPES OF NECKTIES DEFINED: NECKTIE.

neckerchief See SHAWLS, SCARVES, AND HANDKERCHIEFS: TYPES OF SCARVES DEFINED.

necktie See HISTORY AND SIGNIFICANCE OF TIES AND NECKWEAR TO FASHION.

regimental striped tie See TEXTILES IN ACCESSORIES: ADDING COLOR AND DESIGN TO FABRIC: DESIGNS AND SURFACE EFFECTS DEFINED: REGIMENTAL STRIPES.

rep tie/repp tie Tie made from fabric with closely spaced crosswise ribs. Fabric may be made from a variety of fibers.

sailor tie Large square scarf of black silk folded diagonally and worn under square sailor collar and either tied in sailor knot or pulled through strap on front of a middy blouse, which is a type of blouse copied from those traditionally worn by sailors.

sailor tie

scarf See SHAWLS, SCARVES, AND HANDKERCHIEFS: HISTORY AND SIGNIFICANCE OF SHAWLS, SCARVES, AND HANDKERCHIEFS TO FASHION.

seven-fold tie Unlined tie made from an outer fabric that is folded over itself seven times. As a result no lining is required; however, due to the cost of such ties, they are now relatively rare.

shell Outside fabric of a necktie.

sheriff tie See TYPES OF NECKTIES DEFINED: STRING TIE.

shoelace tie See TYPES OF NECKTIES DEFINED: BOLO TIE.

Southern Colonel tie See TYPES OF NECKTIES DEFINED: STRING TIE.

Spitalfield tie (spit′-ahl-field) Necktie made from silk fabric of a type produced in the Spitalfield section of London, England. Fabric has a small, overall pattern that looks like a mosaic. It is usually made in a DOBBY WEAVE. See under TEXTILES IN ACCESSORIES: DIFFERENT TYPES OF FABRIC STRUCTURES: WOVEN FABRICS DEFINED.

string tie Necktie, usually not more than one inch wide, often black, worn in a bow with ends hanging down. Also called *bootlace tie, Southern Colonel tie,* and, in Britain, *sheriff's tie.*

string tie

white tie Man's white bow tie worn for formal occasions with tails, usually hand tied.

Windsor tie Regular man's necktie tied in four-in-hand style with a more complicated knot that is larger. *Der.* Called a *Windsor knot,* after Duke of Windsor who made it popular in early 1920s.

UMBRELLAS

HISTORY AND SIGNIFICANCE OF UMBRELLAS TO FASHION

Used as a protection against the rain or sun; an umbrella is a round, flat, or convex platelike fabric canopy, originally used to shade the person carrying it from the sun. In early Egyptian, Assyrian, Indian, and African civilizations, and in the Catholic Church throughout the Middle Ages, this device was a sign of rank. By the early 16th c., it had also become a fashionable novelty to protect against the sun. Occasional mention is made in the early 17th c. of the umbrella as protection against rain; however, it was only at the end of that century that waterproof umbrellas came into widespread use. By 1800, a distinction was made in English between an **umbrella,** which was waterproof and used against rain, and a **parasol,** which was a sunshade and often highly decorative. Parasols were very important accessories throughout the 19th c. and into the early 20th c., after which they gradually went out of fashion while the utilitarian umbrella continued to be used against the rain. By the end of the 20th c., umbrellas could be highly decorative, made in colors, and printed. Their surfaces also served as a place to promote products and causes. Handles ranged from the practical to the ornamental. *Der.* Parasol derives from *para,* against, *sol,* the sun; umbrella from the Italian *umbra,* meaning shade.

carriage parasol

walking parasol

ANATOMY OF AN UMBRELLA

A modern collapsible umbrella generally consists of a cover, usually made of nylon, polyester, or plastic, mounted on a structure of ribs that are

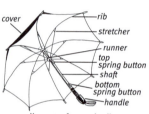
diagram of an umbrella

attached to the top of a long straight shaft. The shaft is generally made of wood, steel, aluminum, fiberglass, or plastic. At the lower end of the shaft, a handle is mounted, which may be simple and plain or decorative. Umbrellas can have from six to sixteen hinged ribs mounted at the top of a handle; however, at the present time they are more likely to have from 8 to 10 ribs. Early versions used lightweight cane ribs. By the 1850s, the ribs were being made of lightweight steel. Today they are usually made of aluminum, steel, or rigid plastic. The hinges permit the top to be opened and closed. A thin metal piece called the stretcher, which is at the middle of each rib, stretches the fabric and attaches to a runner that slides up and down between two springs, one at the top and one at the bottom of the shaft.

Several types of **folding umbrellas** are made in which the pole is in two or more sections, which telescope each inside the others. This makes for a more compact device. The even smaller, **minifolding umbrella** not only has a telescoping handle, but the cover is hinged in such a way that it folds back upon itself, making it very small.

Although parasols are not so widely used as they once were, they are still available. With the emphasis on protection against the sun, some parasols are made of fabrics with a **Sun Protection Factor (SPF)** rating. This is a number that indicates the ability of a sunscreen or fabric to protect the skin from the harmful effects of the sun. The higher the SPF number, the greater its ability to block ultraviolet (UV) radiation. An SPF of 15 is recommended as a minimum to block out most UV radiation.

TYPES OF UMBRELLAS DEFINED

bell umbrella   Dome-shaped umbrella of transparent plastic or of fabric with a plastic window through which to look, which is deeper than most umbrellas and therefore protects the face. Also called a *bell-shaped umbrella* or a *dome umbrella*.

dome umbrella   See TYPES OF UMBRELLAS DEFINED: BELL UMBRELLA.

fashion umbrella   An umbrella with an ornamental cover and handle.

folding umbrella   An umbrella in which the lower part of the shaft telescopes inside the upper part and the ribs of the top fit into a hollow handle in order to make the umbrella smaller and easier to carry. An even smaller MINI-FOLDING UMBRELLA can be made when the cover is hinged to fold back upon itself.

Japanese parasol   Parasol or umbrella made of brightly colored glazed paper with bamboo ribs. Also made of oiled silk for wet weather.

mini-folding umbrella   See TYPES OF UMBRELLAS DEFINED: FOLDING UMBRELLA.

rolled umbrella   An umbrella that when closed can be rolled up tightly. Some rolled umbrellas are also used as walking sticks.

stick umbrellas   An umbrella that is mounted on a straight, long handle.

WATCHES

HISTORY AND SIGNIFICANCE OF WATCHES TO FASHION

A **watch** is a timepiece that is usually carried in a pocket or worn on a band at the wrist. Watches have been fashionable accessories since the 16th c. Before this time, clocks used weights or pendula to move the hands. In the early 1500s, Peter Henlein, a German locksmith, invented a coiled watch spring that he called a **mainspring.** It was successfully used to drive the clock hands, making smaller clockworks possible. Watches of 4 to 5 inches in diameter and about 3 inches in depth became possible.

The earliest watches were usually carried in the hand. As they became smaller, they were put into pockets. The first record of a watch to be worn on the wrist is one that was made for the Queen of Naples in 1810. In the late 19th c., women wore watches that dangled from pins. Wristwatches were a novelty and little used until the 1920s, after World War I. Soldiers fighting in the war found them more convenient than pocket watches, and after the war they were also adopted by the general population. In the 1960s and 1970s, some watches were decorated with novelty straps and face designs and were considered to be costume jewelry. Others were worn on chains around the neck.

Technical developments in recent decades include watches powered by small replaceable batteries, self-winding mechanisms, waterproofing, and shock-resistance. Digital watches have digital printouts which not only show date, time, and seconds, but are also designed with alarms and other technical features that track appointments, read pulses, and tell the temperature.

ANATOMY OF A WATCH

An **analog watch** shows the time on the face of a watch by using hour, minute, and second hands that point to the time. A **digital watch** shows the time in hours, minutes, and seconds in numbers that constantly change.

A watch requires a power source. In some watches, winding the watch with a small exterior knob provides the power; in a **self-winding watch,** the movement of the wearer's arm provides the motion that winds the watch. In a mechanical watch, the power source causes a section of the watch, called the **balance,** to move back and forth. Gears or other devices connect the various mechanical parts of the watch, including the hands on the watch face. Timing of the various movements is carefully adjusted so that the face of the watch will correctly show the time.

A small motor operated by a battery, which usually must be changed about once a year, powers electric watches. Battery-powered watches may use any of several drive systems. Some are mechanical, either having a mechanism similar to that mentioned above or one in which electromagnets move the mechanism. In one electrically powered watch, which may more accurately be called an **electronic watch,** a battery drives a minute tuning fork that vibrates at a very high frequency. This vibration is utilized to supply the power to move the hands in an analog watch or form the display on a digital watch.

TYPES OF WATCHES DEFINED

alarm watch   Wristwatch that rings at a set time; sometimes the alarm is musical and called *musical alarm watch.*

ankle watch   Large watch with wide band worn strapped to the ankle.

bangle watch   See TYPES OF WATCHES DEFINED: BRACELET WATCH.

bracelet watch   Watch with an ornamental band and a face that is sometimes covered with a small hinged piece of metal. Frequently set with stones, it acts as both a decorative bracelet and a watch. Also called *bangle watch.*

bracelet watch

calculator watch   Watch that, in addition to giving the time in eight different time zones of the world, is a stop watch, has an alarm, and will do mathematical problems.

calendar watch   Watch that also shows month and day of year in addition to indicating time.

cartoon watch   Children's watch with trademarked cartoon characters (e.g., Mickey Mouse®, Star Wars® characters, and Smurfs®) popular since 1930s.

chatelaine watch   (shat'-eh-lane)   Watch suspended from a lapel pin. Popular in 19th and early 20th c. and revived intermittently. Also called a *lapel watch. Der.* Keys worn at the waist on a chain by medieval mistress of the castle or "chatelaine."

chatelaine watch

chronograph   A watch with features, such as a perpetual calendar and moon phase repeater, and that has dials which glow in the dark.

chronometric watch   Watch equipped with aviation computer to calculate speed, distance, conversion of miles into kilometers or knots, and fuel consumption. Used when flying, auto racing, and boating. First used by space pioneers in flight of May 1962.

diamond watch   **1.** Wristwatch decorated around the dial with diamonds and other precious gems. Introduced in the 1920s, the watchband was made with diamonds set in a platinum band. **2.** In the 1960s, semiprecious gems (e.g., CARNELIAN, ONYX, or TURQUOISE) (see under GEMS, GEM CUTS, AND SETTINGS: TYPES OF GEMS DEFINED) were used for the face with diamonds set around the edge.

digital watch   A watch that shows the time in hours, minutes, and seconds in numbers which constantly change, rather than having a dial with hands pointing to the time.

digital watch

fashion watch   Watch that is a decorative accessory as well as a functional one. In the 1950s, bracelet, pendant, and ring watches were designed, some set with jewels, others in antique mountings. Previous to this, women owned one watch—now they may own several and wear them as jewelry.

go-go watch   Watch that snaps into very wide interchangeable, colorful bands, matching or contrasting with the costume. Introduced in 1966, they were at first considered a fad, but later influenced the introduction of larger-sized watches and watchbands for women.

hunter watch   Large gold pocketwatch with covered face depicting a hunting scene.

jeweled watch   A watch in which the metal movements have gemstone tips that prevent wear and tear, thereby prolonging the life of the watch. Seventeen jewels will produce a serviceable watch; a 23-jewel watch will outlive its owner by many years.

lapel watch   See TYPES OF WATCHES DEFINED: CHATELAINE WATCH.

LCD quartz watch   Digital watch that displays time and date by Liquid Crystal Display; powered by a small replaceable battery.

pendant watch   Watch suspended from a chain worn around the neck. May be decorated on the back and worn on either side or made with a hinged cover. Made in all shapes and sizes in antique as well as modern designs and in LCD calendar watches.

pocket watch Now rarely seen, a pocket watch is one worn either in the vest pocket or in a small watch pocket in the trousers. Pocket watches went out of fashion after the introduction of wristwatches.

pocketwatch

quartz crystal watch A watch powered by a battery rather than by mechanical movements.

ring watch Watch in ring style—popular in 1960s and 1980s, sometimes decorated with stones and made with hinged cover. Other very simple styles were made of lucite.

self-winding watch A wristwatch that winds automatically as a result of the movement of the wrist.

seventeen-jeweled watch Fine watch using genuine or imitation RUBIES and SAPPHIRES (see under GEMS, GEM CUTS, AND SETTINGS: TYPES OF GEMS DEFINED) at points of friction inside the case. Originally stones were genuine but now synthetic stones are more frequently used.

waterproof watch A watch in a sealed case that prevents the entrance of water.

wristwatch Watch worn on the wrist. Introduced in the late 1800s and gaining in popularity before World War I. Made in all sizes and types of faces, and sometimes with interchangeable bands. Some are set with diamonds and called DIAMOND WATCHES (see under TYPES OF WATCHES DEFINED).

wristwatch wardrobe Women's watch sold with several interchangeable watchbands in several colors.

WIGS *and* HAIRPIECES

HISTORY AND SIGNIFICANCE OF WIGS AND HAIRPIECES TO FASHION

A **wig** is composed of hair, human or artificial, mounted on an elastic net cap or foundation of bands (called a **capless wig**). Wigs are worn stretched over the head to conceal natural hair or baldness and styled in conventional cuts and colors, or in fancy arrangements and colors as fashion dictates. Wigs were important in ancient Egypt, where they were worn over shaved heads. It is thought that this was a practice related to comfort and sanitation in a very warm climate. Actors appearing in theatrical performances in classical antiquity wore wigs as part of their stage costume. In the 17th and 18th c., they were a status symbol of royalty and the upper classes. By the 19th and early 20th c., wigs were no longer worn openly. Those who wanted to hide baldness or hair loss wore wigs secretly.

Whereas wigs cover the entire head and hair, a **hairpiece** is additional hair, either human or synthetic, to supplement natural hair.

hairpiece

ANATOMY OF A WIG

Wigs can be purchased ready-made in adjustable sizes, or may be made to order. If the wig is made to order, the first step in its construction is to measure the head of the wearer. Those measurements are transferred to a wooden wig block and fabric tape is nailed to the wooden block at the points that were measured. A base of cotton lace or nylon or polyester net is placed over the block and pinned to the tapes. The base is cut to the appropriate measurement markings, after which the base is sewn to the tapes. This forms the foundation of the wig.

In mass-produced wigs, the foundation may be made of stretch lace in order to accommodate varying head sizes, or, alternatively, devices to permit adjustment of size may be added to the wig. Once the wig foundation is complete, the "hair" fiber that makes up the outer portion of the wig must be fastened to the base. Wigs may be made of human hair or synthetic fiber such as MODACRYLIC FIBER (see under TEXTILES IN ACCESSORIES: FIBERS AND YARNS: THE BUILDING BLOCKS OF FABRICS: GENERIC AND OTHER MANUFACTURED FIBERS DEFINED). The hair or fiber is knotted to the base by hand in handmade wigs, beginning at the back and working around the sides. A hand-tied wig can be brushed or combed in any direction. Machine-knotted wigs are styled before sale, and the style cannot be changed very much. Another feature that may be included in wigs is **open ear tabs,** adjustable material that will contour to the wearer's face at the temple, thereby making it easier to wear eyeglasses. Some wigs have a **velvet comfort band** placed inside the front rim to make the wig more comfortable.

TYPES OF WIGS AND HAIRPIECES DEFINED

Afro wig Very curly, short-haired wig that fits over the hair, often back-combed so that hair stands on end. Introduced in 1968 when African styles were very influential in fashion.

beach wig   Modacrylic wig sometimes attached to a bathing cap or made in amusing shapes. Worn instead of beach hats at the shore or the swimming pool.

fall   Long straight hairpiece fastened to head with ribbon headband or pinned in place so that it hangs down over natural hair. Popular in late 1960s. Purchased by length; short length fall is called a *mini fall;* shoulder-length fall is called a *maxi fall.*

fall

hairpiece   See under HISTORY AND SIGNIFICANCE OF WIGS AND HAIRPIECES TO FASHION.

human hair wig   Imported genuine hair wig that reacts like regular hair, therefore is harder to care for, must be set more often, and is more expensive than synthetic wigs.

maxi fall   See TYPES OF WIGS AND HAIRPIECES DEFINED: FALL.

mini fall   See TYPES OF WIGS AND HAIRPIECES DEFINED: FALL.

postiche   See TYPES OF WIGS AND HAIRPIECES DEFINED: WIGLET.

put-on   Thick hairpiece, sometimes 18″ long, made of modacrylic fiber that is matched to hair. May be worn as part of many different hairstyles, including ponytails, double braids, buns, chignons, etc.

rug   Slang for wig or hairpiece.

stretch wig   Comfortable cool wig with synthetic hair attached to elastic bands running around and over the head in crisscross fashion.

switch   Long hank of false hair that may be braided in a plait and worn on top of the head as a coronet or twisted into a French braid.

toupee (too-pay′)   Man's small partial wig used to cover baldness.

transformation   Term used in early 20th c. for a natural-looking wig or hairpiece worn by women. The term is still sometimes used by older persons.

wiglet   Small hairpiece worn on the top of the head and usually combed into bangs. Worn as an aid for thinning hair by both men and women. Also a fashion item. Also called *postiche* (pos-teesh′).

OTHER ACCESSORIES

MASKS

A **mask** is a covering for the face. Masks are used in some cultures in rituals and ceremonies. The ancient Greeks and Romans used masks in the theater. In the 16th and 17th c., they were used for purposes of disguise when going out on the street at night, and in the American colonial period, masks were fashionable for protection of face from the sun in the daytime. At present, use of masks is limited. They are used as a disguise for Halloween, at pre-Lenten carnivals such as Mardi Gras, or at masquerade parties. Masks are also worn as a protection for the face for active sports and in industrial or work settings.

TYPES OF MASKS DEFINED

catcher's mask Mask made of wire or plastic covering the face that fastens with strap around the head. Worn in baseball games by the catcher to prevent face injury.

chill mask/cold mask See TYPES OF MASKS DEFINED: HOT MASK.

domino Small mask covering upper half of the face, leaving the mouth exposed; worn for masquerades. Also called a *half-mask*.

domino

false face See TYPES OF MASKS DEFINED: RUBBER MASK.

fencing mask Protective mask of fine wire screening fitting over the face to prevent injury from foil when fencing.

gas mask Mask that covers the face and contains filtration materials that protect the wearer against breathing in poisonous gaseous materials.

half-mask See TYPES OF MASKS DEFINED: DOMINO.

hat mask Hat extending partway down over the face with cutouts for the eyes. Used for beach hats and for helmet-type hats in 1960s.

hot mask Mask shaped like a DOMINO (see under TYPES OF MASKS DEFINED) that ties at back of head. **Chill mask** is used for puffy eyes, tension, or hangover; heat mask is used to relieve sinus pain and stuffy noses. Also called *cold mask*.

industrial mask Large fiberglass mask with clear see-through window. Worn for soldering or doing dangerous industrial tasks.

life mask Mask similar to a surgical mask with carbon filter. Worn on the street as a protection against air pollution and smog.

rubber mask Mask fitting over the entire head, worn for Halloween. Molded of latex and painted various colors in a realistic representation of characters from comic strips, cartoons, stories, films, and television; of grotesque and imaginary creatures; and of animals. Also called *false face.*

sanitary mask Masks worn by healthcare workers and others to protect against the transmission of infection.

scarf mask Fashion item of the early 1970s consisting of a scarf tied across the face revealing only the eyes.

scuba mask See-through mask covering eyes and nose worn when swimming underwater or for scuba diving or snorkeling.

ski mask Knitted hood fitting snugly over the head and neck with openings for the eyes,

ski mask

nose, and mouth. Worn for skiing, winter sports, and in cold climates to prevent frostbite. *Der.* Inspired by similar hoods worn in the mountains of Peru.

sleep mask   Soft cushioned mask fitting closely to eyes and nose made of black fabric with an elastic band fitting around head. Worn when sleeping in daylight to block out the light.

surgical mask   Sanitized cloth mask tied over nose and mouth by physicians and nurses to prevent spread of germs to patients. Sometimes used outdoors by people affected by allergies or air pollution.

FANS

HISTORY AND SIGNIFICANCE OF FANS TO FASHION

A **fan** is a hand-held device that, when waved, creates a breeze. Some are rigid—either wedge-shaped, round, or square and flat. Others are pleated, collapsible, and attached to a handle. Women and men used fans made of carved ivory in early Egypt, China, and Japan. Fans have been in common use mostly by women in the Western world from mid-16th c. and after. The materials used include paper, fabric, lace, tortoise shell, feathers, hand-painted silk, and woven palm. The fan was considered a weapon of coquetry from the

feather fan

17th through 19th c. The rules for flirting with a fan were well established. With the advent of air conditioning, the use of fans has declined. Antique fans have become collectors' items. They are often put on display in homes as an attractive accent in interior decoration.

ANATOMY OF FANS

One of the most common types of fans is the FOLD-ING FAN (see under TYPES OF FANS DEFINED). It consists of a framework of hard materials, called the **monture,** which is made up of **sticks.** The sticks at either end of the fan are called **guard sticks.** Fan sticks can be made from many different materials including real or imitation ivory, wood, mother-of-pearl, plastic, tortoiseshell, etc. When the fan is folded, the guard sticks are visible; therefore, they are often more highly ornamented than the interior sticks. A fan can be made of sticks alone, but is more commonly made of such materials as fabric, paper, lace, feathers, and the like. The material is attached to or stretched between the sticks. This section is called the **leaf.** Fans may be covered by leaves on one or both sides. At the base of the sticks a **rivet** holds the sticks together while also allowing them to move enough to close and open the fan.

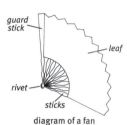

diagram of a fan

TYPES OF FANS DEFINED

brisé fan   A fan composed of sticks alone. The sticks are usually carved. They have a narrower base and a wider top. They are attached one to the other by ribbon or ornamental cord.

cockade fan   A folding fan generally mounted on two sticks that opens to a full 360-degree circle. A **parasol fan** is similar but generally has a single stick.

fixed fan   Fan made from a round or square flat surface that is mounted on a single handle. Also called a *hand screen.*

parasol or cockade fan

folding fan   Half- or quarter-circle fan pleated to close narrowly.

parasol fan   See TYPES OF FANS DEFINED: COCKADE FAN.

folding fan

REMOVABLE COLLARS AND CUFFS

Before drycleaners and automatic washers and dryers were available, removable collars and cuffs were often used on garments as a means of protecting clothing from body soil. These were made of fabrics such as cotton and linen, and were washable. Some fashion designs today may call for removable collars and/or cuffs. These may be used for practical reasons or may be a decorative element of clothing. They are generally made so that they can be tacked into place and removed easily for washing or drycleaning. Others may be made as an accessory item that has the appearance of a collar. Separate collars of fur or fur imitations are also made. The most commonly used designs for removable collars and cuffs are defined below.

STYLES OF REMOVABLE COLLARS DEFINED

asymmetric collar   Any collar that does not appear the same on both sides of center front.

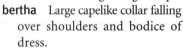
asymmetric collar

Bermuda collar   Woman's shirt collar that opens in front, is small and round, and lies flat. Its corners have a right-angle shape.

bertha   Large capelike collar falling over shoulders and bodice of dress.

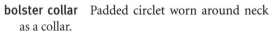
bertha

bishop collar   Large collar, rounded in front, extending almost to shoulder seams.

bolster collar   Padded circlet worn around neck as a collar.

bumper collar   Large fur collar that extends to edges of shoulders when worn flat. Becomes a high rolled collar when ends are hooked in center front.

Buster Brown collar   Medium-sized stiffly starched round white collar first worn by boys in the beginning of the 20th c. and later adopted by women and girls. Often worn with a separate wide, soft bow tie. *Der.* Named for *Buster Brown,* a comic strip character, drawn by Richard F. Outcault in early 20th c.

butterfly collar   Extremely large collar extending to sleeves at shoulders. Front hangs down in two points almost to waist with outer edge having scrolled effect to shoulders, creating the appearance of a butterfly's wings. An innovation of the early 1980s.

cape collar   Large circular-cut collar that extends over the shoulders and upper arms.

carnival collar   Collar made of wide loops of bright printed fabric arranged in an unstarched RUFF (see under STYLES OF REMOVABLE COLLARS DEFINED) as on a clown's costume.

cavalier collar   Broad, flat, lace-edged collar falling over shoulders that is similar to collars worn by Cavaliers, partisans of Charles I, in the early 17th c. Also called a *falling collar.*

choir-boy collar   Flat collar with rounded ends in front, similar to PETER PAN COLLAR (see under STYLES OF REMOVABLE COLLARS DEFINED) only larger, worn over choir robes.

cowl collar   Large draped collar frequently cut on the bias that extends nearly to shoulders in circular style. May be made as a separate item and pulled over the head.

cowl neckline

detachable collar   **1.** Separate collar made with tiny buttonholes at lower edge so that it can be buttoned onto a dress or blouse. Alternatively, the collar may be mounted on a strip of bias fabric that is sewn temporarily to the garment. **2.** A man's separate shirt collar usually fastened with a STUD (see CLOSURES: TYPES OF CLOSURES DEFINED) in back and a collar button in front. Generally used on formal dress shirts.

double collar   Usually a large collar styled with two identical layers of fabric—one slightly larger than the other.

Eton collar   Stiffened boy's collar, similar to a man's shirt collar but twice as wide, with widespread points in front. Worn by underclassmen at Eton College in England until 1967.

jabot (zha-bo′)   Standing band collar with hanging ruffle attached to front of collar.

jabot

middy collar   See STYLES OF REMOVABLE COLLARS DEFINED: SAILOR COLLAR.

Peggy collar   Rounded collar with scalloped ends similar to PETER PAN COLLAR (see under STYLES OF REMOVABLE COLLARS DEFINED).

petal collar   Collar made of several irregularly shaped pieces that look like petals of a flower.

Peter Pan collar   Small round flat collar with rounded ends in front. Worn originally by children, later also adopted by women. *Der.* Copied from costumes worn in play *Peter Pan,* written by James M. Barrie in 1904.

Peter Pan collar

pierrot collar (pee-yehr-oh′)   Small collar made of a double ruffle or ruff. *Der.* From costume of the comedy character in French pantomime called *Pierrot* (little Peter), especially the clown in opera *Pagliacci,* who wore a clown suit with this collar.

pilgrim collar Large round collar extending to the shoulder seams at sides and ending in two long points at center front. *Der.* Copied from early Pilgrim costume.

Puritan collar Square-cut, wide, flat white collar that extends to shoulder seam. *Der.* Copied from early Puritan costume.

rolled collar Any collar that has a roll to it, making it stand up on neck, as differentiated from a flat collar that has no roll and lies flat at base of neck.

rolled collar

ruff A circle of fabric that encompasses the neck, is usually frilled or pleated, can be made in varying widths, and is often edged in or made of lace. A ruff is a contemporary version of an historic collar of the 16th and 17th c.

ruff

sailor collar Large square collar hanging in back with front tapering to a V with dickey inserted. Trimmed with rows of braid and worn on blouses or tops inspired by navy uniforms. Also called *middy collar.*

sailor collar

turtleneck/turtleneck collar High band collar, usually knitted, that fits very close to the neck and rolls over, sometimes twice. Can be made as a separate item that is pulled over the head.

turtleneck collar

REMOVABLE CUFF STYLES DEFINED

detachable cuff Cuff cut out of an additional piece of fabric rather than being an extension of the sleeve and which may be taken off, washed, and reattached to the sleeve.

French cuff Large band cuff that doubles back on itself and is usually fastened with a cuff link. Also called *double cuff.*

French cuff

gauntlet cuff Wide turned-back cuff that slants away from the arm, flaring wide at top and tapering to wrist.

gauntlet cuff

single cuff Band cuff that, in contrast to a FRENCH CUFF (see under REMOVABLE CUFF STYLES DEFINED), has no section doubled back on itself. This cuff is stitched to the sleeve. It usually closes with one or more buttons.

APPENDIX A
TRADE ASSOCIATIONS

Accessories Council, New York, NY
www.accessoriescouncil.org

Accredited Gemologists Association (AGA) San Francisco, CA www.aga.polygon.net

American Apparel and Footwear Association, Arlington, VA www.americanapparel.org

American Diamond Industry Association (ADIA) New York, NY

American Gem and Mineral Suppliers Association (AGMSA) Middletown, CT

American Gem Society, Las Vegas, NV www.ags.org

American Gem Trade Association, Dallas, TX www.AGTA.org

American Luggage Dealers Association, Santa Barbara, CA www.luggagedealers.com

American Watch Association, Washington, D.C.

American Watchmakers and Clockmakers Institute, Harrison, OH www.awi-net.org

Associated Fur Manufacturers (AFM), New York, NY

Athletic Footwear Association, North Palm Peach, FL www.sgma.com

Carolina Hosiery Association, Raleigh, NC www.carohose.com

Council of Fashion Designers of America (CFDA), New York, NY www.cfda.com

Cultured Pearl Association of America (CPPA), New York, NY

Diamond Council of America (DAC), Nashville, TN www.diamondcouncil.org

Diamond Manufacturers and Importers Association of America (DMIAA), New York, NY

Embroidery Trade Association, Dallas, TX www.embroiderytrade.org

Fashion Footwear Association of New York (FFANY) New York, NY www.ffany.org/

Fashion Jewelry Association of America (FJAA), Providence, RI

Footwear Distributors and Retailers of America (FDRA), Washington, D.C. www.fdra.org

Fur Information Council of America, Herndon, VA www.fur.org

Fur Institute of Canada, Ottawa, ON. Canada www.fur.ca/

Gemological Institute of America (GIA), Carlsbad, CA www.gia.org

Headwear Information Bureau (HIB), New York, NY www.hatsny.com/HIB/index.html

High Fashion Italian Footwear Consortium, Milano, Italy www.highfashionshoes.com

Hosiery Association, The (THA), Charlotte, NC www.nahm.com

Independent Jewelers Organization, Norwalk, CT ijo.polygon.net

Jewelers of America, New York, NY www.jewelers.org

Jewelry Manufacturers Association (JMA), New York, NY www.jewelry.org.hk

Jewelry Information Center (JIC), New York, NY www.jewelryinfo.org

Leather Apparel Association (LAA), New York, NY www.leatherassociation.com

Leather Industries of America (LIA), Washington, D.C. www.leatherusa.com

Luggage and Leather Goods Manufacturers of America (LLGMA), New York, NY www.travel-goods.org

Manufacturing Jewelers and Suppliers of America (MJSA) www.mjsainc.org

Metal Findings Manufacturers Association (MFMA), Providence, RI www.mfma.net

Narrow Fabrics Institute (NFI), Roseville, MN www.narrowfabrics.com

National Fashion Accessories Association (NFAA), New York, NY www.accessoryweb.com

National Shoe Retailers Association (NSRA), Columbia, MD www.nsra.org

Neckwear Association of America (NAA), New York, NY www.apparel.net/naa

Schiffli Lace and Embroidery Manufacturers Association (SLEMA), Fairview, NJ www.schiffliusa.com

Shoe Service Institute of America (SSIA) www.ssia.info/default2.asp

Silver Users Association, Washington, D.C. www.silverusersassociation.org

Society of North American Goldsmiths (SGMA), Naperville, IL www.snagmetalsmith.org

Sunglass Association of America (SAA), Norwalk, CT www.sunglassassociation.com

Surface Design Association (SDA), Sebastopol, CA www.surfacedesign.org

Watchmakers of Switzerland Information Center (WOSIC), Rochelle Park, NJ www.fhusa.com

Women's Jewelry Association www.womensjewelry.org

APPENDIX B
BIBLIOGRAPHY

BOOKS

GENERAL REFERENCES

American Heritage Dictionary of the English Language, 3rd edition. Boston: Houghton Mifflin Company, 1992.

Calasibetta, C. *Fairchild's Dictionary of Fashion,* 2nd edition Revised. New York: Fairchild Publications, 1998.

Chase, D. *Terms of Adornment.* New York: Harper Collins Publishers, 1999.

Chenoune, F. *A History of Men's Fashion.* Paris: Flammarion, 1993.

Diamond, J., and E. Diamond. *Fashion Apparel and Accessories.* Albany, NY: Delmar Publishers, 1994.

———— *The World of Fashion.* New York: Fairchild Publications, 1997.

Feldman, E. *Fashions of a Decade: The 1990s.* New York: Facts on File, 1992.

Key Moments in Fashion. London: Hamlyn, 1998.

Lomas, C. *20th-Century Fashion: The 80s & 90s.* Milwaukee: Gareth Stevens Publishing, 2000.

Oxford English Dictionary. Oxford, England: Oxford University Press, 1971.

Schoeffler, O. E., and W. Gale. *Esquire's Encyclopedia of 20th-Century Men's Fashions.* New York: McGraw-Hill, 1973.

Tortora, P., and K. Eubank. *Survey of Historic Costume.* New York: Fairchild Publications, 1998.

Webster's New International Dictionary, 2nd edition. Springfield, MA: G. & C. Merriam Company Publisher, 1953.

COMPONENTS OF ACCESSORIES

Amaden-Crawford, C. *Guide to Fashion Sewing,* 3rd edition. New York: Fairchild Publications, 2000.

Biddle, S., and M. Biddle. *Making Flowers in Paper, Fabric, and Ribbon.* Newton Abbot, Devon, England: David and Charles, 1991.

Collier, B., and P. Tortora. *Understanding Textiles.* Upper Saddle River, NJ: Prentice Hall, 2001.

Cudlip, E. *Furs.* New York: Hawthorn Books, 1978.

Dubin, L.S. *The History of Beads.* New York: Harry N. Abrams, 1987.

Gostelow, M. *Mary Gostelow's Embroidery Book.* New York: E. P. Dutton, 1978.

Proddow, P., and M. Fasel. *Diamonds: A Century of Spectacular Jewels.* New York: Harry N. Abrams, 1996.

Schwab, D. E. *The Story of Lace and Embroidery and Handkerchiefs.* New York: Fairchild Publications, 1957.

Tortora, P., and R. Merkel. *Fairchild's Dictionary of Textiles,* 7th edition. New York: Fairchild Publications, 1996.

ACCESSORIES

Albrizio, A. *Classic Millinery Techniques.* Asheville, NC: Lark Books, 1998.

Armstrong, N. *The Book of Fans.* New York: Mayflower, 1978.

Baseman, A. *The Scarf.* New York: Workman Publications, 1989.

Borland, K. K., and H. R. Speicher. *Clocks, from Shadow to Atom.* Chicago, IL: Follett Publishing Company, 1969.

Braun-Ronsdorf, M. *A History of the Handkerchief.* Leigh-on-Sea, Britain: F. Lewis, 1967.

Campione, A. *Men's Hats.* San Francisco, CA: Chronicle Books, 1995.

Chaille, F. *The Book of Ties.* Paris/New York: Flammarion, N.D.

Cheskin, M. P. *The Complete Handbook of Athletic Footwear.* New York: Fairchild Publications, 1987.

Clark, E. *Hats.* London: B. T. Batsford, 1982.

Collins, C. C. *Love of a Glove.* New York: Fairchild Publcation, 1947.

Cox, J. S. *An Illustrated Dictionary of Hairdressing and Wigmaking.* New York: Drama Book Publishers, 1984.

Crawford, T. S. *A History of the Umbrella.* New York: Taplinger Publishing Company, 1970.

Cummings, V. *Gloves.* New York: Drama Book Publishers, 1982.

Ellsworth, R. *Platform Shoes.* Atglen, PA: Schiffer Publishing Ltd., 1998.

Ettinger, R. *Handbags,* 2nd edition. Atglen, PA: Schiffer Publishing Ltd., 1998.

Evans, C. *Jewelry.* Worcester, MA: Davis Publications, 1983.

Farrel, J., and A. Riberio. *Socks and Stockings.* London: B. T. Batsford Ltd., 1992.

Fider, R., and J. M. Glasman. *Socks Story.* Paris: Logos Designs, 1992.

Folding Fans in the Collection of the Cooper Hewitt Museum. Washington, DC: Smithsonian Institution, 1986.

Foster, V. *Bags and Purses.* London: B. T. Batsford, 1982.

Gibbings, S. *The Tie: Trends and Traditions.* Hauppauge, NY: Barron's Educational Series, Inc., 1990.

Ginsburg, M. *The Hat.* Hauppauge, NY: Barron's Educational Series, Inc., 1990.

Grass, M. N. *History of Hosiery.* New York: Fairchild Publications, 1955.

Gross, K. J., and J. Stone. *Accessories,* lst edition. New York: Knopf, 1996.

Hart, A. *Ties.* New York: Costume and Fashion Press, 1998.

Jonas, S., and M. Nissonson. *Cuff Links.* New York: Harry N. Abrams, 1991.

Jewelry: 7,000 Years. New York, Harry N. Abrams, 1987.

Josephson, J. P. *Umbrellas.* Minneapolis, MN: Caroirhoda Books, 1998.

Lawlor, L. *Where Will This Shoe Take You?* New York: Walker and Company, 1996.

Mackrell, A. *Shawls, Stoles, and Scarves.* London: B. T. Batsford, 1986.

Marly, P. *Spectacles and Spyglasses.* Paris: Editions Hoebke, 1988.

Mascetti, D., and A. Triossi. *Earrings: From Antiquity to the Present.* New York: Harry N. Abrams, 1987.

——— *The Necklace: From Antiquity to the Present.* New York, Harry N. Abrams, 1997.

Mason, A. and D. Packer. *An Illustrated Dictionary of Jewellery.* New York: Harper and Row, 1974.

Manual of Shoemaking. Clarks Ltd. Printing Department, 1980.

Mosconi, D. *The Book of Ties: 188 Knots for Necks.* London: Tie Rack Ltd., 1985.

O'Keefe, L. *Shoes. A Celebration of Pumps, Sandals, Slippers, and More.* New York: Workman Publishers, 1996.

Packing: Bags to Trunks. New York: Alfred A. Knopf, 1994.

Pattison, A. *A Century of Shoes.* Edison, NJ: Chartwell Books, 1997.

Reilly, M. *Hot Shoes: 100 Years.* Atglen, PA: Schiffer Publishing Ltd., 1998.

Scarisbrick, D. *Rings: Symbol of Wealth, Power, and Affection.* New York: Harry N. Abrams, 1993.

Steele, V. *Shoes. A Lexicon of Style.* New York: Rizzoli, 1999.

Tolkien, T., and H. Wilkinson. *A Collector's Guide to Costume Jewelry.* Willowdale, Ontario, Canada: Firefly Books, 1997.

Wilcox, C. *A Century of Bags: Icons of Style in the 20th Century.* Edison, NJ: Chartwell Books, 1997.

Worthington, C. *Accessories.* New York: Alfred A. Knopf, 1996.

PERIODICALS

Only those periodicals devoted specifically to accessories or materials used in accessories are listed. Other general fashion periodicals such as *Women's Wear Daily, Daily News Record, Vogue, Harper's Bazaar,* and the like regularly include features about accessories and can also be consulted.

Accessories, 185 Madison Avenue, 5th Floor, New York, NY 10016

American Shoemaking, Shoe Trades Publishing, 61 Massachusetts Avenue, Arlington, MA 02474

Arpel Fur, Ars Arpel Group s.r.l., Via Nievo 33, 20145 Milano, Italy

Bags and Accessories Collezioni, Zanfi Editori, via Emilia Ovest 954, 41100 Modena, Italy

FN—Footwear News, Fairchild Publications, Inc., 7 West 34th Street, New York, NY 10001-8191

Fur Age, 2 Main Street, Roslyn, NY 11576

Metalsmith, SNAG/Metalsmith, Business Office, 710 E. Ogden Avenue, Suite 600, Napierville, IL 60563-8603

Ornament, P.O. Box 2349, San Marcos, CA 92079-2349

Travelware, 185 Madison Avenue, New York, NY 10010

Watch and Clock Review, Golden Bell Press, 2403 Champa Street, Denver CO 80205

World Footwear, Shoe Trades Publishing Co, 140 58th Street, Suite 2B, Brooklyn, NY 11220-2521